GLOBALIZATION AND THE HUMAN FACTOR

GLOBALIZATION AND THE HUMAN FACTOR

Globalization and the Human Factor

Critical Insights

Edited by
E. OSEI KWADWO PREMPEH
JOSEPH MENSAH
SENYO B.-S.K. ADJIBOLOSOO

ASHGATE

Published by
Ashgate Publishing Limited
Gower House
Croft Road
Aldershot
Hampshire GU11 3HR
England

Ashgate Publishing Company
Suite 420
101 Cherry Street
Burlington, VT 05401-4405
USA

Ashgate website: http://www.ashgate.com

British Library Cataloguing in Publication Data
Globalization and the human factor : critical insights
    1.International economic relations - Social aspects
    2.Globalization - Social aspects
    I.Prempeh, E. Osei Kwadwo II.Mensah, Joseph
    III.Adjibolosoo, Senyo B-S. K.
    303.4'82

Library of Congress Cataloging-in-Publication Data
Globalization and the human factor : critical insights / [edited] by E. Osei Kwadwo Prempeh, Joseph Mensah, Senyo B.-S.K. Adjibolosoo.
        p. cm.
    Includes bibliographical references and index.
    Index 0-7546-4292-5
    1. International economic relations--Social aspects. 2. Globalization--Social aspects. I. Prempeh, E. Osei Kwadwo, 1960- II. Mensah, Joseph, 1960- III. Adjibolosoo, Senyo B-S. K.

    HF1359.G581713 2004
    303.48'2--dc22

                                                2004015404

ISBN 0 7546 4292 5

Printed & Bound in Great Britain by MPG Books Ltd, Bodmin, Cornwall

Contents

List of Contributors

Senyo B.-S.K. Adjibolosoo is full Professor of Economics at Point Loma Nazarene University, San Diego, California, USA. He is the founder and Executive Director of the International Institute for Human Factor Development (IIHFD) and the Editor-in-Chief of the journal, *Review of Human Factor Studies* (RHFS), which is the journal of the IIHFD. His publications include numerous journal articles, books, book chapters and book reviews.

Francis Adu-Febiri is the Chair of the Social Sciences Department, Camosun College, Canada, and Adjunct Professor at the University of Victoria, British Columbia, Canada. He has presented and published extensively on tourism, human factor development, globalization, diversity, racialization, ethnicity and Canadian First Nations. He is the President of the Canadian Chapter of the International Institute for Human Factor Development (IIHFD).

Joseph Mensah is an Assistant Professor of Human Geography at the School of Social Sciences, Atkinson Faculty of Liberal and Professional Studies at York University, Toronto, Ontario, Canada. He has written several journal articles and contributed to chapters to a number of books. He is the author of *Black Canadians: History, Experience and Social Conditions.*

Randy Moore is a Professor of Biology at the University of Minnesota. His most recent book is *Evolution in the Courtroom: A Reference Guide.*

Victor Ngonidzashe Muzvidziwa is an Associate Professor in the Department of Sociology, University of Zimbabwe. His publications in journals and book chapters cover areas of culture and theory, the human factor in development and social policy, family and gender studies.

E. Osei Kwadwo Prempeh is an Associate Professor of Political Science; and Sociology and Anthropology at Carleton University, Ottawa, Ontario, Canada. He has published numerous articles and book chapters on the human factor, globalization and the politics of resistance to globalization.

Korbla P. Puplampu teaches at Grant MacEwan College in Edmonton, Alberta, Canada. He has published articles in academic journals such as *African Studies Review, Review of African Political Economy, Canadian Journal of Development Studies and Review of Human Factor Studies.* He edited with Wisdom J. Tettey and Bruce J. Berman, *Critical Perspectives on Politics and Socio-Economic Development in Ghana.*

Wisdom J. Tettey is Associate Professor at the Faculty of Communication and Culture, University of Calgary, Calgary, Alberta, Canada. He co-edited (with Bruce J. Berman and Korbla P. Puplampu) *Critical Perspectives on Politics and Socio-Economic Development in Ghana*. He has also written on globalization, information technology and the diasporization of civil society in various edited volumes and journals.

Acknowledgements

The Editors wish to acknowledge debts of gratitude to several people who made this book possible with dedication and a sense of purpose. The reviewers and staff at Ashgate Publishing, especially Kirstin Howgate and Donna Hamer, provided invaluable support and encouragement at all stages. Diane Dodds at the Department of Political Science, Carleton University, did a remarkable job editing and producing the final camera-ready copy. We are extremely grateful to all of them.

Some of the chapters in this book are based on previously published articles. We are grateful to the International Institute for Human Factor Development (IIHFD) for permission to draw on these articles which they hold under copyright and which first appeared in the special issue of *the Review of Human Factor Studies on Globalization and the Human Factor*, Volume 8, Number 1, June 2002.

E. Osei Kwadwo Prempeh dedicates this book to his late mother and brother Obaapanin Kaakyire Amma Boakyewaa and 'Godfather' Osei Kwadwo Anane-Binfoh respectively; his spouse Anna Nsiah-Sarkodie and their four children Eva, Greg, Stephanie and Christopher. He also gratefully acknowledges the financial support of the Deans of the Faculty of Public Affairs and Management and the Faculty of Arts and Social Sciences, Carleton University and the funds made possible by a Carleton University Teaching Achievement Award for 2001.

Joseph Mensah dedicates this book to his parents, Mr. M.Y. Mensah and Madam Gladys Gyan in Techiman, Ghana; his wife Janet Ann Mensah and to the loving memory of his mother-in-law, Ms. Gwendolyn Thomas Jeffers.

Senyo B.-S.K. Adjibolosoo dedicates this book to Sabina Adjibolosoo.

E. Osei Kwadwo Prempeh, Ottawa
Joseph Mensah, Toronto
Senyo B.-S.K. Adjibolosoo, San Diego

Introduction

The Globalization-Development Debate: The Need for a Paradigm Shift

E. Osei Kwadwo Prempeh,
Joseph Mensah and Senyo B.-S.K. Adjibolosoo

Introduction

Since about the early 1980s, the world has experienced an unprecedented push towards economic, political, social, and cultural integration, which – in its totality or in various permutations – has come under the rubric of globalization. A resurgent neo-liberal economic and political agenda has been the driving force behind the globalizing trend, unleashing structural changes of profound complexity and magnitude worldwide. As a phenomenon with dramatic consequences, globalization has engendered extraordinary response that at once engages the attention of both advocates and critics alike. A good deal of the prevailing response revolves around the tensions and conflicts inherent in globalization, with much emphasis on political economy, but little attention, if any, to what the economist Senyo Adjibolosoo calls the human factor (HF) in development theorization, notwithstanding attempts to make globalization more human-centered.

This book clarifies some of the tensions inherent in making globalization more anthropocentric, by inserting a new, even controversial, theme into the debate. *Globalization and the Human Factor: Critical Insights* suggests that globalization is a process that is not only contested, but also has significant human factor implications. The human factor, as used in this book, connotes a wide range of personality attributes and other dimensions of human performance (e.g., a discipline labour force, rule of law, and political harmony) which facilitate the successful functioning of socio-economic and political institutions over time (Adjibolosoo, 1993, p. 142).

As a cross-disciplinary exercise, this book brings together scholars from diverse backgrounds to probe the potentials and limits of globalization with respect to the human factor theoretical framework. While there are many books on globalization – indeed, some would even argue far more than is necessary – none has successfully grappled with the important role of the human factor either in a hegemonic or counter-hegemonic context. This book inserts the human factor into the debate, and argues that this hitherto marginalized concept holds one of the keys to providing a holistic understanding and contestation of globalization. The focus is on how particular human variables shape, and are shaped, by specific phenomena within the context of globalization.

While there are nuanced and sophisticated differences, all the authors are unified in highlighting the marginalization of the human factor in the globalization debate and in making the case for providing some critical reflections on the economic, political, social, and cultural consequences of globalization from a human factor perspective. The overriding concern is to examine the extent to which globalization has enhanced or undermined the human factor. We forcefully argue against the tendency to equate globalization with western values and the market, and highlight the need to respect indigenous cultures and to promote global harmony in all spheres of human endeavor. Using the human factor as the organizing framework, the contributors draw attention to what has been missing in the globalization debate, and address some of the main gaps in the existing literature.

Our main rationale, therefore, for writing yet another book on globalization is three-fold:

- To use the human factor construct to critically engage and interrogate the hegemonic processes of globalization.
- To examine the role and significance of the human factor in global change from an interdisciplinary perspective.
- To provide an accessible account of the possible nexus between globalization and the human factor in the theorization of uneven development across the globe.

In contrast to the many and burgeoning literature on globalization, this book presents a more holistic analysis, which is at once mindful of the powerful thrust of globalization in its various dimensions, yet moves beyond the existing tendency to conceptualize globalization in restrictive, technical, and economic terms, thereby overlooking the important issues raised by the human factor perspective. By introducing the concept of the human factor, the collection aims to broaden the globalization debate – at the very least, making it more human-centered. Students interested in exploring the ramifications of globalization outside the existing orthodoxy will particularly find this book a welcome addition to their collection.

Defining Globalization

Due to the diverse disciplinary backgrounds of the authors, we conceptualize globalization as a broad, multifaceted phenomenon with wide ranging economic, political, cultural, and social ramification worldwide. A sampling of the prevailing definitions of globalization would certainly help set the stage for our analysis. The British social theorist Anthony Giddens (1990, p. 64) captures the long reach of globalization in the following words: '[globalization] is the intensification of worldwide social relations which link distant localities in such a way that local happenings are shaped by events occurring many miles away and vice versa'. The emphasis here is on the compression of time and space and the decreasing importance of distance. This serves as the nub of Roland Robertson's claim that 'globalization refers both to the compression of the world and the intensification of the consciousness of the world' (Robertson, 1992). Implicit in these are arguments about the 'end of geography'. It is worth noting that while Robertson's definition stresses the cultural aspects of globalization, Giddens' is more concerned with the links between globalization and (post)modernity and their attendant technological implications.

Economic deterministic arguments, on the other hand, tease out the widening reach of global markets in an interdependent world. Herbert Stocker, for instance, cites the Organization for Economic Cooperation and Development's views on globalization as a process 'by which markets and production in different countries are becoming increasingly interdependent due to dynamics of trade in goods and services and the flows of capital and technology' (1998, p. 103). The saliency of these interconnections and increased flows of transnational relations is further elaborated in suggestions about a 'borderless world' (Ohmae, 1990), which situate the concepts in a much broader sense insofar as it encompasses a trend towards cultural, economic, social, and political integration. As Tabb (1999, p. 1) shrewdly puts it: 'globalization refers to the process of reducing barriers between countries and encouraging closer economic, political, and social interaction'.

The chapters in this volume emphasize these diverse conceptualizations of globalization in one way or the other, and provide nuanced critiques from cultural, political, technological, and social perspectives, using examples from Africa and other parts of the developing world, for the most part. These critiques point to the economic determinism of the prevailing definitions and stress the need to explore the political, social, and cultural consequences of globalization. Along these lines, Ethan Kapstein points out that:

> In most of the popular and journalistic accounts of "globalization", the emphasis is usually placed on the allegedly deterministic forces of technical change that are now creating a world without borders. These analyses miss a central point: that globalization is fundamentally a political phenomenon. It did not arise "naturally", but rather was the product of policy decisions taken after World War II among the Western allies (1999, p. 17).

Here, Kapstein reinforces the power of politics and, implicitly, of the human agency and the human factor. There is little doubt that globalization has so far engendered both negative and positive outcomes, the essence of which is best captured by James Mittelman's observation that:

> [Globalization] offers major benefits, including gains in productivity, technological advances ... [and] widespread dissemination of information and knowledge ... Yet there is a price for integrating in this global framework and

adopting its practices. Expressed or tacit acceptance of being encompassed in globalization entails a lessening, or in some cases, a negating, of the quantum of political control exercised by the encompassed, especially in the least powerful and poorest zones of the global political economy (2000, p. 5).

This collection explores these diverse issues in the globalization-development debate from an alternative perspective, namely, the human factor.

An Alternative Approach

The point of entry for our alternative approach to the prevailing debate on globalization is underpinned by the seminal work of Senyo Adjibolosoo on the importance of the Human Factor (HF) in development discourse. We use insights from Adjibolosoo's work not only to contribute to the debate on globalization, but also to cast it in a more holistic and anthropocentric mode of thinking. A note of caution is appropriate at this juncture: while our adoption of the human factor (HF) as a touchstone is a way to extend and shed a different light on the debate, it is important to note the HF perspective is just one, albeit critical way, of injecting human-centeredness into the globalization discourse.

In his pioneering study 'The Human Factor in Development', published in *The Scandinavian Journal of Development Alternatives* (1993), Adjibolosoo explored why the mainstream development theories have failed to reverse years of decline in the 'Third World' in general and Africa in particular. He traced the failure to what he termed the human factor decay and/or underdevelopment. His notion of human factor connotes human qualities, attributes, and traits which foster the efficient functioning of people and institutions in relation to economic, social, political and cultural activities. Adjibolosoo cautions us not to relegate the human factor to the background, as we strive to improve the human condition around the world. In his view,

> the attainment of true and lasting progress requires people who have acquired the HF. Attempts to find solutions to social, economic, political, cultural and intellectual problems need to address HF decay and/or underdevelopment in society (1996, p. 21).

How important is this conceptualization of the HF for the globalization-development debate? We contend that globalization and development theorists have so far ignored the HF implications of their policies and opted instead to rely almost exclusively on overly technical assessments of rationality, notwithstanding the mounting evidence questioning the basis of these assumptions. With the aid of the HF perspective, this volume offers a reappraisal of the prevailing discourse on globalization and development, placing more emphasis on global harmony, environmental sustainability, and the moral dimensions of human well-being. As Korbla Puplampu points out in this collection, 'the overall essence of the concept of the Human Factor is the crucial role of human beings and their relationship to their environment in a manner that would bring about genuine human development. Human factor development therefore undertakes a critical analysis of how culture and development institutions interact, analyzing the interaction as both a means and an end'.

Part I, *Conceptualizing Globalization and the Human Factor*, sets the intellectual and theoretical foundation for this critical engagement between globalization and the human factor in bold, maybe controversial terms. E. Osei Kwadwo Prempeh, in the first chapter, *Globalization and the Human Factor: Some Preliminary Observations*, draws attention to the economic globalization thesis' focus on a narrow set of issues, its technical approach, and the fact that it pays too much attention to the perceived efficiency of the self-regulating market. Missing in this theoretical analysis, he argues, are questions about the HF that are central to comprehending the process and impacts of globalization. The chapter brings the HF into the debate and points out that this marginalized concept offers fresh new insights into the globalization – development debate. The overarching framework for his analysis is provided by global economic integration, which he points out has unleashed powerful economic, political, social, cultural and technological changes unprecedented in the global economy. In a more direct way, he notes that 'this reshaping of the contemporary economic system is unfolding within the overarching structure of the process of globalization'. The changes inherent in the configurations and transformations now in vogue under the impact of the forces of globalization point to new challenges for global society and the development policy debate. At the core of this debate is the view that globalization enhances development and thus has a positive impact on overall development.

The second chapter which examines issues of *Globalization and the Human Factor*, addresses some of the economic dimensions of globalization specifically around issues of global participation and gain-sharing. Senyo Adjibolosoo in, *Tapping into and Benefiting from the Forces and Agents of Globalization: Creating an Integrated Vehicle for Global Participation and Gain-Sharing*, critiques the tendency of the forces of globalization to tip the rules and scales of gain-sharing in favour of the inhabitants of the developed world. The question that provides the structure for this analysis is set in a straightforward manner and in line with earlier contributions from dependency theorists about the possibility of 'Third World' countries delinking from the global capitalist economy: should the residents of the developing countries totally disengage themselves from the rest of the world in an attempt to avoid the negative implications of globalization? His response is that total disengagement is not a sustainable solution. Instead, he argues, it is only through the development of the appropriate human factor that the poor people of the world could stand a greater chance of benefiting from the forces and agents of globalization.

Part II, *Globalization, the Human Factor and Cultural Identities*, analyzes the cultural and social dimensions of globalization from a HF perspective. The contributions highlight a contradiction within globalization: on the one hand, globalization has opened up space for local cultures; on the other hand, there seems to be a move underway towards a totalizing effect with its attendant privileging of

Western attitudes and cultures. Joseph Mensah's *Integrating Culture in Globalization and Development Theory: Towards a Human Factor Approach* probes the inadequate treatment of culture and human factor attributes in the prevailing literature on globalization and development. Picking on a familiar theme in the globalization discourse, Mensah reminds readers that the rise of market-oriented global networks has provided the developed countries and multinational corporations with additional power to subjugate and dominate the less developed countries. The author laments the loss of whatever little power and influence 'Third World' countries had prior to the ascendancy of contemporary globalization.

Victor Ngonidzashe Muzvidziwa's *African Culture and the Social Implications and Consequences of Globalization* examines how and the extent to which globalizing processes have and continue to influence African culture. In his view, globalization has produced a phenomenal global response that engages African culture and traditions in a supportive and antagonistic way all at once. These tensions and conflicts inherent in the globalization processes have implications for the development of African values, traditions and culture. His chapter seeks to present a critical reflection of the consequences of globalization on African culture and the extent to which it enhances and undermines African culture.

Chapter 5 by Francis Adu-Febiri picks up on some of the issues of identity that inform Mensah and Muzvidziwa's analysis. In his *Globalization and Diversity in the Tourism Industry: A Human Factor Perspective*, Adu-Febiri posits that at the interface of globalization and tourism is a natural diversity in the areas of demographic and cultural representations. However, as he points out, the tourism industry tends to push this diversity to the margins with the assumption that cultural cloning at the core of the industry would maximize the bottom-line. He argues that this assumption is faulty and agrees with postmodernist thinking that tourism can optimize productivity/profit, enhance social justice, enrich cultures, and motivate environmental conservation when it facilitates rather than destroys diversity. The chapter also affirms the postmodernist position that diversity can be successfully facilitated in tourism in spite of the homogenizing tendencies of globalization. However, contrary to the perspective of postmodernism, the chapter does not problematize globalization. This is because, as the author points out, globalization is not the problem; the problem is human factor decay and/or underdevelopment. Therefore, he argues, the key to successful facilitation of diversity in tourism is not the halting of globalization and/or multiculturalism policies and diversity management as many postmodernists believe but rather the application of appropriate human factor.

Part III, *Globalization, the Human Factor and Science and Technology* takes on the science and technology implications of globalization. The authors explore the transformations of the science and technology revolution and its impact on human factor dynamics. Korbla P. Puplampu's *National Agricultural Research Systems, the Biotechnology Revolution, and Agricultural Development* reminds readers of how recent strides in technology have revolutionized agricultural production, marketing, and consumption systems worldwide. The chapter is particularly interested in how biotechnological innovations have changed the nature of agricultural production. The debate is set in the context of Africa, a continent where the agricultural sector continues to anchor its development prospects. Puplampu argues that biotechnology either presents a real possibility for transforming the agricultural sector and with that agricultural and national development or as yet another false start for African development. He examines the extent to which biotechnology can bring about some improvements in agricultural development in Africa by focusing on institutional capabilities of national agricultural systems in Africa, questions of ownership and transfer of technology within the context of the globalization of agriculture.

Wisdom J. Tettey's *Globalization, Diasporization and Cyber-Communities: Exploring African Transnationalism* revisits the issue of transnational migration which has assumed unprecedented global proportions as we begin the new millennium. At the same time as this process of global migration gathers momentum, the world has also seen an unprecedented increase in the development of information technologies, which have allowed diasporic communities to emerge in cyberspace and to interact beyond the confines of geographic space. The chapter is based on an analysis of African discussion forums, chat rooms, and websites over the last year. It explores how Africans, living abroad, are using the internet as a vehicle for the construction of ethnic, cultural, and national identities; the advancement of home-diaspora linkages for the purposes of socio-economic development at home; and engagement in political discourse.

The final chapter in this section, Randy Moore's *Human Factor Decay, American Exceptionalism, and the Exclusion of Women and Minorities from Science and Science-Driven Globalization* brings attention to how during the recent decades, globalization has often been driven by interactions of the human factor with democracy, science, and technology developed in and exported by the United States. Ironically, however, this chapter points out that the United States – which promotes itself as 'the land of opportunity' – continues to be an exception to its own claims, for human factor decay often excludes women and ethnic minorities from the science and technology that has driven globalization. The chapter analyzes how human factor decay has produced and perpetuated the exclusion of women and minorities from science, and how the increased access of women and minorities to science and science-driven globalization has correlated with changes in the human factor.

The final section, Part IV, on *Globalization, the Human Factor, Democracy and Governance* seeks to address the political dimensions of the globalization-development and human factor interaction. The objective is to underscore the importance of politics in the debate as a way to 'bring politics back in'. Political Scientist E. Osei Kwadwo Prempeh tackles the issues head-on. In *Globalization, Governance and the Human Factor*, Osei Kwadwo Prempeh, adopting an analysis steeped in Richard Falk's approach, makes the case that the exclusionary practices of the process of 'globalization-from-above' has elicited a strong grassroots counter-hegemonic response of 'globalization-from-below' which seeks to bring democratic governance to the processes of globalization. The chapter explores the nature of this governance critique of globalization and makes the case for widening it. The human factor school of thought, it is pointed out, might seem well positioned to contribute to this. Central to this is the development of a two-step strategy of governance supplemented by positive HF engineering.

The final chapter – *Democracy as Political Counterpart to Globalization: Wither the Human Factor?* – by E. Osei Kwadwo Prempeh identifies a different aspect of the globalization-governance-democracy debate and subjects it to critical scrutiny. The author sets the stage by making the case that the foundation of neoliberalism is provided by an ideological component with political and economic manifestations. The economic manifestation is the free market while the political is democracy. However, the multi-faceted process of globalization is producing a global political environment in which a particular vision of democracy prevails. Indeed, Western liberal democracy seems to be the political counterpart to globalization. The chapter subjects this vision of democracy to intense debate from a HF perspective. He argues that in the presence of HF underdevelopment and/or decay, political institutions will fail to function effectively.

References

Adjibolosoo, Senyo B.-S.K. (1996), "Human Factor Engineering: The Primary Mission of Education and Training", in Senyo B.-S.K. Adjibolosoo (ed.) *Human Factor Engineering and the Political Economy of African Development*, Westport, CT. and London: Praeger.

Adjibolosoo, Senyo B.-S.K. (1993), "The Human Factor in Development", *The Scandinavian Journal of Development Alternatives*, 12 (4): 139-149.

Giddens, Anthony (1990), *The Consequences of Modernity*, Cambridge: Polity Press.

Kapstein, Ethan (1999), *Sharing the Wealth*, New York: W.W. Norton.

Mittelman, James H. (2000), *The Globalization Syndrome: Transformation and Resistance*, Princeton, NJ.: Princeton University Press.

Ohmae, Kenichi (1990), *The Borderless World: Power and Strategy in the Inter-Linked World Economy*, New York and London: Harper Collins.

Robertson, Roland (1992), *Globalization: Social Theory and Global Culture*, Newbury Park, CA.: SAGE.

Stocker, Herbert (1998), "Globalization and International Convergence in Incomes" in Johnren Chen (ed.) *Economic Effects of Globalization*, Aldershot, UK: Ashgate.

Tabb, William (1999), "Progressive Globalism: Challenging the Audacity of Capital", *Monthly Review*, 50 (9): 1-10.

PART I:
CONCEPTUALIZING
GLOBALIZATION AND THE
HUMAN FACTOR

Chapter 1

Globalization and the Human Factor: Some Preliminary Observations

E. Osei Kwadwo Prempeh

Introduction

There has been a qualitative increase in global economic integration in the last two decades leading to a dramatic and unprecedented pace of change in the global economy. This reshaping of the contemporary economic system is unfolding within the overarching structure of the process of economic globalization. Underpinned by a neoliberal theoretical perspective, the process of globalization has acquired added significance by unleashing forces affecting the economic, political, social and cultural aspects of everyday life. Hailed by its proponents as a forward-looking process for rapid economic growth and criticized by opponents as the source of inequality and instability, globalization has resulted in powerful shifts in both domestic and international balances of social, economic, and political forces and consequent transformations and configurations in inter-state and intra-state relations.

Attempts at understanding the specific features of this configuration now taking place under the rubric of globalization have proliferated over the years to the extent that to invoke Hirst and Thompson's point, the term has become 'a fashionable concept in the social sciences, a core dictum in the prescriptions of management gurus, and a catch-phrase for journalists and politicians of every stripe' (Hirst and Thompson, 1996, p. 1). Such configurations and transformations under the impact of forces of globalization highlight not only the extent of transnational flows and networks, but also the new challenges for global society and the development policy debate. Indeed, one of the most fascinating debates in contemporary times is the impact of globalization on development.

This chapter is a critical response to the ever-expanding literature on globalization that emphasize its positive impact. The attempt here is to add a critical new voice to the debate through the introduction of the Human Factor (HF). Conceived as a theoretical intervention in the debate on globalization and development, the paper challenges globalization's claim to opening up a unique opportunity for sustained and long-term equitable economic growth and development. The central argument is that the globalization thesis avoids critical discussion of the HF basis for development. The globalization thesis underestimates the importance of the HF and exaggerates globalization's growth potential. In so doing, the paper seeks to create spaces for the construction of a HF alternative to enhance possibilities of respect for human dignity, social welfare and equitable growth. It is proposed that the insights of the HF school of thought can fruitfully serve as a useful touchstone in development policy. Despite its marginalization within development theory, the HF is capable of addressing some of the central concerns of development studies in this era of globalization in an open, sophisticated and interdisciplinary fashion.

A growing body of literature exists that addresses globalization's impact on inequality. This work acknowledges these contributions but also provides a new insight by bringing in new scholarship of substantive issues. This introductory piece, therefore, sets the terrain of critical engagement between globalization and the HF in bold, maybe controversial terms. It is beyond the scope of this paper to pursue all of the processes underpinning the transformation engendered by globalization. Instead of offering a catch-all analysis short on detail, emphasis is placed on exploring the theoretical basis of globalization which is underpinned by neoliberalism and offer a HF challenge and counter-critique. The discussion begins with a review of some of the recent literature on globalization. The ways in which the discourses of the HF school of thought can provide useful, alternative insights is then examined.

Economic Globalization: Central Theoretical Assumptions

What is globalization? Hurrell and Woods' definition is worth considering here. In the face of definitional and conceptual problems, they set themselves a more limited task:

> The term 'globalization' is often invoked to describe the process of increasing interdependence and global enmeshment which occurs as money, people, images, values, and ideas flow ever more swiftly and smoothly across national boundaries. It is assumed to be a process driven by technological advance which will lead to a more and more homogeneous and interconnected world. In the new globalized world economy, it is argued, states will cooperate more and international institutions will flourish. All of this draws on the 'liberal interpretation of globalization' ... The term liberal is used to characterize both a market-liberal interpretation of the increasing interconnectedness of world markets, and a broader liberal interpretation of the political and social aspects of globalization (1995, pp. 447-448).

At the core of the economic globalization thesis is a belief that the process is reconstituting national economies. Globalization, in this exposition, is therefore associated with transforming national economies in a positive way. The dominant, though not uncontested, orientation of the literature on globalization is therefore, broadly speaking, economic. As Held et al. point out:

Despite divergent ideological convictions, there exists a shared set of beliefs that globalization is primarily an economic phenomenon; that an increasingly integrated global economy exists today; that the needs of global capital impose a neoliberal economic discipline on all governments such that politics is no longer the 'art of the possible' but rather the practice of 'sound economic management' (1999, p. 4).

In other words, the transformational process consists of economic agents, hence the predominant view that globalization is an economic process. In Falk's words, globalization is 'a new alignment of forces that is being crystallized by a constellation of market, technological, ideological and civilizational developments …' (1997, p. 125).

As an economic phenomenon, globalization has three manifestations: international finance, international investment and international trade. Viewed in these terms, globalization encompasses the spread and expansion of economic transactions and the organization of economic activities across national boundaries. As such, it is associated with growing economic interdependence, increasing interconnectedness and deepening economic integration between countries in the global economy. The nature of these interconnections and interdependence wrought by these manifestations of the economic processes of globalization are captured by this powerful statement from Deepak Nayyar thus:

Economic *openness* is not simply confined to trade flows, investment flows, and financial flows. It also extends to flows of services, technology, information, and ideas across national boundaries. But the cross-border movement of people is closely regulated and highly restricted. Economic *interdependence* is asymmetrical. There is a high degree of interdependence among countries in the industrialized world. There is considerable dependence of the developing countries on the industrialized countries. There is much less interdependence among countries in the developing world. It is important to note that a situation of interdependence is one where the benefits of linking and the costs of delinking are about the same for both partners; where such benefits and costs are unequal between partners, it implies a situation of dependence. Economic *integration* straddles national boundaries as liberalization has diluted the significance of borders in economic transactions. It is, in part, an integration of markets (for goods, services, technology, financial assets, and even money) on the demand side, and, in part, an integration of production (horizontal and vertical) on the supply side (2000, p. 7).

As a market driven process, albeit with wider implications and different dimensions, globalization, seen in this way, emphasizes the saliency of interconnections and increased flows of transnational relations and the move towards an interdependent world. Also to be discerned from this is the creation of a global market through the amalgamation of national markets. For Hans-Peter Martin and Harald Schuman, 'globalization is understood in terms of the creation of a global market. Advances in communication, falling transportation costs and unrestricted trade is leading to the creation of a single global market' (1998, p. 5). For McGrew,

> Globalization is the multiplicity of linkages and interconnections that transcend the nation-state (and by implication the societies) which make up the modern world system. It defines a process through which events, decisions, and activities in one part of the world can come to have significant consequences for individuals and communities in quite distant parts of the globe (McGrew, 1992, pp. 13-14).

Picking up on this theme, but from a distinctly Marxist perspective, Ankie Hoogvelt writes of globalization as:

> A new social architecture of cross-border human interactions. It breaks down the old international division of labour and the associated hierarchy of rich and poor countries. In this process the integrity of the national territorial state as a more or less coherent political economy is eroded, and the functions of the state become re-organized to adjust domestic economic and social policies to fit the exigencies of the global market and global capitalist accumulation (1997, p. 67).

The sense one gets from these definitions which emphasize the economic aspects of globalization is of a multidimensional process or processes which integrates production, markets and national financial systems on a global scale such that the national is subsumed under the global.

Taking a cue from this and at the risk of being accused of economic and technological determinism, I proceed to outline the neoliberal economic globalization thesis. This should not, however, be construed to imply that globalization as an economic project unfolds only in the economic sphere. In fact, the preceding remarks clearly demonstrate the extent and reach of the process and its impact on the political, social and cultural spheres as well. Globalization results in the enmeshment of economies and societies in social, political and cultural terms. Given the multifaceted dimensions and nature of the process of globalization, it is not surprising that Cerny refers to it as a highly complex phenomenon 'given its scale and scope, its many levels of interaction and types of actors, and its complex iterated character: globalization generates *multiple equilibria*' (2000, p. 435).

The standard orthodox, neoliberal conception of globalization articulates a position based on a theoretical faith in market forces as the quintessential mechanism for efficient allocation of resources and a harbinger for positive economic growth. This dominant neoliberal theory of globalization celebrates the universality of 'modernity' and human progress propelled by economic growth. The approach emphasizes reliance on private and free, unregulated mechanisms and deregulation. The economic principles of liberalization, stabilization and privatization are its defining element (Stiglitz, 1998).

The market is assumed to be a self-generating, self-disciplining system which operates through its own internal dynamics. This market fetishism has been rightly identified by Soros as 'market fundamentalism [which] is today a greater threat to open society' (Soros, 1998, p. xxii). In more specific terms, Soros points out that 'the disenchantment with politics has fed market fundamentalism and the rise of market fundamentalism has, in turn, contributed to the failure of politics. One of the great defects of the global capitalist system is that it has allowed the market mechanism and the profit motive to penetrate into fields of activity where they do not properly belong' (Soros, 1998, p. xxiii). In this view, the market mechanism, regulated by the invisible hand leads to economic growth and efficiency.

The crux of the prevailing dynamic of neoliberal economic globalization philosophy is captured by Hurrel and Woods in this poignant statement:

> The liberal orthodoxy posits a world economy in which a global increase in transactions is driven by technological advance and by self-maximising decisions of private actors. On this view, states and governments are bystanders to globalisation: the real driving forces are markets. Furthermore, the emergence of global markets improves efficiency. In the first place, the free movement of capital and goods across borders produces a more *efficient allocation of resources* around the globe ... In the second place, global markets ensure a more *efficient production of goods* in the world economy through the gains of trade ... Finally, a global world economy with freely exchangeable currencies and open markets ensures an *efficient distribution of goods and services* in a world in which price mechanisms operate globally (1995, p. 448).

This globalizing neoliberalism is underpinned by an ideological component with political and economic manifestations: democracy and the capitalist free market.

The momentum of the current globalization dynamic is so far-reaching that it has acquired hegemonic status in both theoretical and policy considerations. The self-regulating, self-disciplining market has usurped all other institutions. The market-driven logic of the process of globalization has altered the balance of political and social forces through its imposition of the so-called discipline of global market forces. The operation of these global market forces in such laissez faire terms is seen as generating efficiency benefits. Economic growth, generated as a result of this unfettered operation of the market, will result in broader economic and social rights and improve material well-being. This market-driven logic embodied in the neoliberal consensus is an extremely ideological process and driven by pressures towards competition and economic restructuring.

This, in more respects than one, constitutes a 'rediscovery of the market', serving as an attack on state intervention and the welfare state. The rules of the game are set by the requirements of this global marketplace. As Teeple (1995, pp. 79-80) rightly points out:

> The proponents of the free market argue that it has positive political and economic implications. They say it is the source of capitalism's purported political liberties and freedom of opportunity and is the most neutral, or non-political, way to provide for the needs of society ... The market is also presented as an alternative to government ownership and regulation of the economy, an alternative that is

'successful' and that 'delivers'. It is touted as the very reality of society itself; that is, humans are mere exchangers of goods and services, and not products of socialization.

These theoretical claims of the globalization thesis is summed up succintly by Frankel thus:

> Seeking to rule out all sector-specific intervention is the most effective way of discouraging rent-seeking behaviour. Globalization increases the number of competitors operating in the economy. Not only does this work to reduce distortionary monopoly power in the marketplace (which is otherwise exercised by raising prices), it can also reduce distortionary corporate power in the political arena (which is exercised by lobbying). Most important, new trade theory offers reason to believe that openness can have a permanent effect on a country's rate of growth, not just the level of real GDP. A high rate of economic interaction with the rest of the world speeds the absorption of frontier technologies and global management best practices, spurs innovation and cost-cutting, and competes away monopoly (Frankel, 2000, p. 60).

In the final analysis, the broad picture of the world economy painted by the economic globalization thesis is that of a global marketplace in which goods, services and capital flow across national borders without much problem; a global marketplace where an integrated trade and financial system provides considerable opportunities. This global expansion and spread of market forces, it is pointed out, ensures prudent macroeconomic management.

As Bill Watson points out, 'the race to the bottom – the idea that ever-deepening economic integration or globalization, as it is more popularly known, will cause all the world's countries to become more and more alike in their tax rates, regulation, and public spending – is as close to an article of faith as can be found in the otherwise mainly unbelieving 1990s' (1999, p. ix).

To what extent does this account presented by the economic globalization thesis reinforce the hegemonic credentials of this process as being beyond doubt? As Friedman notes in his description of what happens when countries confront what he terms the Golden Straitjacket:

> Two things tend to happen: your economy grows and your politics shrinks ... The Golden Straitjacket narrows the political and economic policy choices of those in power to relatively tight parameters ... Once your country puts on the Golden Straitjacket, its political choices get reduced to Pepsi or Coke – to slight nuances of tastes, slight nuances of policy, slight alterations in design to account for local traditions, some loosening here or there, but never any major deviation from the core golden rules (1999, p. 87).

It is important at this juncture to touch briefly on a by-product of economic globalization, that is, the cultural dimension. As indicated earlier, the market-driven globalization under discussion is understood as a process that integrates not only national economies and technologies, but also cultures. Perhaps

Tomlinson captures this potential move toward a global culture and society best when he claims that:

> The huge transformative processes of our time that globalization describes cannot be properly understood until they are grasped through the conceptual vocabulary of culture; likewise ... these transformations change the very fabric of cultural experience and, indeed, affect our sense of what culture actually is in the modern world (1999, p. 1).

Writing from a sociological perspective, David Harvey calls attention away from economic determinist definitions and stresses other changes that flow from globalization. For Harvey, globalization has led to 'an intense phase of time-space compression that has had a dis-orienting and disruptive impact upon political-economy practices, the balance of class power, as well as upon cultural and social life' (1989, p. 284). Harvey is very much interested in explaining and understanding the time-space compression in the post-modern condition.

The conceptualization of globalization above suggests a reordering of time and space and gives credence to discussions of 'placelesness' or 'the end of geography'. This is the essence of Eleonore Kofman and Gillian Youngs' explicit point that:

> Globalization is frequently analyzed in terms of flows and networks, whether of media, communications, technology or finance. These flows are assumed to be placeless and disembedded, such that transmission takes place instantaneously and real time obliterates space. The result is an indeterminate juxtaposition of heterogeneous and disparate elements. Places supposedly no longer matter in the operation of global economy and culture. Thus one of the spatial discourses emanating from the West, with universal pretensions akin to the 'end of history' thesis, is the 'end of geography' (1996, p. 7).

This compression and the associated increased interpenetration of national societies have the potential to subvert not only national economies but also national cultures. After all, if globalization results in linking the local to the globa, it is conceivable that social and cultural relations would no longer be seen solely in local terms. Social and cultural relations would be structured and embedded in global networks. This is consistent with Anthony Giddens observation that globalization entails 'intensification of worldwide social relations which link distant localities in such a way that local happenings are shaped by events occurring many miles away and vice versa' (Giddens, 1990, p. 64). This 'compression of the world' aided by technological advances has had an enormous impact at the cultural level leading to a globalization at the cultural level.

The globalized society outlined here increasingly provides grounds for homogenization of societ and cultures. Aided by a global technological and communications revolution, globalization is not only eroding the divide between local, national and international boundaries, it is also helping in the rapid sinking of the world into a global village. This global village, however, is achieved at the expense of the given cultural particularities and specificities of societies, in favour of a global, Western standard. Viewed from this perspective, therefore, cultural globalization is increasingly conceptualized in terms of a worldwide assimilation of cultural values. Such a narrative of globalization tends to gravitate towards uniformity and forces local communities and nations into a global arena which ignores local historical and cultural characteristics.

The need to incorporate culture into analyses of globalization is beyond doubt. What is questionable is the way it is done under the prevailing discourse. Including culture in globalization discourse need not reinforce globalization thesis' homogenizing project, but as a way to call attention to cultural heterogeneity. M. Featherstone critizes current globalization discourse's propensity to ignore this heterogeneous aspect and argues that one consequence of globalization is not just the production of homogeneity but also familiarization with greater diversity, the knowledge that there is an extensive range of cultures (Featherstone, 1993, p. 169). On this basis, Roland Robertson makes the case for culture to be written into analyses of globalization, albeit from a more critical perspective that recognizes the importance of local cultures:

> I believe that it is directly necessary to adopt a cultural focus to what is often called world politics ... We have come increasingly to recognize that while economic matters are of tremendous importance in relations between societies and in various forms of transnational relations, these matters are ... subject to cultural contingencies and cultural coding (1992, p. 4).

In this way, both Robertson and Featherstone provide a postmodern and poststructuralist narrative highlighting cultural oppression as a consequence of globalization.

The advocates of globalization celebrate its transformative potential to bring about modernity, by which they mean the export of Western values and its universalization. The basis of this universal civilizational agenda is the Enlightenment. In this respect, neoliberal market-driven globalization is as much about the spread of universal cultural values (read Western) as it is about trade and finance. The result is the imposition of the hegemonic values and philosophy of the market and social and cultural forms.

Contemporary globalization is therefore linked to modernization, which is synonymous with the Westernization of cultural institutions, beliefs and practices. It incorporates a move away from the local to a highly narrow view of cosmopolitanism as an aspect of a move towards universalism. This suggests a reincarnation of a narrative of Enlightenment principles based on a universal civilization and a common destiny for humankind. Jan Aart Scholte prompts us to take stock of such claims on behalf of globalization by this succinct account:

> In liberal eyes, contemporary globalization offers the prospect of at least fully realizing the promise of modernity. Released from the shackles of traditionalism, colonialism and communism – so this account goes – market forces, electoral multiparty democracy, techno-scientific rationality, national self-determination

and international cooperation have the opportunity to work their complete magic, and to the benefit of all humanity (1996, p. 51).

The significance of this point about prioritizing the universal accounts of modernity is illustrative in Francis Fukuyama's argument that progress is reflected within fairly standard notions of development and modernization, and the political as well as economic relationship of individuals to such ideas. The unifying forces of modernization are presented in almost evangelical terms. Globalization can therefore be seen as the enlargement of Western notions of modernity and progress into a global design for human well-being. Such thought and postulation unfolds without due regard for specific local, national and cultural narratives and experiences.

Moreover, it has been suggested that Western values and practices may flourish within societies, along with an explicit and renewed commitment to extending this to the global level on the assumption that it has universal applicability. Proponents of this view claim that these liberal values set standards for the international community about the nature, consequences and definition of modernity. Such universal, liberal values must of necessity apply not only in Western societies but throughout the globe for the benefit of all humanity. As Gillian Youngs explains, 'Liberal economics and liberal politics are viewed very much as open frameworks offering seemingly endless opportunities for individual material gain and a social sense of self. Quite simply, they are seen as meeting human needs, 'material' and 'non-material' (1996, p. 66). These claims on behalf of globalization are highlighted by David Held et al. in these quotes:

> Such a view of globalzation generally privileges an economic logic and, in its neoliberal variant, celebrates the emergence of a single global market and the principle of global competition as the harbingers of human progress (1999, p. 3). Accordingly, for many neoliberals, globalization is considered as the harbinger of the first truly global civilization, while for many radicals it represents the first global 'market civilization' (1999, p. 4).

Such sweeping generalizations about the universalizing of modernity need to be challenged for their narrow interpretation and failure to accommodate specificities of values, and of development. To uncritically accept the progressive and homogenizing power of the Western narrative of progress and modernity is at best limiting, and at worst, triumphalism at its extreme. Again, Youngs' reminder of the limits of this discourse and Fukuyama's claims for the 'triump of capitalism' is appropriate here:

> It is also associated with universalistic qualities which allow for a sense that questions have been answered, ultimate solutions reached. But, as indicated in this discussion of the thesis, its universalism is highly particularistic. These particularities need to be addressed in spatial and temporal as well as ideological terms. As a discourse of globalization, it is fundamentally state-centric, West-

centric, and presents an overtly idealized view of liberal democracy and economic liberalism, especially concerning their interrelationship (1996, p. 65).

Cultural globalization, carried to its extreme, entails in the final analysis, a potential homogenization of culture. Local cultures get subsumed by the hegemonic Western culture which is the embodiment of globalization. As local cultures come into direct contact with the hegemonic culture inherent in the process of globalization, the possibility that the local will get lost is reinforced. One gets a constant reminder of this in the spread of U.S. popular culture: images, television (CNN), and film:

> Other aspects of national culture gradually succumb, first to the commodification of all social needs, of life-experience itself, and then to globally produced products and services that are distributed around the world. The result is an increasing degree of cultural homogenization or hybridization at the global level. Once commodified, all that comprises national identities is increasingly a caricature of previously meaningful historical phenomena (Gary Teeple, 2000, p. 21).

The globalization of culture under the influence of economic factors and the technology revolution is altering cultural practices and global consciousness. Whether these transformations are beneficial or even democratic is an issue not addressed in the prevailing hegemonic logic of globalization. Benjamin Barber raises these concerns in this perceptive analysis: 'a culture of advertising, software, Hollywood movies, MTV, theme parks, and shopping malls hoped together by the virtual nexus of the information superhighway closes down free spaces, such a culture is unquestionably in the process of forging a global something: but whatever it is, that something is not democratic' (Barber, 1995, p. 276).

A Human Factor Critique

The neoliberal philosophy underpinning globalization outlined in the preceding section relies on a set of assumptions which are suspect at best. One of the most important assumptions draws heavily on the notion of rationality. The crux of this position is that policy is shaped, mediated and formulated by a rational, technocratic core of policy makers with knowledge and expertise. The contributions of Held and McGrew to this debate is worth elaborating on here:

> Adjustment to the international economy – above all, to global financial markets – becomes a fixed point of orientation in economic and social policy. The 'decision signals' of these markets, and of their leading agents and forces, become a, if not the, standard of rational decision-making. This position is linked, moreover, to the pursuit of distinctive supply-side measures – above all, to the use of education and training as tools of economic policy. Individual citizens must be empowered with cultural and educational capital to meet the challenges of increased (local,

national, regional, global) competition and the greater mobility of industrial and financial capital (2000, p. 34).

This position is taken without any reference or regard to the HF attributes of these policy makers. There is a complete failure to recognize the HF dynamic, choosing to emphasis instead a highly technical, apolitical and agency-free approach. Indeed, as Young points out, 'what has always lain at the heart of the liberal endeavour is the claim to be able to uncover a 'universal standpoint' – the 'view from nowhere' – in abstraction from the concrete characteristics of human communities and societies, by reference to a natural level of human existence which is accessible to logical and quasi-scientific modes of reasoning' (Tom Young, 1995, pp. 528-529). This predisposition towards technocracy at the expense of human factor attributes calls into question the fundamental soundness of the economic globalization thesis. If we accept Reich's insights that 'each nation's primary assets will be its citizen's skills and insights' (Reich, 1991, p. 3) in this period of globalization, failing to probe the HF dimension which at core addresses personality traits and human skills constitutes a major oversight and source of controversy in neoliberal thought.

In more ways than one, the economic globalization thesis fails to analyze in great detail one of its supposed core assumptions. While this is by no means fatalistic it, at the minimum, exposes a fundamental gap in their thinking and opens them up to a sustained critique. In so doing, neoliberal philosophy ignores an important dimension which is crucial to an understanding of the nature and impact of globalization: the HF.

Furthermore, the argument that this market fetishism and free competition is either inevitable or desirable or that it can be equated to economic efficiency, welfare and social progress is not a strong one and, again, clearly overstated. Here, mention must be made of Polanyi's critical rebuke of the claims to a pure market system as a 'utopian abstraction' (Karl Polanyi, 1957).

In effect, economic globalization brings into the open the contradiction between the institution of the market and that of the individuals who operate it and the state that regulates it. The market and economic preeminence overshadows the HF. The HF is underestimated because it is relatively intangible while more tangible and measurable economic variables are overstated. Yet some social scientists are beginning to draw attention to the importance of the HF in generating sustained development. People provide the essential human agency which is required for the operation of the market, hence the need to examine the HF basis for efficient market operation.

It is crucially important to stress that the market is an institution and as such functions only in so far as it is regulated formally by the state and informally by humans. These humans, acting as policy makers and as buyers and sellers, play an important role, a role which cannot be divorced from the operation of the market. Indeed, the HF stresses the fundamental importance of humans as neither markets nor any other economic variable by itself can function; it is human beings responding to economic variables that can make or unmake the market.

Adjibolosoo's call for a careful examination of both economic and human factor dynamics is worth recalling here:

> The interaction and simultaneous mixing of these factors [economic and human factors] determines the direction of economic development, creating the stage for either adequate levels of development or underdevelopment. If the mix that results from the interaction is unfavourable to development, the economy will perform poorly, leading to underdevelopment. Alternatively, if both economic and human factors are combined in a favourable fashion, the stage for economic development would be set. Orthodox economic development theory has ignored this fact for many decades, and this neglect has misled many development theorists to propound policies and economic programs that have been ineffective (Adjibolosoo, 1994, p. 27).

As Bonsu notes,

> A fundamental flaw inherent [in the models] is that they all assume the existence of a knowledgeable, supportive and dedicated work force that is anxious to see changes in the system. This work force is also assumed to be willing to use its skills in productive ventures for the benefit of society as a whole and to take business risks by adopting and investing in innovative ideas. Work ethics and development ethos of these kinds do not occur naturally; they are learned responses that can be hindered or facilitated by sociocultural and historical factors (Bonsu, 1999, pp. 146-147).

Without appropriate HF development, market institutions, programs or technology will fail to function effectively. Progress and development, according to Adjibolosoo, 'requires improvements in the simultaneous performance and functioning of its people and institutions in relation to the social, economic, political, cultural and intellectual aspects of human life and activities' (1996, pp. xi-xii). In other words, the efficiency gains and growth attributed to economic globalization will not be recognized without the requisite HF. For Adjibolosoo, 'the attainment of true and lasting progress requires people who have acquired the HF' (Adjibolosoo, 1995).

The HF school of thought articulates a human-centered approach to development through the insertion of the HF as the basis for the 'development of the whole person'. The HF is seen as the sine qua non for the development of the required human qualities for effective performance. The individual cannot perform efficiently and effectively without appropriate and optimal HF. The HF is defined as:

> The spectrum of personality characteristics and other dimensions of human performance that enable social, economic, and political institutions to function and remain functional, over time. Such dimensions sustain the workings and application of the rule of law, political harmony, a disciplined labour force, just legal systems, respect for human dignity and the sanctity of life, social welfare, and so on. As is often the case, no social, economic or political institutions can

function effectively without being upheld by a network of committed persons who stand firmly by them. Such persons must strongly believe in and continually affirm the ideals of society (Adjibolosoo, 1993, p. 142).

As is obvious from this comprehensive and integrated definition, the HF holds the key and provides one of the foundations for realizing the economic globalization thesis' sought after and claimed gains. It provides the foundation of not only the effective institutional structures, both formal and informal for the effective operation of the market, but it also addresses the least developed aspect of the globalization thesis. This least developed aspect is the human qualities of the individuals who establish the rules for the market and who participate in those markets. Without individuals participating in the market, the latter institution has no life of its own. Individuals make institutions: 'the caliber of people every society needs for its survival in a competitive global marketplace are individuals who have acquired the relevant HF. This is what society must be fully committed to' (Adjibolosoo, 1996, p. 26).

HF characteristics such as integrity, accountability and responsibility play a significant role in helping sustain the effective functioning of markets. The HF, so defined and articulated, serves as a catalyst for promoting socioeconomic growth. Harnessing the appropriate HF levels will determine the extent to which socioeconomic and political factors interact to facilitate the development of the market and enhance the spread of economic, social, cultural, and technological change in an equitable and self-sustaining manner.

Another assumption inherent in the economic globalization thesis is the view that the process of globalization facilitates the promotion of a universal set of values. The set of values that are articulated are Western based and reflected in the Enlightenment project of constructing a universal civilization. This raises a dilemma, given the propensity to reify a particular tradition of the Enlightenment project, a universal civilization based on the assumed rationality of individuals unencumbered by parochial interests and values. On the question of how such a project comes to terms with and explains or captures the dynamics of diversity, the globalization thesis is again silent. And here again, the HF school comes to its rescue.

A careful reading of the theoretical basis of the economic globalization thesis reveals its strong links to modernization theory. Indeed, it has been argued that globalization is an extension of modernization. To the extent that this is accurate and globalization is seen as a new variant of modernization theory, there seems to be an in-built bias for a teleological belief in progression from 'traditional to modern', a predetermined outcome/goal. The underlying assumptions are linked to their origins in Western thought, with an emphasis on the principles of the Protestant ethics which, it is argued, have formed the basis of economic, political and social institutions. This same Protestant ethic is presented as a universalizing approach because of its alleged efficiency attributes.

In drawing our attention to this phenomenon, Tettey points out that, 'some of the assumptions on which the paradigm was based, such as the superiority of western cultures, still hold sway across the continent, thereby stifling indigenous cultures and blinding policy makers to the need to engage in decision making that is relevant to the context of their societies' (1995, p. 50). While not calling into question the importance of the Protestant ethic in the development of western institutions, values and ethos, it is equally important to articulate the view that there is considerable specificity in modes of organization in other non-western societies. It is thus critically necessary not to expect these societies to adopt blindly the same western ethos. The point about local and national specificity provides an opening to analyze the specific national characteristics without falling prey to the economic globalization thesis' universalizing tendencies. While the HF approach is designed to recognize the importance of a strong work ethic, it rejects the tendency within the globalization thesis to generalize and universalize. In the HF analysis, local dimensions of change receive attention. The creation of locally specific and conditioned HF attributes of integrity, communal spirit, responsibility, transparency and accountability serves as a catalyst for socioeconomic development.

Conclusion

This introductory chapter on the HF contribution to the globalization debate has necessarily been exceedingly brief. It is meant to set the context for the broader discussion that unfolds in the remaining papers. It teases out for the reader some of the main HF school of thought critique of globalization by providing a framework for conceptualizing and understanding the HF dimension in the globalization process. The subsequent papers pick up on specific issues/problematiques and offer a HF response, challenging us to think of the human dimension to globalization and how to bridge the gap between the different perspectives.

References

Adjibolosoo, Senyo B.-S.K. (ed.) (1996), *Human Factor Engineering and the Political Economy of African Development*, Westport, CT: Praeger.

Adjibolosoo, Senyo B.-S.K. (1995), *The Human Factor in Developing Africa*, Westport, CT: Praeger.

Adjibolosoo, Senyo B.-S.K. (1994), 'The Human Factor and the Failure of Economic Development Policies in Africa', in Fidelis Ezeali-Harrison and Senyo B.-S.K. Adjibolosoo (eds.) *Perspectives on Economic Development in Africa*, Westport, CT and London: Praeger.

Adjibolosoo, Senyo B.-S.K. (1993), 'The Human Factor in Development', *The Scandinavian Journal of Development Alternatives*, 12 (4): 139-149.

Barber, Benjamin (1995), *Jihad vs. McWorld*, New York: Ballatine Books.

Bonsu, Samuel K. (1996), 'The Human Factor in Marketing and Development in the LDCs', in Senyo B.-S.K. Adjibolosoo (ed.) *Human Factor Engineering and the Political Economy of African Development*, Westport, CT: Praeger.

Cerny, Philip G. (2000), 'Political Agency in a Globalizing World: Toward a Structurational Approach', *European Journal of International Relations*, 6 (4): 435-463.

Falk, Richard (1997), 'State of Siege: Will Globalization Win Out?', *International Affairs*, 73 (1): 123-136.

Featherstone, M. (1993), 'Global and Local Cultures', in J. Bird et al. (eds.) *Mapping the Futures: Local Cultures, Global Change*, London: Routledge, pp. 169-187.

Frankel, Jeffrey (2000), 'Globalization of the Economy', in Joseph S. Nye, Jr. and John D. Donahue (eds.) *Governance in a Globalizing World*, Washington, D.C.: Brookings Institution Press.

Friedman, Thomas G. (1999), *The Lexus and the Olive Tree: Understanding Globalization*, Farrar, Straus and Giroux.

Fukuyama, Francis (1992), *The End of History and the Last Man*, London: Penguin.

Giddens, Anthony (1990), *The Consequences of Modernity*, Cambridge: Polity Press.

Harvey, David (1989), *The Condition of Postmodernity*, Oxford: Basil Blackwell.

Held, David and McGrew, Anthony (eds.) (2000), *The Global Transformations Reader: An Introduction to the Globalization Debate*, Cambridge: Polity.

Held, David, McGrew, Anthony, Goldblatt, David and Perraton, Jonathan (1999), *Global Transformations: Politics, Economics and Culture*, Stanford, California: Stanford University Press.

Hirst, Paul and Thompson, Grahame (1996), *Globalization in Question: The International Economy and the Possibilities of Governance*, Cambridge, UK: Polity Press.

Hoogvelt, Ankie (1997), *Globalization and the Postcolonial World*, Baltimore: Johns Hopkins University Press.

Hurrell, Andrew and Woods, Ngaire (1995), 'Globalization and Inequality', *Millennium: Journal of International Studies*, 24 (3): 447-470.

Kofman, Eleonore and Youngs, Gillian (1996), 'Introduction: Globalization – The Second Wave', in Eleonore Kofman and Gillian Youngs (eds.) *Globalization: Theory and Practice*, New York: Pinter, pp. 1-8.

Martin, Hans-Peter and Schumann, Harald (1998), *The Global Trap: Globalization and the Assault on Prosperity and Democracy*, Montreal: Black Rose Press.

McGrew, T. (1992), 'A Global Society', in S. Hall, D. Held and T. McGrew (eds.) *Modernity and Its Futures*, Cambridge: Polity Press.

Nayyar, Deepak (2002), 'Towards Global Governance', in Deepak Nayyar (ed.) *Governing Globalization: Issues and Institutions*, Oxford: Oxford University Press, pp. 3-18.

Polanyi, Karl (1957), *The Great Transformation: The Political and Economic Origins of Our Time*, Boston, MA.: Beacon.

Reich, Robert (1991), *The Work of Nations: Preparing Ourselves for 21st-Century Capitalism*, London: Simon and Schuster.

Robertson, Roland (1992), *Globalization: Society Theory and Global Culture*, Newbury Park, CA.: Sage.

Scholte, Jan Aart (1996), 'Beyond the Buzzword: Towards a Critical Theory of Globalization', in Eleonore Kofman and Gillian Youngs (eds.) *Globalization: Theory and Practice*, New York: Pinter, pp. 43-57.

Soros, George (1998), *The Crisis of Global Capitalism: Open Society Endangered*, New York: Perseus Books.

Stiglitz, Joseph E. (1998), *Towards a New Paradigm for Development: Strategies, Policies and Processes*, Prebisch Lecture Series. UNCTAD.

Teeple, Gary (2000), 'What is Globalization?', in Stephen McBride and John Wiseman (eds.) *Globalization and Its Discontents*, New York: St. Martin's Press.

Teeple, Gary, (1995), *Globalization and the Decline of Social Reform*, Toronto: Garamond Press.

Tettey, Wisdom J. (1995), 'The Media Dimension of the African Development Malaise', in Senyo B.-S.K. Adjibolosoo (ed.) *The Significance of the Human factor in African Economic Development*, Westport, CT: Praeger.

Tomlinson, John (1999), *Globalization and Culture*, Chicago: University of Chicago Press.

Watson, William (1998), *Globalization and the Meaning of Canadian Life*, Toronto: University of Toronto Press.

Young, Tom (1995), 'A Project to be Realised: Global Liberalism and Contemporary Africa', *Millennium: Journal of International Studies*, 24 (3): 527-546.

Youngs, Gillian (1996), 'Dangers of Discourse: The Case of Globalization', in Eleonore Kofman and Gillian Youngs (eds.) *Globalization: Theory and Practice*, New York: Pinter, pp. 58-71.

Chapter 2

Tapping into and Benefiting from the Forces and Agents of Globalization: Creating an Integrated Vehicle for Global Participation and Gain-Sharing

Senyo B.S.-K. Adjibolosoo

Introduction

Given current events, it can be argued that the forces of globalization work to connect and intensify the degree of interconnectedness among different groups of people in the Global Village. Its patterns of interaction and flows know no political boundaries. The escalating pace of global interconnectedness has tremendous implications for the degree of intensity of global interactions among various people through modern transport and telecommunications systems and the diffusion of ideas and information. The volume and frequency of the movement of the factors of production, goods, and services continue to skyrocket.

Held, McGrew, Goldblatt, and Perraton (1999) carried out an extensive research program to discover the extent to which the forces of globalization and regionalization collude to alter the existing economic order of the world, national sovereignty, and internal autonomy.[1] Starting of with their definition for the concept of globalization, Held et al. (1999) noted that:

> Globalization reflects a widespread perception that the world is rapidly being molded into a shared social space by economic and technological forces and that developments in one region of the world can have profound consequences for the life chances of individuals or communities on the other side of the globe. For many, globalization is also associated with a sense of political fatalism and chronic insecurity in that the sheer scale of contemporary social and economic change appears to outstrip the capacity of national governments or citizens to control, contest or resist that change. The limits to national politics, in other words, are forcefully suggested by globalization ... Globalization may be thought of initially as a widening, deepening and speeding up of worldwide interconnectedness in all aspects of contemporary social life, from the cultural to the criminal, the financial to the spiritual (pp. 1 and 2).

To Held et al. (1999, p. 15), therefore, globalization is about the great implications the stretching of social, political, and economic activities exerts on the way of life of a people in their own environment. Globalization reveals the interconnectedness within and across regions of the world due to the growing networks made up of social, economic, and political activities of different groups. It reveals the extent to which the actions of one group of people could either exert significant positive or negative impact on the practices of another group of people. The complete comprehension of the primary sources and implications of globalization requires clearer and deeper insights into the intellectual foundation of the process of globalization and its future trajectories.

Globalization is perceived to be a process or set of processes that alter social relations and transactions in terms of their extensity, intensity, velocity, and impact. As a set of processes, globalization generates networks, interactions, the exercise of power, and massive social, economic, and political activities on transcontinental or interregional basis (Held et al., 1999, p. 16). In addition to these, the moment-by-moment flows and movements of artifacts, human practices, information, and many others are significant aspects of globalization. In most cases, these flows exhibit regularized patterns of global interactions, exchanges, and transfers between people living in different regions of planet earth.

Aninat (2002, p. 1) sees globalization to be the 'process through which an increasingly free flow of ideas, people, goods, services, and capital leads to the integration of economies and societies'. He points out further that the process of globalization continues to forge trade expansion, technological diffusion, continuing migration, the cross-fertilization of cultural traditions, unprecedented volumes of capital flows, and growing information exchange and storage. In his view, therefore, as the process of globalization escalates, the issues of primary concern, yet not central to the mandates of the International Monetary Fund (IMF) and the World Bank, include the environment, labor rights, migration, and human rights.[2]

In light of these perceptions of the concept of globalization, various scholars continue to debate as to whether the process of globalization is a real life phenomenon or an intellectual conception aimed at the achievement of certain objectives of global capitalists and Western leaders (Carr, 1981; Gilpin, 1987; Ruigrok and Tulder, 1995; and Krugman, 1996).

In general, it can be argued that the process of globalization seems to be forcing the whole world into what we now refer to as the *global village*. Writing about the concept of the global village, Adjibolosoo (1998a, pp. 117 and 119) observed:

> As many of us are aware, the world is gradually being transformed into a global village. Technological developments and advancements, improved electronic devices, the electronic mail system and its accessories and well-organized transport and telecommunications systems continually remind humanity that we are more of a well-joined together global village, rather than scattered and severely disjoined countries. Disasters in one country have the tendency of

impacting the economies and lives of other nations ... Humanity is, therefore, reminded day by day by natural and humanly created events (i.e., earthquakes, famine, floods, wars, oil spills, environmental degradation, ethnic strife, etc.) that its many habitats are intricately intertwined. In view of these observations, it can be argued that the realization that naturally and/or artificially created events in one nation can affect every facet of life in other countries creates the feeling that the many habitats of humanity are, therefore, little fragments of a whole. This perception sets in motion an evolutionary process which calls for concerted group (joint) efforts which in turn lead to the creation of various means for either adapting to or solving the problems and dealing with the numerous concerns of all humanity. It is this realization which is shrinking the size of the world in terms of time, space and distance, and hence promoting the development of the global village.

Evident in this quotation is a deeper perception of globalization – a phenomenon through which humans from different parts of the world are doing their best to derive social, economic, and political benefits from all the four corners of the world. As many human events and activities suggest, the available gains to be derived from the process of globalization are of greater benefits to those in the developed rather than the developing countries.

This conclusion underscores the search for answers as to how people of the developing countries could derive real benefits from the forces and agents of globalization. In what follows, I argue that any attempts aimed at improving the chances of these people to benefit from globalization must begin with the channeling of the critical minimum level of human energy and the necessary financial resources into the development of the appropriate HF without which these people would always contribute to but never able to derive any substantial and sustained benefits from contemporary globalization. To fully comprehend this line of thought, it is important that one understands the true meaning of the HF. The HF refers to:

The spectrum of personality characteristics and other dimensions of human performance that enable social, economic and political institutions to function and remain functional, over time. Such dimensions sustain the workings and application of the rule of law, political harmony, a disciplined labor force, just legal systems, respect for human dignity and the sanctity of life, social welfare, and so on. As is often the case, no social, economic or political institutions can function effectively without being upheld by a network of committed persons who stand firmly by them. Such persons must strongly believe in and continually affirm the ideals of society (Adjibolosoo, 1995, p. 33).

This definition for the HF addresses the key issue head on in that it highlights the significance of the HF to human endeavors, efforts, and activities.

This chapter tells a synthesized but compact version of the story of globalization, the forces and agents driving it, implications for governance, and the sovereignty of the nation state in the poor areas of the world. The remainder of this chapter is presented in the following sequence. The next section spells out briefly the sources of contemporary globalization. Next, the views of the various schools of thought on globalization are outlined and briefly discussed. While following this is a presentation on the implications of contemporary globalization from a HF perspective. Finally, there are some concluding remarks and propositions for public policy.

The Sources of Globalization: Orthodox Conceptions

Globalization is a multifaceted phenomenon in that its many tentacles reach out into all areas of human endeavor in both developed and developing countries. For example, in every country, the forces and agents of globalization exert tremendous impact on the cultural, social, economic, political, and educational, life of a people. In every country, each of these aspects of human life is being stretched in both positive and negative ways in most countries – some much more than others. It is, therefore, important that when one presents a discourse on the sources of globalization, one must of necessity highlight the extent to which globalizing forces propel continuing transformation in each of these areas of human endeavor.

The experience of war in ancient times, the evolution of industrialized warfare techniques in the modern era, and the prevailing geopolitical competition have together led to the escalation of the globalization of military conflict and rivalry in the twentieth century. During this era, the world experienced two major wars (i.e., World War I and II) and also a devastating Cold War. During the decades when the Cold War intensified, technological advancement led to the birthing of the Nuclear Age. This era in human history was an epoch dominated with the development and production of lethal weapons of mass destruction. The easy availability of these technological implements of war brought home to most people the reality of how humans could easily annihilate themselves off the face of planet earth. The world military order in terms of its evolution, structure, dynamics, the changing geography, and historical patterns of global military relations have also contributed tremendously to the processes of globalization.

Trade has not only become one of the primary vehicles for moving goods and services from one area to another, but also the means for technology transfer from one location to another. Through trading ventures and activities, domestic markets have become highly interconnected with international and global markets. Strong trade links have made it possible for people – especially from the developed countries – to gain access to almost any commodity they desire. Their supermarkets are always stocked with desirable commodities from all over the world – all year round. From this perspective, people hardly notice the seasonality that used to be the case when certain commodities were in and out of season. That is, scientific and technological advancement has made it possible to bring in commodities from all over the world to the places they are needed on continuing basis. Trade globalization refers to the prevalence of high levels of continuing interregional trade activities that make local markets get stocked with commodities from all over the world. Global trade has, therefore, become a system of regularized but unequal exchange of goods and services among different people's groups from all over the world.

The development and functioning of global financial systems and markets were made possible through the evolution of new financial instruments, the deregulation of national financial markets, growth of international banking, and many other financial institutions. Discussing the phenomenon of the globalization of finance, Häusler (2002, p. 1) observes that:

> During the past two decades, financial markets around the world have become increasingly interconnected. Financial globalization has brought considerable benefits to national economies and to investors and savers, but it has also changed the structures of markets, creating new risks and challenges for market participants and policy makers.

Häusler argues further due to today's forces and agents of financial globalization, it is possible for local manufacturers to borrow funds from elsewhere to finance their domestic business and manufacturing operations. In his estimation, some of the main factors that continue to promote the globalization of finance include the following:

- Advances in information and computer technologies.
- The globalization of national economies.
- The liberalization of national financial and capital markets.
- Competition among the providers of information services.

From Häusler's perspective, therefore, the key participants in the process of financial globalization include investment banks, securities firms, asset management groups, mutual funds, insurance companies, specialty and trade finance companies, hedge funds, and telecommunications, software, and food companies. Häusler (2002, p. 3) points out that in light of the ongoing emergence of these global business organizations:

> Banks have been forced to find additional sources of revenue, including new ways of intermediating funds and fee-based businesses, as growing competition from nonblank financial intermediaries has reduced profit margins from banks' traditional business – corporate lending financed by low-cost deposits – to extremely low levels. This is especially true in continental Europe, where there has been relatively little consolidation of financial institutions. Elsewhere, particularly in North America and the United Kingdom, banks are merging with other banks as well as with securities and insurance firms in efforts to exploit economies of scale and scope to remain competitive and increase their market shares.

Today corporate power and global production networks continue to transform the world. The role of transportation infrastructure, telecommunications systems, and institutions that support global labor markets and the migratory flow of labor are tremendous and expanding. Globalizing forces brought significant changes to different countries of the world in the 1980s and 1990s (Boughton, 2002).

Cultural globalization is centuries old. The issue of instantaneous reporting of news and other events all across the globe simultaneously contributes to the speed of cultural globalization. In business, corporation trademarks have become powerful symbols of cultural globalization. In general, cultural globalization is reflected in the existence of trans-regional, trans-civilization, and transcontinental flows of cultural practices and institutions. The basic vehicle for the globalization of culture is the design and use of corporate infrastructure and business activities. This infrastructure, Held et al. (1999) maintained, made available producers and networks that made use of technological and linguistic infrastructures with the contents they supply. According to Held et al. (1999, p. 370),

> The deepening of global markets for films, recorded music, news and television programming has been accompanied by the development of multinational culture industries, multinational telecommunication corporations and a variety of all alliances and projects that link them to each other as well as to MNCs in computer, software and electronic hardware. To these shifts we can also add the massively expanded infrastructure of international travel. Combined, these infrastructures, irrespective of their cultural consequences or content, have made for large increases in the circulation of ideas, artifacts and images at global and regional levels. They allow for the movement of images and objects over enormous distances with greater intensity, volume and speed. They have made interaction between distant places cheaper and easier. They have also contributed to an increase in the symbolic density of social life. This has significantly altered the institutional context in which more local or national cultural projects of all kinds develop, and the costs and benefits of national policies of cultural autonomy or political control and censorship.

There exist numerous conceptualizations of globalization. Among these, the views of three schools of thought on globalization are prominent. In what follows, the beliefs of each of these schools of thought regarding the concept of globalization are briefly presented.

The Three Schools of Thought on Globalization

As noted in the preceding section, globalization permeates every sphere of human life. Therefore, to fully comprehend its propelling forces and impact, it is imperative to recognize that social, economic, political, cultural, and educational factors play tremendous roles in determining the course of globalization. Over the years various scholars have tried to provide meaningful insights into the causes of globalization. The attempts made by various scholars to isolate the forces of globalization in order to make them easier to comprehend and harness led to the development of different perceptions and views about the meaning of globalization and the factors that drive it. Such discussions are most frequently filled with debates and pronouncements as to what globalization is and whether or not it is intensifying or dissipating over the decades. Though scholars of globalization agree on the intensification of global interconnectedness, heated debates still rage on – ringing loud through the corridors of conference halls and seminar rooms and on the pages of academic journals, magazines, and books regarding how to conceptualize globalization, its causal dynamics, and how to characterize its imminent short-term impact and long-term implications. The participants of these debates are classified into three different schools of thought, namely the *hyperglobalizers, skeptics,* and *transformationalists.* Proponents of each of these schools hold unique and sometimes opposing views on the forces, direction, and implications of globalization for all humanity, especially those in the developing world. In what follows, the views of each of these schools of thought are presented.

The Hyperglobalizers

The Hyperglobalizers[3] believe that contemporary globalization creates a new era in which people from all over the world are continuously subjected to the forces of demand and supply in the global marketplace. In their view, globalization is a reflection of a new era in human history in which 'traditional nation-states have become unnatural, even impossible business units in a global economy' (Held et al., 1999, p. 3). The proponents of this view posit and argue further that in a single global market, competition is the major force that propels human progress. To the hyperglobalizers, therefore, the denationalization of economies through transnational production networks, trade, and finance is a result of economic globalization. In the borderless economy, *the hyperglobalizers* argue, national governments are nothing more than conduits of global capital transfer. They are, however, powerless in most cases as far as the sovereignty of the nation-state is concerned. For example, today, indigenous institutions are being paralyzed by the more powerful local, regional, and global mechanisms of governance. The impersonal market forces are becoming more powerful than states that supposedly wield power – hence losing their relevance, significance, and authority.
    In the views of the hyperglobalizers, therefore,

> The emergence of institutions of global governance, and the global diffusion and hybridization of cultures are interpreted as evidence of a radically new world order, an order which prefigures the demise of the nation-state … the conditions facilitating transnational cooperation between peoples, given global infrastructure of communication and increasing awareness of many common interests, have never been so propitious. In this regard, there is evidence of an emerging 'global civil society', (Held et al., 1999, pp. 4-5).

To the hyperglobalizers, therefore, economic globalization continues to create a new division of labor that leads to the polarization between the winners and losers.

The Transformationalists

The Transformationalists[4] argue that current patterns of globalization are historically unprecedented to such an extent that states and societies all over the world continue to experience tremendous transformations in their attempts to face and also deal with the challenges of an uncertain world. To the transformationalists, the central force behind the rapid social, economic, and political transformations in the world today is globalization. In their views, therefore, the strength and significance of the forces of globalization continue to drag along and also force government leaders and their people to find ways and means whereby they can successfully cope with the forces that continue to erase the glaring distinctions between domestic/internal and international/external affairs.

From this perspective, therefore, the transformationalists maintain that globalization is a powerful force that is continuously shaking the very foundations of social, economic, and political life of people in their own nation-state and/or society. As such, the forces and agents of globalization are now reconstituting and re-engineering the power, functions, and authority of national governments.

The Skeptics

The Skeptics[5], contrary to the views of the hyperglobalizers, maintain that the idea of globalization is a manufactured myth aimed at obscuring the fact that the international economy is being gradually demarcated into three powerful regional blocks within which national governments still continue to be powerful – Europe, Asia Pacific, and North America.[6] Using statistical data on the flow of world trade, investment, and labor for the nineteenth century as the fact on which to predicate their position, the skeptics maintain that current levels of economic interdependence are not necessarily new and as such are not any different from those known in human history. The skeptics believe, therefore, that new trade data do not necessarily reveal or confirm any new trends. To them, the new historical evidence merely substantiates the increased magnitude of internationalization – nothing more than basic interactions between predominantly national economies.

The skeptics argue further that present levels of economic integration are also not ideal. In their view, therefore, the magnitude of contemporary globalization is highly exaggerated. Commenting on the views of the skeptics, Held et al., (1999, p. 5) observed:

> In this respect, the skeptics consider the hyperglobalist thesis as fundamentally flawed and also politically naïve since it underestimates the enduring power of national governments to regulate international economic activity. Rather than being out of control, the forces of internationalization themselves depend on the regulatory power of national governments to ensure continuing economic liberalization.

To the skeptics, therefore, the new evidence on economic activity reveals nothing more than the extent to which the global economy is becoming more and more regionalized into three major financial and trading blocks as noted earlier in this section. Unlike the hyperglobalists, the sceptics maintain that governments still have significant powers and authority and as such, are not necessarily passive victims of internationalization. In conclusion, the sceptics believe that the concepts of cultural globalization and global culture are all techniques of propaganda aimed at ensuring the primacy of the West in world affairs.

Having thoroughly reviewed and analyzed the positions of the three schools of thought on globalization, Held et al., (1999) argued further that regardless of the intensity of the debates among the proponents and members of these schools, their perspectives reveal certain common conclusions about globalization in terms of conceptualization, causal dynamics, socio-economic consequences, implications for state power and governance, and historical trajectory.

Based on the views of the proponents of these schools of thought, Held et al., (1999) derived four types of globalization. These are:

- *Type 1: Thick globalization* (i.e., extensive reach of global networks with high intensity, high velocity, and high impact propensity across all facets of social life).
- *Type 2: Diffused globalization* (a combination of high extensity, high intensity, and high velocity. These, however, exert low impact propensity).
- *Type 3: Expansive globalization* (its characteristics are high intensity of global interconnectedness with low intensity, low velocity, and high impact propensity. Its reach and impact rather than the velocity of flows defines this form of globalization better).
- *Type 4: Thin globalization* (i.e., in this type, high extensity of global networks is not matched by similar intensity, velocity or impact. These are usually low in this case).

Based on the thought experiments used to generate these four types of globalization, the authors point out that such a process could generate a range of other possible outcomes – of unlimited nature. Using these observations, the authors argue that globalization is neither a singular condition nor a linear process. It is, therefore, better to think about it as a diverse phenomenon that encompasses every sphere of human life – social, economic, political, cultural, factor movements, and so on.

Though these observations and conclusions are meaningful, however, our task in the remainder of this paper is not to determine which of these schools of thought are accurate in their views about globalization. Instead, our goal is to point out that regardless of these conceptions about globalization and its infinite number of trajectories, people who dwell in the poor nation states can successfully re-position themselves to benefit from the forces and agents of contemporary globalization. Let us now turn to this view and flesh it out in detail.

Implications of Contemporary Globalization: A Human Factor Persepctive

In this section, I present some ideas regarding whether or not the forces of contemporary globalization could lead to either the demise or enhancement of the authority of those who wield state power and the real welfare of the inhabitants of the developing countries.

The Plight of the Poor and Directions for the Future

Regardless of what one's views are concerning the full implications of contemporary globalization two key questions arise. These are:

- Can one successfully argue that the forces and agents of contemporary globalization impose new limits to what the citizens of the developing countries can do to make a successful transition through its prevailing storms and devastations?
- Is it possible for people living in poor nation states to tame and nurture the forces and agents of globalization to derive the full benefits from their contributions to the various economies of the global village?

To provide answers to these questions, it is imperative to point out that in the presence of severe HF decay (HFD), orthodox policies and programs will never lead to any gains and improvements in the social, economic, and political conditions of the poor people. To Adjibolosoo (2001), HFD:

> Refers to the phenomenon of negative attitudes, behaviors, and actions as evidenced in personal lack of accountability, integrity, honesty, responsibility, and caring. In its severest form, those who suffer from severe HFD engage in attitudes, behaviors, and actions that are contrary to principle-centeredness, moral injunctions, and ethical standards. People who suffer from this syndrom find it too difficult to make their development plans, policies, programs, and projects to function as effectively as expected. This is the case because these people are usually unable to successfully create, administer, and manage the development program. In addition, the people lack the requisite HF to support continuing economic growth and sustained human-centered development. To minimize problems of underdevelopment a people must begin with the appropriate education and training programs aimed at improving the quality of the HF.

Obviously, orthodox development policies and programs that will always fail in the presence of severe HFD include but not limited to the following:[7]

- Opening markets in the developing countries to business organizations from the developed countries so they can increase and channel more foreign direct investment into these ailing economies.
- Intensifying and fostering transnational business activities aimed at the promotion of ongoing economic growth in the poor countries.

- Encouraging the developing countries to produce and export more primary raw materials to the advanced countries.
- Integrating the developing countries into global capital markets and also liberalizing their capital accounts.
- Increasing the stability of financial markets, capital flows, and also stimulating investment and technical progress by promoting financial development in the poor countries.
- Opening the local financial sector in the developing countries to international capital flows and competition.
- Giving full access to the people living in the poor nation states so they can acquire a much larger pool of capital with which to finance their local development.
- Speeding up the process of capital accumulation and the absorption of foreign technologies in the poor nation states.
- Assisting the developing countries to participate in and also sustain stabilization policies and structural adjustment programs.
- Promoting and fostering stable global macroeconomic environment.
- Donating computers to the poor nations and having them properly installed – be they either used or brand new or both. In addition, it is important to increase the activities of the global soup kitchen – providing food aid, disaster relief, and so on.

Fortunately, however, in light of the queries presented above, it is imperative to perceive that there exist two critical activities through which the poor peoples of the world can benefit from globalization. These activities must be engaged in in a simultaneous fashion to successfully harvest the good fruits of globalization.

First, these people must of necessity concentrate on the development and applications of the positive HF. Until this objective is achieved and sustained the people of the developing countries stand little chance of successfully traveling the highway of globalization to wealth-creation through the effective appropriation of their unique niches in the global marketplace. Second, the leaders and intelligentsia of these countries, working hand-in-hand with their citizens, must precisely identify the social, economic, business, and political activities they must engage in to create commodities and services that would command higher marginal utilities and values and, therefore, greater financial remuneration – both at home and abroad.

The people of the poor nation states must of necessity be mindful that when they continue to focus solely on the production of goods and services based on what someone else wants and dictates to them to produce and sell in the global marketplace, they could perpetuate long-term global imbalances in gain sharing. That is, they would not only be saddled with the burden of channeling their scarce resources into producing and exporting raw materials that command little value in the global marketplace, but also be pushed into activities that make them drawers of water and hewers of wood – effectively assisting others to build and furnish their dwellings while they languish at the courts of hunger, disease, and starvation. Worst of all, they would also fail to improve the poor quality of their existing social, economic, and political conditions in the long-term.

Today, people living in different parts of the world and so far away from the location of the headquarters of companies in the industrialized countries are still unable to escape the tentacular influences of the social, economic, and political activities going on in the various marketplaces of the advanced countries and elsewhere in the global village. The people who operate gigantic corporations and their activities directly and indirectly exert tremendous impact on the social, economic, and political lives of the poor. The plight and fate of the poor people, therefore, seem to be intricately and irrevocably intertwined with the fortunes of the owners, shareholders, and stockowners of advanced country corporations. For this reason, the local infrastructure (i.e., communications systems, transportation networks, social organization, indigenous industries, food sources, environment, education, etc.) and economic activities in the poor countries are either being dominated or annihilated. The poor people seem to be losing their abilities and rights to economic survival and self-determination. Similarly, their power base, authority, and the capability to enhance their livelihood and well being are being continuously weakened and eroded away in the long-term.

It is currently evident that for centuries, natural and humanly created phenomena continuously unleash globalizing forces and agents that shape the social, economic, and political lives of all people. The artificial forces are initiated and propelled into motion by and revealed in the attitudes, behaviors, and actions of human beings. Existing national income statistics and financial records of corporations show clearly how the forces and agents of globalization tip the rules and scales of gain sharing in favor of the people in the developed countries. One of the primary reasons why this is the case is that the people of the developed countries do not only lead the way in scientific and technological advancement, but also determine the rules of the game and the positioning of the goalposts.[8] By so doing, the inhabitants of the developing countries do not only feel helpless, but also become convinced that their economies depend solely on those of developed nations and that all they (i.e., the poor people) could do is to straddle along – following the direction of the currents and forces of change released by the people in the advanced countries and doing according to external desires and directives.

After having studied and analyzed the impact of the power, authority, and force of these globalizing agents, it makes intuitive sense to argue that the citizens of the developing countries have no way of successfully participating and benefiting from the forces and agents of globalization. This conclusion, however, does not only create the scary feeling of not being able to improve the conditions of the poor people, but also leads to the perpetual helplessness and hopelessness in these people.

In light of these observations, I argue in the remainder of this paper that through HF development programs, the people of the developing countries stand a greater chance of benefiting from the forces and agents of globalization. It is maintained, however, that calling for, crafting, and signing international conventions alone would do little to improve the ability of people in the developing countries to derive optimal benefits from globalization. Instead, the road to effective emancipation and gain sharing is intensive HF development and strong commitment to getting involved with and engaging people in the developed countries in various human endeavors that could lead to the creation and securing of the sources of the wealth of the poor nation states.

Human Factor Development: The Only Hope and Road to Emancipation and Gain Sharing

Contemporary globalization, though forging tremendous global transformations, will not necessarily lead to the demise of the nation-state and its power – except in the presence of severe HF decay and/or underdevelopment.[9] The various intergovernmental activities, programs, alliances, and the contributions of members of civil society groups aimed at civilizing and democratizing globalization will fail to accomplish their intended objectives if the appropriate HF is non-existent. From the HF perspective, therefore, it is arguable that the strength and quality of democracy depend more on the quality of the HF of all citizens and everyone else involved in the decision-making process than excellent blueprints of plans, policies, programs, and projects. Though these may be useful, their availability or unavailability is not necessarily the primary source of either bad or good governance in the poor nation states. Similarly, the poor people do not lack social, economic, and political institutions. Instead, every institution the poor people need to enhance their welfare already exists in their nation states. Unfortunately, however, these institutions are unable to achieve their intended objectives because those who lead, manage, and run them suffer from severe HF decay and/or underdevelopment.

From the HF perspective, therefore, the view that the quality of democracy is a function of the public's deliberation and decision-making process is misleading and deceptive. Anyone who believes that the process of deliberation and decision-making determines the quality of democracy is oblivious to the view that the primary foundation for the success of any human activities, programs, social networks, and institutions (i.e., religious, political, economic, social, etc.) is the quality of the people's HF (see Adjibolosoo, 1995 and 1998a). Humans create democracy, a social institution. Viewed from this light, democracy has no life of its own. Similarly, the quality, efficiency, and effectiveness of any government are direct reflections of the quality of the HF of the people who form the government and its political bureaucracy by which it operates.

Viewed in this light, it stands to reason that if people in the developing countries are interested in enhancing the quality of the due process of democracy and the performance of governmental bureaucracy in terms of efficiency and effectiveness, they must assist every citizen involved in leadership and other vital positions to acquire and exercise trust, responsibility, accountability, integrity, love, caring, and such like. That is, those who desire to improve the performance effectiveness of the democratic process must focus on how to assist everyone to develop the appropriate HF. By working hard in a step-by-step fashion to accomplish this objective, everything else will fall in place in the long-term.

Unfortunately, however, due to the many decades of wrong thinking and theorizing, people in the developing countries have been misled and also wasted precious time and energy hoping that they could reform their governments and their associated mammoth bureaucracies at various levels. Yet regardless of the countless number of attempts they made in the past and still continue to make today to bring *democratization and good governance* to the developing countries, they have always failed to comprehend that to be successful in reforming any institutions in the developing countries, they must first help these people to improve the quality of their HF without which none of their programs would work as effectively as the people have always hoped for.

In light of this reality, neither the pursuit of *laissez faire* economic policies, programs, and projects nor democratization nor empowerment nor girl-child education would enhance the gain people could receive from globalization in the developing countries. Instead, it is the quality of the HF of people that makes the primary difference as far as welfare enhancement is concerned. That is, in the presence of well-developed HF, the people of the developing countries would be better prepared to tame and nurture the forces of globalization to their best advantage. based on this conclusion, Wriston's (1974) perspective on the significance of the quality person in running programs, institutions, cities, and business ventures is right on. Writing on this issue, Wriston (1974, p. 16) observed: [10]

> I believe that the only game in town is the personnel game. If you have the right person in the right place, you don't have to do anything else. If you have the wrong person in the job, there's no management system known to man than can save you ... Basically, if the fellow you have running London is a highly intelligent and charged up person, with brains and judgment, he will do a fantastic job. If he is dumb and lazy, you can write him all the memos you want and nothing will happen.

Those who recognize and understand better this view have a much greater chance of positioning their plans, policies, programs, and projects to achieve their intended objectives than their counterparts who do not. Without any doubts and questions, Wriston's (1974) view reveals that in the absence of the right caliber of people who are willing and ready to take charge and function effectively and efficiently, no institutions, organizations, businesses, cities, societies, and nations will function and remain functional as expected over time. Truly, it is people who are able to successfully create, implement, establish, and operate *responsibility centers* that make sustained progress happen in the nation state.

Setting Up and Operating Responsibility Centers

In the search for techniques and procedures through which the poor people could tame and benefit from the forces and agents of globalization, it is imperative to recognize that a certain preliminary program of activities has to be initiated and implemented. First and foremost, it is critical to set up appropriate educational and training programs aimed at developing the positive HF. The individuals in charge of the whole operation must select people with well-developed HF and set them in unique groups – *responsibility centers* (RCs). Members of each group must elect one of their own to serve as the leader and/or manager. Each of these groups must be viewed as a vital nerve center for the whole nation. A responsibility center is usually constituted of a team of quality, knowledgeable, and skilled people with a set person who is fully responsible for all the activities of the group (see Anthony and Herzlinger, 1975, pp. 17-18). Within each responsibility center are units, sections, departments, branches, and divisions. Members of each of these responsibility centers are assigned specific tasks that must be performed simultaneously toward the accomplishment of the intended goals and objectives. Anthony and Herzlinger (1975, p. 17) noted that:

> Except for those at the bottom of the organization, these responsibility centers consist of aggregations of smaller responsibility centers. The entire organization is itself a responsibility center. One function of top management is to plan, coordinate, and control the work of all these responsibility centers; this is the management control function.
>
> In the developing country set up, a specific responsibility center must concentrate on and accomplish critical objectives that are required for the whole population to benefit from the forces and agents of globalization. Whatever the members of each responsibility center do must be viewed as necessary but not sufficient alone in itself for the whole nation to successfully harness and civilize the forces of globalization. It is important that the overall objectives of the nation state be outlined and popularized right from the outset by the leaders and people acting together as one unit.
>
> These responsibility centers must concentrate on social, economic, and political activities through which the citizens of the nation state could create commodities and services of tremendous social, economic, business, and political value to their own citizens and people from other nations – both developed and developing countries.

At the initial stages, the pursuit of these activities must be based on *the principle of least cost and locally available technology. Appropriate, affordable, and sound foreign scientific practices and technology must be brought in as the need arises.* The primary reason is that such activities would be easier for the inhabitants of the developing countries to engage in without having to be faced with tremendous costs and advanced technologies they may neither afford nor successfully use.

Using these conclusions as springboards and also taking into account the social, economic, and political activities in the global economy, the people of the poor nation states could develop and engage in unique value creating activities and services in which they process tremendous comparative advantage. Areas of great significance in the creation and development of responsibility centers could include but not limited to the following:

- Developing the appropriate human factor.
- Producing staples and other products for domestic consumption.
- Selecting and developing indigenous technology foundries charged with the primary task of evolving relevant scientific and technological methods and also applying their inventions and innovations to produce goods and services to meet local needs in the short-term and external demand in the long-term (see details in Adjibolosoo, 1996, pp. 39-59).
- Getting into key international sporting and athletic events (e.g., golf, basketball, baseball, cricket, soccer, football, etc.) and competing effectively so as to share in the windfall gains associated with these activities.
- Initiating and promoting value creating cross-cultural touristic activities and successfully marketing these to the local people as well as global tourists.
- Forging internal and external piecemeal integration (see Adjibolosoo, 1998b, pp. 131-150).
- Creating, for example, documentary films on indigenous music, drama, drumming, and dancing and making these products available to everyone who desires it in the global marketplace.
- Setting up and operating local and national dance troupes whose services would be patronized locally and internationally.
- Developing social, economic, and political infrastructure required for progress to take place in the long-term.

However, a people's ability to tame the forces and agents of globalization is determined by the extent to which they can effectively and efficiently apply their HF to create, develop, perfect, and use social, economic, business, political, and environmental action programs – cultural practices – to their best advantage. The achievement of this objective requires knowledge, understanding, and wisdom that are necessary for the initiation and establishment of certain areas of excellence (i.e., the actual comparative advantages enshrined in the members of each responsibility center) that would be of tremendous interest to the people of the advanced countries.[11] Unfortunately, however, in the midst of severe HF decay, the people of the developing countries stand to lose from the forces and agents of globalization in the long-term.

Concluding Remarks and Propositions for Policy

As far as the social, economic, and political problems of the poor people are concerned, whether or not one believes in the reality of the forces and agents of contemporary globalization is irrelevant. One thing that is true, though, is that the poor people continue to suffer from hunger, starvation, disease, hopelessness, and helplessness. The social, economic, and political forces that shape life in the advanced countries also continue to impact the welfare of the poor people in the developing countries. Since these forces seem to be acting like unstoppable military troupes that are on the march to conquer and subdue enemy forces, the poor people, given the current condition and plight of their HF, cannot easily halt the moment-by-moment advances of the agents and forces of globalization.

Fortunately, however, the poor people can develop the requisite ability to harness, tame, and harvest the fruits of contemporary globalization. The way to go about doing so is to begin with appropriate programs aimed at continuing development of the positive human factor.

In addition to human factor development, the pursuit and incorporation of the following testable propositions into policies, plans, programs, and projects is imperative. Deeper insights into the significance of each of these propositions would lead the poor people to build their own unique ladders through which they can also climb to the top of the tree of contemporary globalization to harvest some of its desirable fruits to enhance their social, economic, and political welfare.

- Without making the conscious and calculated effort to channel sufficient human energy and financial resources into the development of the positive human factor, people in the poor nation states stand a greater chance of losing out as the forces and agents of contemporary globalization slip deeper into and permeate their social, economic, and political activities.
- By not blindly following policy and program recommendations of the people from the advanced countries but thoroughly studying, investigating, and understanding their long-term implications, the inhabitants of the developing countries could successfully discover their real strengths and weaknesses and then act together to discover and work to their greatest advantage the economic and business activities of those in charge of their responsibility centers.
- No people from the poor nation states can derive any benefits from the forces and agents of globalization by being forced to serve as conduits for what goes on in terms of social, economic, and political progress in the developed nations. Instead, the people who stand the greater chance of successfully transitioning through the transformative waves of globalization are those who relentlessly hone their positive human factor as they work to master the fundamentals of how to compete effectively in the global marketplace.
- Those who know precisely what their needs, strengths, and weaknesses are and are willing and ready to work toward the transformation of their weaknesses into strengths and lacks into plenty have the capability to work around their existing hindrances and difficulties to improve their own social, economic, and political life.

By incorporating these propositions into public policy – social, economic, and political – and doing exactly as they suggest, the leaders of the developing countries stand a much better chance of taking their nations on to higher levels of progress over time. They would also be positioned to successfully harvest some of the fruits of contemporary globalization. Any other development activities that fail to take the wisdom embedded in each of these propositions into account would lead to long-term failures as have been the real life experience from the distant past to the present. In truth, the inability to focus on and develop the positive human factor is an excellent recipe for continuing retrogression and total failure in the long-term. In this regard, there would be little hope for the poor people as far as deriving benefits from globalization is concerned.

Notes

[1] The inspiration for this chapter is drawn from my detailed review of the world of Held et al., (1999). In this paper, I drawn extensively on the research of these scholars as far as the meaning of globalization is concerned. Moreover, their research, a synthesized multidisiplinary work, presents some interesting seminal ideas on the concept, forces, and impact of globalization.

[2] See other definitions for globalization in Modelski (1972); Giddens (1990); Ohmae (1990 and 1995); McFail and Goldeier (1992); Wriston (1992); Redwood (1993); Gill (1995); Guehenno (1995); Hirst and Thompson (1996); Amin (1997); and Rosenau (1997).

[3] Some of the leaders of this school of thought on globalization include Gray (1998); Greider (1997); Albrow (1996); Strange (1996); Cos (1996 and 1997); Gill (1995); Ohmae (1995); Guehemno (1995); Wriston (1992); Reich (1991); Luard (1990).

[4] Contributors to this school of thought on globalization include Giddens (1990); Rosenau (1990); Scholte (1993); Cammileri and Falk (1992); Linklater and MacMilan (1995); Castells (1996); and Sessen (1996).

[5] Among the scholars who advocate the skeptical thesis are: Weiss (1998); Hirst (1997); Boyer and Drache (1996); Hirst and Thompson (1996); Krugman (1996); Ruigrok and Tulder (1995); Gilpin (1987).

[6] It is not surprising to recognize that Africa is not listed in this enumeration. This omission is a precise illustration of the belief most Western scholars, politicians, businessmen and women hold as to the irrelevance of the African continent in terms of the contributions Africans can make to the process of globalization. Worst of all, it also reveals the unspoken conclusion that Africans are unable to derive any significant benefits from globalization.

[7] These policy and program suggestions appear in Aninat (2002) as well as in many neoclassical economic discussions on the role of free markets in economic development. Unfortunately, the developing countries have tried most of these policies and programs with dismal results to date. That is, these policies and program have led to absolutely no known sustained positive results as far as the social, economic, and political conditions in the poor countries are concerned.

[8] These changes are usually initiated in the foreign policies of the developed countries. In certain cases, policy changes desired by the advanced countries are forced on the developing countries through tied aid programs, the voices of civil society leaders and their members, bilateral and multilateral agreements, the crafting and signing of international conventions, and so on. See examples of such international conventions in US Congress (1991); UN (1998); UNEP (1993); UNFPA (1994); and UNHCR (1993 and 1994).

[9] As I proceed to discuss ideas regarding how the poor people could benefit from globalization, I must point out that I do not believe that in the post-modern era knowledge and science will maintain and even strengthen the role of the nation state in world competition and global politics. Whether or not the nation state will fight for the control of information as they did in the past to gain control over territories as argued by Lyotard (1984, p. 5) is irrelevant. I am, however, convinced that in the presence of severe HF decay, a people's ability to derive gains from globalization will not be enhanced by merely acquiring more knowledge/information and the necessary skills to practice science. In the past, it was this view and many others like it that led to the design of misguided educational

programs for the poor people – especially those in African countries. Over six decades now, people from the developing countries still reap the negative fruits of and also suffer from the outcomes of the policies aimed at transporting educational and training programs from the advanced countries. Rather than channel their scarce resources into pursuing knowledge acquisition and science at this point in time, I argue that the people from the developing countries would be far better off if they concentrate on HF development at the present moment. Over time, a people with well-developed HF would be capable of generating, learning, acquiring, and borrowing the necessary information they need to improve their standard of living and welfare. Above all, a people who possess the necessary HF will also have the required capability and knowledge to practice and benefit from science.

[10] See Walter Wriston, Chairman of the Board and Chief Executive Officer of Citicorp, the holding company for First National City Bank. An interview reported in *The Harbus News* (April 4, 1974) (quoted in Anthony and Herzelinger, 1974, p. 16).

[11] This view does not endorse the believe that the poor people must engage in and tie their scarce resources to the production of raw materials to service industrial and economic activities in the advanced countries. Instead, through their own responsibility centers, the people from the poor nation states must identify activities and services they believe they do not only have resources to engage in, but also have the capability to effectively compete against their counterparts in the developed countries. When they are successful in doing so, they would avoid the danger of being forced into business and economic activities that have limited potentials for the creation of significant values added.

References

Adjibolosoo, Senyo B.-S.K. (1995), *The Human Factor in Developing Africa*, Westport, CT: Praeger.

Adjibolosoo, Senyo B.-S.K. (1996), 'Enhancing the Efficiency and Performance of Indigenous Industrial Technology Transfer Foundries and Centers', *Review of Human Factor Studies*, 2 (2): 39-59.

Adjibolosoo, Senyo B.-S.K. (1998a), *Global Development the Human Factor Way*, Westport, CT: Praeger.

Adjibolosoo, Senyo B.-S.K. (1998b), 'Achieving a Cooperative Integration in Sub-Saharan Africa: A Voluntary Piecemeal Harmonization Process', in Senyo B.-S.K. Adjibolosoo and B. Ofori-Amoah (eds.) *Addressing Misconceptions About Africa's Development: Seeing Beyond the Veil*, Lewiston: The Edwin Mellen Press, pp. 131-150.

Albrow, Martin (1996), *The Global Age*, Cambridge: Polity Press.

Amin, Samer (1997), *Capitalism in the Age of Globalization*, London: Zed Press.

Aninat, Eduardo (2002), 'Surmounting the Challenges of Globalization', *Finance and Development*, 39 (1): 4-7.

Boughton, James M. (2002), 'Globalization and the Silent Revolution of the 1980s', *Finance and Development*, 39 (1): 40-43.

Boyer, Robert and Drache, Daniel (eds.) *States Against Markets*, London: Routledge.

Cammilleri, Joseph A. and Falk, Jim (1992), *The End of Sovereignty? The Politics of Shrinking and Fragmented World*, Aldershot: Edward Elgar.

Carr, Edward H. (1981), *The Twenty Years Crisis 1919-1939*, London: Papermac.

Castells, Manuel (1996), *The Rise of the Network Society*, Oxford: Blackwell.

Cox, Robert (1997), 'Economic Globalization and the Limits to Liberal Democracy', in A. G. McGrew, (ed.) *The Transformation of Democracy? Globalization and Territorial Democracy*, Cambridge: Polity Press.

Cox, Robert (1996), 'Globalization, Multilateralism and Democracy', in Robert Cox (ed.) *Approaches to World Order*, Cambridge: Cambridge University Press.

Giddens, Anthony (1990), *The Consequences of Modernity*, Cambridge: Polity Press.

Gill, Stephen (1995), 'Globalization, Market Civilization, and Disciplinary Neoliberalism', *Millennium*, 24.

Gilpin, Robert (1987), *The Political Economy of International Relations*, Princeton: Princeton University Press.

Goldeier, James M. and Michael McFaul (1992), 'A Tale of Two Worlds: Core and Periphery in the Post-Cold War Era', *International Organization*, 46.

Gray, John (1998), *False Dawn, The Delusions of Global Capitalism*, New York: New Press.

Greider, William (1997), *One World, Ready or Not: The Manic Logic of Global Capitalism*, New York: Simon and Schuster.

Guehenno, Jean-Marie (1995), *The End of the Nation-State*, Minneapolis: University of Minnesota Press.

Haüsler, Gerd (2002), 'The Globalization of Finance', *Finance and Development*, 39 (1): 10-12.

Held, David, McGrew, Anthony, Goldblatt, David and Perraton, Jonathan. (1999), *Global Transformations: Politics, Economics and Culture*, Stanford, California: Stanford University Press.

Hirst, Paul and Thompson, Grahame (1996), *Globalization in Question: The International Economy and the Possibilities of Governance*, Cambridge: Polity Press.

Linklater, Andrew and MacMillan, John (1995), 'Boundaries in Question', in John MacMillan and Andrew Linklater (eds.) *Boundaries in Question*, London: Francis Pinter.

Lyotard, Jean-Francois (1984), *The Postmodern Conditions: A Report on Knowledge*, Minneapolis: The University of Minnesota Press.

Luard, Evan (1990), *The Globalization of Politics*, London: Macmillan.

Modelski, George (1972), *Principles of World Politics*, New York: Free Press.

Ohmae, Kenihi (1995), *The End of the Nation State*, New York: Free Press.

Ohmae, Kenichi (1990), *The Borderless World*, London: Collins.

Redwood, John (1993), *The Global Marketplace*, London: HarperCollins.

Reich, Robert (1991), *The Work of Nations: Preparing Ourselves for Twenty-First Century Capitalism*, New York: Simon and Schuster.

Rosenau, James (1997), *Along the Domestic-Foreign Frontier*, Cambridge: Cambridge University Press.

Ruigrok, Winfred and van Tulder, Rob (1995), *The Logic of International Restructuring*, London: Routledge.

Sassen, Saskia (1996), *Losing Control? Sovereignty in an Age of Globalization*, New York: Columbia University Press.

Scholte, Jan Aart (1993), *International Relations of Social Change*, Buckingham: Open University Press.

Strange, Susan (1996), *The Retreat of the State: The Diffusion of Power in the World Economy*, Cambridge: Cambridge University Press.

United Nations (1988), *Human Rights: A Compilation of International Instruments*, New York: United Nations.

UNEP (1993), *Report of the United Nations Conference on Environment and Development*, – Volumes 1, 2, and 3, New York: United Nations.

UNFPA (1994), *The State of the World's Population*, New York: United Nations Fund for Population Activities.

UNHRC (1993), *Populations of Concern of Concern to UNHCR*, Geneva: United Nations High Commission for Refugees.

UNHRC (1994), *The State of the World's Refugees: The Challenge of Protection*, New York: Penguin.

US Congress – Office of Technology Assessment (1991), *Arms Trade 1991*, Washington, DC: USGPO.

US Department of Commerce (1972), *Historical Statistics of the United Nations: From Colonial Times to 1970*, Washington, DC: US Department of Commerce.

Weiss, L. (1998), *State Capacity: Governing the Economy in a Global Era*, Cambridge: Polity Press.

Wriston, W. (1992), *The Twilight of Sovereignty*, New York: Charles Scribners Sons.

PART II:
GLOBALIZATION, THE HUMAN FACTOR AND CULTURAL IDENTITIES

Chapter 3

Integrating Culture into Globalization and Development Theory: Towards a Human Factor Approach

Joseph Mensah

Introduction

The inadequate treatment of culture in the prevailing narratives on globalization and development is the concern of this paper. The rise of market-oriented global networks has augmented the ability of advanced capitalist nations and their multinational corporations to subjugate the countries of the developing world. Indeed, the little economic 'power' that the developing countries wielded prior to the *con*temporary globalization has all but dissipated.

As social scientists strive to account for the development challenges wrought by globalization upon the nations of the South, the emphasis has, until quite recently, been on the intricacies of political economy, with little or no attention paid to the cultural dimensions of the issues involved. However, in addition to their overarching capacity for economic, political, and military domination, the West exercises tremendous hegemonic control in the global production of knowledge, meanings, and ideas, and, consequently, has the ability to transform the worldviews of non-Westerners.

To better understand the impact of globalization on 'Third World' development, we need to go beyond the economic and geopolitical manipulations of the West, and probe into how the non-West has been compelled to participate in an epistemology that prioritizes western knowledge and culture, and the attendant commodity fetishism, over its own knowledge base and cultural traditions. Arguably, more than the production and consumption of material goods, it is in the creation of knowledge that the West seeks to sustain its hegemonic grip on 'Third World', under a purportedly value-neutral development discourse. This chapter examines the concepts of globalization, development, culture, and the human factor, and explores their subtle and not-so-subtle imbrications. It also shores up the Eurocentrism in the prevailing globalization development thinking, and argues, from the human factor perceptive, for the insertion of culture in a (post)development theory. Of the four major concepts mentioned so far – culture, development, globalization, and the human factor – the latter deserves immediate clarification, as it is relatively new in the development literature. The human factor denotes positive personality attributes such as honesty, concern for others, and perseverance, the presence of which allows societies to function and progress over time. The human factor concept would be further elucidated in due course, for now let us turn our attention to globalization, a term that is known to almost everybody except the 'experts'.

Understanding Globalization

While global analysis is nothing new in academic discussions, especially among geographers, globalization entered popular imagination in the 1960s when the Canadian media scholar Marshall McLuhan coined the term "global village" in his *Understanding Media* (1964). 'In its relatively short career', writes John Tomlinson (1997, p. 22), 'globalisation has accumulated a remarkable string of both positive and negative connotations without having achieved a particularly clear denotation'. The phenomenon has convoluted implications for individuals and groups across the globe. It affects the (Nederveen Pieterse, 1995, p. 45). Indeed, as Frederic Jameson (2001, p. xi) conjectures, 'there is something daring and speculative, unprotected, in the approach of scholars and theorists to this unclassifiable topic, which is the intellectual property of no specific field'.

Globalization is broader than mere internationalization. It entails deeper integration of societies, and has a significant interchange with development theory and the ongoing cultural turn. To some analysts, globalization is really nothing new (Hirts and Thompson, 1996); to others it is imperialism in disguise (Tomilinson, 1995, p. 175), or the return of modernization in a new dress (Nederveen Pieterse, 1995). Still to people like the late Vincent Tucker (1997, p. 15) the concept is just another 'quasi-geographic metaphor that needs to be unpacked' for in the real world, 'there is no such place as global ... there is no disconnected global sphere floating above or outside 'local', 'traditional', or 'indigenous' societies'.

Notwithstanding the proliferation of spatial metaphors and geographic terms (e.g., global village, global neighbourhood, distanciation, etc.) in the discussion of globalization, and perhaps because of the time-space compression associated with the phenomenon, some analysts are asserting the 'end of geography'. Without a doubt, technological innovations in transport and communication and the global marketing of standardized goods seem as if they might dissolve spatial variations and wash away the distinctiveness of places to create *placelessness*, to borrow Ralph's (1976) term for a moment. However, despite its homogenizing effects, differences between places are still a significant component of globalization. As Dicken (2000, p. 316) points out, '[t]he particular character of individual countries, of regions and localities interacts with the larger-scale general processes of change to produce quite specific outcomes'. Similarly, in his spirited attack on the growing emphasis on the homogenizing, (or westernizing) effects of globalization, Appadurai (1990, p. 328) noted that '[w]hat these arguments fail to consider is that at least as rapidly as forces from various metropolises are brought into new societies they tend to become indigenized in one or another way'.

In the context of development discourse, it bears stressing that neither the benefits nor the risk of globalization are evenly distributed; they vary from place to place, and on the basis of gender, age, race, and other social locations (Massey, 1994). Ironically, the space-time compression and the enhanced mobility of people and products across the globe have somehow added to the significance of place and geography. Knox and Marston (1998, pp. 16-17) encapsulate this point in the following words:

> The more universal the diffusion of material culture and lifestyles, the more valuable regional and ethnic identities become ... The faster the information highway takes people into cyberspace, the more they feel the need for a subjective setting ... that they can call their own. The greater the reach of transnational corporations, the more easily they are able to respond to place-to-place variations in labour markets and consumer markets ... The greater the integration of transnational governments and institutions, the more sensitive people have become to localised cleavages of race, ethnicity, and religion.

The multidimensional nature of globalization makes it not only difficult to find a logical point of departure for its analysis, but also to even come up with an all-inclusive definition. Consequently, after defining the concept as 'the rapidly developing process of complex interconnections between societies, cultures, institutions and individuals worldwide', Tomlinson (1997, p. 22) took pains to remind reader that his definition is sufficiently general, abstract, and flexible enough to capture much of the concept's complexities. The multidimensional and interactional nature of globalization resonates through the work of McGrew (1992, p. 23) who defines the concept as ' ... the process by which events, decisions, and activities in one part of the world can come to have significant consequences for individuals and communities in quiet distant parts of the globe'.

A recurrent theme in the discussion of globalization is the assertion that much of the ongoing stretching and deepening of global processes occurs in the sphere of economics, based on ideologies and configurations of production and consumptions orchestrated by multinational corporations (Knox, 1995, Dicken, 2000). The work of Knox (1995, pp. 4-5) indicates that the automobile industry – and to some extent, the pharmaceutical and steel industries – has been at the forefront of this economic globalization, 'with a history of translational joint ventures, personal exchanges, cross-licensing research, and production partnerships' (p. 4).

According to Clairmont (1997, p. 16; quoted in Sutcliffe, 1999, p. 145) 'the share of transnational capital in the world GDP grew from 17% in the middle of the 1960s to 24% in 1982 to reach more than 30% in 1995. Similarly Reich (1991, 114 quoted in Sutcliffe 1999, p. 145) notes that 'in 1990 more than half of America's import, by value, were simply the transfers of such goods and related services within global corporation'. And after comparing the GNP of some nations and the sales of leading transnational corporations, Knox and Agnew (1998, p. 42) noted that:

> ... all of the top 50 transnational corporations – including the likes of Exxon, General Motors, Ford Motor Company, Matsushita Electronics, IBM, Unilever, Philips, ICI, Union Carbide, ITT, Siemens and Hitachi – carry more economic clout than many of the world's smaller LDCs [Less Developed Countries], while the very biggest transnationals are comparable in size with national economies of countries like Greece, Ireland, Portugal, and New Zealand.

Even though there are indications, at least from the work of Sutcliffe (1997) and Glyn and Sutcliffe (1992), that some of the claims and empirical evidence on the extent of economic globalization and the power of transnational corporations have been exaggerated, few will deny that there has been heightened integration of the global, since about the mid-1980s, to date it conservatively.

The increasing economic integration has led to a 'jumbled up world' (Tucker, 1997, p. 16) in which the 'Third World' has appeared in the 'First World' and *vice versa* (Dirlik, 1994, p. 352), making it difficult to theorize about the interconnections between globalization, development, and culture. Indeed, the much touted cultural turn, and the attendant ascendancy of post-modern, poststructural, post-colonial, and post-development discourses, is keenly associated with the 'crisis in understanding' engendered by globalization (Tucker, 1997, p. 16). What exactly are the cultural dimensions of globalization? Can we rightly talk of an emerging global culture? Can we realistically disentangle culture from the political, economic, social spheres of life in this discussion? What are the pros and cons of globalization for the development of the 'Third World'? We examine some of these issues in the subsequent sections.

Development in the Age of Globalization

Like globalization, development is a multidimensional concept that denotes different things to different people. As Tucker (1997, p. 4) puts it: 'Development does not mean the same thing for the director of the International Monetary Fund as for a Zambian worker who has had his wages reduced and currency devalued; it does not mean the same for the Iranian Muslim as for the employee of USAID; nor for a Tibetan monk and a Peking government official'. Development is neither a transcultural concept nor a natural process with universal validity. The work of Rist (1990, p. 12) even suggests that there is no a corresponding or equivalent concept to development in some non-Western languages.

Over the years, the study of development has been highly Eurocentric; for the most part, Western views have been presented, either consciously or unconsciously, as though they were universal. This trend has undermined any polycentric analysis of the concept. Not surprisingly, critics such as (Escobar (1995), Tucker (1997, 1999) and Sardar (1997) see development as part of the western 'social imagery' and ideology that seeks to proselytize the superiority of western science and culture and the inferiority of non-Western societies – from which the west hardly admits it has anything worthwhile to learn, notwithstanding the non-Western roots of many of the Western cultural and scientific innovations.

In its most common usage, development refers to a collection of attributes related to modernization, economic growth, material production, and advances in science and technology, together with their corresponding socio-cultural and political changes. In keeping with its positivist tradition, various statistical measures of production, energy consumption, urbanization, population growth, income, education etc., – the so-called development indicators – are used to establish the level of development among nations. However, at a higher, and arguably better, level of abstraction, development connotes a situation where people have control over their destinies and histories under conditions of their own choosing. Clearly, by this conceptualization, no society is really developed, or worse still 'no society has ever engaged in a process of development' (Lee, 1986, p. 103). Yet development is commonly used to ascertain the conformity of non-Western societies to the socio-economic structures and worldviews of the West. We thus find Escobar arguing in his *Encountering Development* (1995) that development discourse is just another chapter of the long history of the hegemonic expansion of western knowledge.

There is now a growing literature of post-development discourse, from the likes of Vandana Shiva, Ziauddin Sarder, Jan Nederveen Pieterse, and Robert Biel, which sees development as a flawed, Eurocentric concept in need of deconstruction. These critics caution us to be vigilant of the unequal power relations in the production of knowledge that undergird much of the categorizations, binary oppositions, Othering, and totalizing tendencies of *con*temporary development theory. Even the basic conception of time in the development discourse seems to be colonized by the West's power to define. As Sarder (1999, p. 46) points out: 'The present of the non-West is the past of the developed world. The future of the developing countries is the present of the West. When the non-West reaches the point of arrival where it becomes 'developed', it has already become the past of the West [Thus] ... with a single definitional category, the West can, and indeed has, written off the past, present and the future of the non-West'.

Clearly, the 'development race' is so fixed, to put it bluntly, that the non-West can never catch-up with the West. Overpowered by the hegemonic discourse of the west, non-Western societies are invariably stunted in their ability to articulate their own intellectual perspectives (Tucker, 1999, p. 13), thereby reinforcing the common misconceptions and false binaries of First/Third Worlds; modern/traditional societies; and core/peripheral regions. Quite disturbingly, Eurocentrism and its attendant deployment of value-loaded binary opposites are rampant among non-Western intellectuals, many of whom almost always use yardsticks of the West to assess socio-economic and political progress in their own societies (Sardar, 1999).

Over the years, as with globalization, development theory has overemphasized the economic, and to some extent the political, dimensions of life, and relegated the spheres of culture to the background. Development for many in not only the West but also the developing world is primarily an economic concept, characterized by industrialization, technological advances in production, and increases in economic variables such as annual growth rates and GNP per capita. The fact that the development blueprints, or the so-called D-Plans, of most developing countries are dominated by technical economic issues, framed in the discourse of development economics, attests to the privileged rank of economics in development thinking.

This economic tilt associates development with modernization, a movement away from non-Western values, generally considered inferior, to a perceived higher state characterized by Western values, which are deemed superior. Like development, modernization has been conceptualized as a unilinear, Eurocentric concept that feeds into the fetishism of Western values and denigrates resistance and counter-discourse from the non-West, under the rubric of 'traditional' or 'primitive'. The implication of the modernization project is that the developing world has little or no real history or culture of its own, and as Blaut (1992) argues, this is a classic example of a racist view of the world. The modernization school of thought posits that the developing world would sooner or later modernize/develop through the magic of trickle-down economics, if it follows the path prescribed by the West under the auspices of the United States and its allies.

However, after nearly three decades of development planning and practices based on the tenets of this 'pervasive economism' (Gidwani and Sivaramakrishnan 2003, p. 187), many developing countries are hardly better off today than before: malnutrition, poverty, unemployment, and socio-economic inequality remain prevalent across Africa, Asia, and Latin America. There is no denying that some developing countries, especially in Asia and Latin America, have perhaps benefited from the processes of development and globalization. Yet many others, notably in Africa, have been exceedingly marginalized by both processes, as the recent works of Appadurai (2000), Beck (2000), Bauman (2000) and many others clearly show.

Unfortunately, the dependency theory, consolidated in Latin America in reaction to the modernization school, has not yielded a better result either. Cast in a Marxist perspective, the dependency theory explains underdevelopment primarily in terms of the super-exploitation of the developing world by developed countries. It certainly unravels the imperialistic undertones of modernization theory. Yet, like the modernization theory it sought to unseat, it focused primarily on the economic – and, to a limited extent on the social and political – dimensions of development, and neglected the cultural aspects of Western domination. The dependency theorists saw development as economic growth, and, consequently, bought into its linear and evolutionary connotations. According to Tucker (1999, p. 12), '[d]ependency theorists were profoundly modern in their worldview'. The apparent overlap and the inadequate treatment of culture culminated in the much-publicised impasse in development theory (Booth, 1994; Sklair, 1988).

In an attempt to negotiate their way out of the theoretical cul-de-sac engendered by this impasse, many analysts are now incorporating culture, and related concepts, such as hybridity, indigenous knowledge, locality, and heterogeneity, in a new globalization and postdevelopment manifesto (Escobar, 1995; Sachs, 1992; Fagan, 1999; Rahnema, 1997). In what follows, we examine the introduction of a cultural gaze to the sprawling literature on development and globalization.

Adding Culture to Globalization and (Post) Development Theory

The call to incorporate culture in globalization and development thinking has emanated not only from several academicians who are increasingly realizing the inadequacies of the existing emphasis on politics and economics situations (Amin, 1989; Skelton, 1997; Gidwani and Sivaramakrishnan, 2003; Tucker, 1997, 1999; and Wolsley, 1984), but also from development practitioners such as Thierry Verhelst (1990), a senior project officer of the Belgian Development Agency, who once identified culture as the forgotten element in development practice. Granted that these critics are not merely asking us to 'add culture and stir', (Nederveen Pieterese, 1995, p. 184), what does the call really mean? What is the best way to integrate culture in our understanding of development and globalization? What is the impetus behind this drive towards culture? And, given the multiplicity of connotations assigned to culture over the years, how do we conceptualize it in this context?

Culture is a complex, dynamic concept with a variety of meaning to different people. Thus, no single definition of the concept is apposite for all cultural analyses. The best way to proceed, therefore, is to identify its relevant themes as a way of grounding the concept for the present discussion. With theoretical inspiration from the likes of Mitchell (2000), Norton (2000), Shurmer-Smith (2002), and Crang (1998), the meaning of culture that is foregrounded here sees it as a contextual, socially construction concept, with individual experience and creation of it varying on the basis of social locations such as race, class, and gender. Culture is used not as a superorganic entity with its own agency, physical existence, or objective reality over and above what is socially construction, but rather as shared sets of 'beliefs and values that give meaning to ways of life and produce (and are reproduced through) material and symbolic forms' (Crang, 1998, p. 2). The (re)production of meaning and knowledge always involves power dynamics. Consequently, culture invariably entails social relations in which dominance/subordination are negotiations, apprehended, resisted, and transformed (Jackson, 1989). Thus, for all practical purposes, the cultural is inseparable from the political.

In the context of globalization and development thinking, culture ' … essentially has to do with people's control over their destinies, their ability to name the world in a way which reflects their particular experience …' (Tucker, 1997, p. 4). Over the years, the West has so successfully controlled the production of knowledge that perspectives from other intellectual traditions, such as African philosophy and Islamic theology and economics, are routinely seen as strange or unorthodox, and strategically (or self-servingly) ignored. The historic lack of attention to such alternative voices is particularly disturbing, especially if one agrees with Tucker's view that culture is nothing beyond a group's control over its own affairs.

Stiglitz (2003) in his masterpiece *Globalization and its Discontent* severely chides the IMF's tendency to impose its 'expert' views on the developing world. As he rightly puts it, '[t]he developing world now has its economists – many of them trained at the world's best academic institutions. These economists have the significant advantage of lifelong familiarity with local politics, conditions, and trends'. Certainly, the IMF is not alone when it comes to intellectual imperialism, as any cursory reading of Edward Said's classic work, *Orientalism,* will quickly reveal.

Since the mid-1980s, however, the intellectual balance of power has been shifting, with the West's power to define and control knowledge coming under increasing subversion and forms of Gramscian counterhegemonic practices. In a way, such subversions are not surprising, for, as Tucker (1999, p. 14) points out with insights from Mark, '[w]hether in visible or invisible forms, resistance is always present, even in the most repressive of situations. *Hegemonic situations always contain the seed of their own liberation*' (my emphasis). In a similar vein, Comaroff and Comaroff (1991, p. 30) assert that hegemony is inherently unstable as it has 'the capacity to generate new substantive practices along the surfaces of economy and society'. Yet, until quite recently much of the counterhegemonic scholarship on development and globalization has been eclectic and haphazard. Again this is hardly surprising, for, as Gramsci (1971) contends, subaltern theory and practice are often fragmentary.

Notable examples of critical (post)development scholarship emanate from the works of members of the Delhi Center for Developing Societies.[1] Others are from Muslim scholars, such as Sardar (1997; 1977), who are increasingly popularizing the concepts and theories of Islamic economics; and from Chinese scholars, such as Wang Tai Peng (1994) who are now using traditional Chinese concepts and categories to undermine the Eurocentrism in mainstream development theory. The long-standing contribution of Latin American scholars in critical development thinking deserves no further introduction here. And, since the early 1990s, several African scholars, including many of the contributors to this monograph, have promoted the notion of human factor in Africa's development.

The incorporation of culture in the study of development and globalization is, among other things, an attempt to empower subaltern groups and those who espouse alternative intellectual traditions, mostly from the developing world, to assert their own meanings, social imaginaries, and cultural identities in the production of knowledge. It is reasoned that the inclusion of culture would help us better understand the intricate recursivity between globalization, development, and knowledge (re)production in the developing world, and, hopefully, help destabilize the Eurocentric and economistic meta-narratives that undergird much of the available research in this area.

The growing interest in the cultural ramifications of development and globalization is neither accidental nor isolated. It is part of the cultural turn in the social sciences which seeks to highlight the role of culture in our understanding of human affairs. Advocates of this intellectual shift invoke postmodern, poststructural, postcolonial, and postdevelopment arguments to promote their projects. The anti-foundationalism, anti-authouritarianism, anti-positivism, and the anti-domination inherent in these new discursive practices have blown both the theoretical and empirical doors wide open for the inclusion of non-Western categories and subaltern lifeworld[2] in the study of development and globalization. Not surprisingly, notions of hydridity, juxtaposition, and global melange are now at the forefront of most academic works on globalization and development. How else could we explain the dramatic ironies in such situations as having 'Thai boxing by Moroccan girls, Asian rap, Irish bagels, Chinese tacos … or Mexican schoolgirls dress in Greek toga dancing in the style of Isidora Duncan' (Nederveen Pieterse, 1994, p. 8). As a result of these cultural admixtures, many are those who are beginning to see culture not so much as something people possess, but rather as something people perform, what people do and not necessary what they own (Shurmer-Smith, 2002).

Some Noteworthy Proposals

Several scholars, including Tucker (1997; 1999), Nederveen Pieterse (1995), Fagan (1999), and Escobar (1995; 1994), have suggested ways to add a cultural gaze to the study of development and globalization. We examine their proposals, before making the case for the incorporation of the human factor concept into the equation.

Tucker asks us to avoid treating the local and the global as separate entities in our attempt to add culture to development studies. As he puts it, 'the local and global are not separate spheres but rather they represent different but complementary perspectives' (Tucker 1997, p. 14). In a similar vein, Nederveen Pieterse (1995) calls for a balance between the local and the global, so as to avoid the fetishism of the local in our zeal to repudiate the Eurocentric scholarship and accentuate traditional cultures in development (and globalization) thinking. This suggestion is intuitively appealing since the everyday lives of many people, even in the so-called Third World, are now heavily influenced by global event disseminated through television and other mass media images.

Escobar (1995) and Tomlimson (1997) for their part, caution us against the temptation of drawing a hard-and-fast line between cultural, economic, political, and social spheres of life. Given that the 'cultural turn' in the social sciences was prompted by the common, and quite artificial, separation of political economy from cultural analysis – and a corresponding elevation of the former to the status of a master paradigm in development theorizing, to the virtual neglect of the latter – some may be tempted to swing the intellectual pendulum towards a compartmentalized notion of culture, or, perhaps, to replace political economy with culture. But as Escabor (1995) and Tomlinson (1997) point out, for all practical purposes, culture is neither separable from the economic nor the political dimensions of our existence. Still 'to argue [pertinently]', writes Tomlinson, (1997, p. 23) 'we have to make, albeit artificial, distinctions whilst not losing sight of the points at which processes and logics in other realms become significantly determining: for example the point at which cultural experiences depend on material resource distribution'.

Honor Fagan (1999), in a thought-provoking paper, challenges us to make a shift from a mere cultural analysis to cultural politics, in our bid to undermine Eurocetrism with a postdevelopment discourse. In her view, it is only with this theoretical shift can we sufficiently situate the marriage between culture and development in the appropriate power dynamics. Fagan is concerned that the deconstruction of development has led to the virtual rejection of its political trajectories. In her view, cultural politics is the best way to produce meaningful interpretation of subaltern lifeworlds, and to explore the relationship between culture and power (Fagan, 1999, p. 186). Furthermore, Fagan and other analysts, notably Leyshon (1995), are concerned that issues of poverty and inequality are being neglected in the wake of the cultural turn. According to Fagan (1999), '[t]he critique of development as a modernist discourse creates a concern that in the 'era of posts' a post-development scenario might involve a conceptual disarticulation of questions concerning inequalities and disadvantage' (pp. 178-180). And with insights from Crush (1995), Fagan writes that 'a second related tension is that the poststructuralist focus on language may lead to a replacement of the 'material' with 'representation' in explanations of politics' (Fagan, 1999, p. 180). Leyshon (1995) raised a similar alarm when he talks about the fact that no lesser collection than the third edition of the *Dictionary of Human Geography* (1994) had no entry on 'poverty'; this omission was, however, corrected in the fourth edition (Johnston et al., 2000).[3]

The basic lesson that could be distilled from Fagan's presentation is not much different from Frederic Jameson's (1981, p. 18) earlier call for us to pay greater attention to political interpretations in reading any narrative; Nederveen Pieterse's (1994, p. 9) insistence that we take due cognizance of "the terms under which cultural interplay and crossover take place'; and Tucker's (1997, p. 17) observation that '[t]raits do no simply travel and mix like some global cultural DNA; they are shaped by power relations which include political, military and economic imperatives'. Clearly, cultural politics is highly pertinent in any robust insertion of culture into development and globalization theory.

The Human Factor Approach

Now let us augment the leads offered by Fagan (1999), Nederveen Pieterse (1994), Escobar (1995), and others with the introduction of human factor construct into the discussion. The primary intention here is to highlight the 'human factor' as a blind spot in the prevailing attempts to insert culture into the development and globalization debate. The human factor is seen as human personality traits, such as discipline, resourcefulness, honesty, and perseverance, which enable societies to progress over time. Obviously, the advocacy here is for positive human factor attributes, the absence of which amounts to human factor degradation or decay. As noted throughout this volume, the human factor concept was coined and popularized by Senyo Adjibolosoo who, in a number of books and scientific paper (e.g., Adjibolosoo, 2000; 1998; 1993), chides the long-standing neglect of moral issues in development thinking.

'From the human factor perspective', writes Adjibolosoo (1998, p. 162), 'each society's ability to accomplish relevant task lies in people who have been properly nurtured to live and uphold the higher moral and ethnical principles that nurture, enhance, and promote human life'. Implicitly, any society would find it hard to progress in the absence of the appropriate human factor attributes. Yet, over the years, globalization and development theorists have paid virtually no attention to the moral and human factor implications of the policies they espouse, and have chosen to rely almost religiously on economic assumptions, such as 'perfect competition', 'rationality', and 'profit maximization', notwithstanding the mounting evidence discrediting these assumptions (Stiglitz, 2003; Chomsky, 2001).

The basic argument, quite simply, is that without due attention to human factor attributes our attempts to situate the discourse on development and globalization in a cultural analysis, or cultural politics, will not amount to much. Every culture is imbued with both positive and negative human factor attributes, and it stands to reason that we consciously identify, and, indeed, accentuate the positive human factor attributes in our attempts to incorporate culture into globalization/development theory and practice. We cannot carry our entire cultural baggage into the development and globalization equation and expect to succeed.

While the human factor perspective, as presented by Adjibolosoo (2000; 1998), seem to favour the absolute, as against relative, conception of morality, it is here argued that the actual configuration of what constitutes appropriate human factor attributes at any point in time will vary from culture to culture, and from place to place. With this in mind, the subsequent presentation only offers general guidelines on how to integrate culture into development and globalization theory from the standpoint of a human factor hypothesis. The use of 'hypothesis' here is deliberate; it is to signify that what follows is neither a robust nor a coherent theory, but rather a loosely joined suppositions, encapsulated under three related arguments or mini-theses.

Firstly, efforts to insert culture in development and globalization theory should place people at front and center, and strive to improve not only the quality of life of people, but also enhance their human factor attributes. This will entail a radical reappraisal of development and globalization theory to accord due deference to the hopes, aspirations, and moral principles of indigenous people around the world.

The second thesis, which flows directly for the preceding, relates to need to acknowledge the ability of non-Westerners to define their own concepts, imageries and categories, and, ultimately, produce their own knowledge. From the human factor perspective, this demands a respect for the intrinsic humanity of people and their cultural traditions and moral principles. The call here is hardly about a romanticized notion of indigenous culture, but rather about a resistance to the prevailing Eurocentrism; the need to give conceptual validity to traditional knowledge; and a demand for a dialogical cultural interchange between Western and non-Western societies. Islamic economists, notably (Sardar, 1999; 1996), have taken the lead here, by introducing and popularizing several Islamic concepts, such as *tazkiyah* (growth through purification), *ijma* (consensus), *istislah* (public interest), and *shura* (cooperation) in a move to subvert the Eurocentrism in development theory. Similar moves have been made by Chinese, Indian, and many other non-Western scholars from various academic perspectives (Tai Peng Wang, 1994; Kang, 2001; and Sinha, 1999).

In the context of the human factor hypothesis espoused here, notable examples of traditional values that demand renewed attention in our attempt to insert culture in development and globalization thinking include self-reliance, communalism, environmental sustainability and stewardship, and the principle of non-violence. The works of Alvares (1992), Sardar (1997), and many others suggest that development, and implicitly globalization, has been a violent process over the years. Alvares (1992, p. 5) even goes as far as asserting an intrinsic link between development and violence. The violence perpetrated in the name of development and globalization is both direct and indirect. It has not only deprived many subalterns of their livelihood and undermines their self-respect and basic humanity, but has also wreaked havoc on their natural environment. It is, however, refreshing to note that many people are now deploying traditional values in an attempt to reduce the violence wrought by the process of development (and globalization). Sardar (1997) sums up this trend in the following words:

> Relief from the violence of development has often come from traditional sources: from the indigenous agricultural practices that produce better yield, are ecologically sound and far superior to imported 'modern' methods ...; from traditional and generic medicines that are accessible to poor rural folks ...; from banking practices that rely on the traditional notion of communal trust rather than the imported idea of collateral; and from indigenous institutions, including religious institutions, that have not only provided support for the poor but defended their dignity and rights in the face of ruthless development policies (p. 37).

As with their (post)modern counterparts, traditional cultures are imbued with configurations of power. With this in mind, the third mini-thesis seeks to extend the primarily psycho-ethical formulation of the human factor concept, espoused by Adjibolosoo (1998; 1993), to incorporate issues of politics. In fact, while the existing literature on the human factor concept stresses the connection between psychological and ethical principles and improved economic performance or development, it pays little attention to power dynamics in society. The existence of positive human factor attributes is routinely singled out as the main ingredient for development; few will dispute this basic argument. However, unless one situates the human factor framework in the context of power, then only half of the story is told, as society is inherently an arena of socio-economic and political contestation. Put differently, the human factor concept cannot be devoid of conflict, social contestation, cultural resistance, and the microphysics of power, and still claim to be realistic. Consequently, in attempting to link culture with development and globalization, we need to include civic politics and socio-cultural contestation as valuable forces for innovation and change in society.

Conclusion

This chapter has focused on the incorporation of culture into the analysis of development and globalization, using the human factor construct. Three broad questions were examined: First, what are the relationships between development and globalization? Second, how do we go about integrating culture in development and globalization theorizing? And, finally, what cultural traditions and human factor attributes deserve our analytical attention in our attempts to add a cultural gaze to this area of research? These questions relate in very important ways to the impasse in development theory; the ongoing cultural turn; and, more importantly, to the enduring Eurocentrism in the study of globalization and development and the growing counter-attacks mounted from the standpoint non-Western cultural traditions and scholarship.

The preceding analysis suggests that only with blind parochialism and utter negligence can we downplay the need to integrate non-Western cultural traditions and values into our understanding of development in this age of globalization. Quite expectedly, many of those who have taken the lead in this intellectual endeavour have relied mostly on postmodernist, poststructuralist, and postcolonial discourses, while others have called for renewed emphasis on the tenets of political economy. These theoretical perspectives have obviously broadened our insight into the intricate links between culture, development, and globalization. As a complement to these insights, this chapter has proposed a human factor hypothesis, which stresses the need to put people front and center in the debate; to respect indigenous cultural traditions and moral principle; and to contextualize our cultural gaze in the study of development and globalization in its proper civil politics and social contestation.

Notes

[1] Notable members of the Delhi Centre for Developing Societies include Rajni Kothan, Shiv Vishvanathan, and Ashish Nandy. This centre has been called the new Frankfurt School (Dallmayer, 1996) because of their critical postdevelopment thinking.
[2] Lifeworld derives from German phenomenology as Lebenwelt; it refers to 'the totality of an individual person's involvement with the places and environments experienced in ordinary life' (Cosgrove, 2000, p. 449).
[3] The 3rd edition of this dictionary was edited by pre-eminent geographers including R.J. Johnston, Derek Gregory, and David M. Smith.

References

Adjibolosoo, Senyo B.-S.K. (ed.) (2000), *The Human Factor in Shaping the Course of History and Development*, Lanham: University Press of America.

Adjibolosoo, Senyo B.-S.K. (1998), *Global Development: The Human Factor Way*, Westport, Connecticut: Praeger.

Adjibolosoo, Senyo B.-S.K. (1993), 'The Human Factor in Development', *Scandinavian Journal of Development Alternatives*, 12 (4): 139-149.

Alvares, Claude (1992), *Science, Development and Violence*, New Delhi: Oxford University Press.

Amin, Samir (1989), *Eurocentrism*, London: Zed Books.

Appadurai, Arjun (1990), "Disjuncture and difference in global cultural economy", in Patrick Williams and Laura Chrisman (eds.) *Colonial Discourse and Post-Colonial Theory: A Reader*, New York: Harverster Wheatsheaf.

Appadurai, Arjun (2000), "Grassroots globalization and the research imagination", *Public Culture*, 12 (1): 1-19.

Bauman, Zygmunt (2000), *Liquid Modernity*, Cambridge, UK: Polity Press.

Beck, Ulrich (2000), *What is Globalization?*, Cambridge, UK: Polity Press.

Biel, Robert (2000), *The New Imperialism: Crisis and Contradictions in North-South Relations*, New York: Zed Books.

Blaut, J.M. (1992), "Fourteen ninety-two", *Political Geography*, 11: 335-386.

Booth, D. (ed.) (1994), *Rethinking Social Development*, London: Methuen.

Chomsky, Noam (2001), "Free trade and free market: pretense and practice", in Fredric Jameson and Masao Miyoshi (eds.) *The Cultures of Globalization*, Durhan, North Carolina: Duke University Press, pp. 356-370.

Collins, Jane, L. (1997), "Development theory and the politics of location: An example from North Eastern Brazil", in Vincent Tucker (ed.) *Cultural Perspectives on Development*, London: Frank Cass, pp. 56-70.

Comaroff, Jean, and Comaroff, John (1991), *Of Revelation and Revolution: Christianity, Colonialism and Consciousness in South Africa*, vol. 1. Chicago: University of Chicago Press.

Cosgrove, Denis (2000), "Lifeworld", in R.J. Johnston et al., (eds.), *The Dictionary of Human Geography*, Oxford: Blackwell, p. 449.

Dallmayr, F. (1996), "Global Development?", *Alternative*, 21; 259-282.

Dicken, Peter (2000), "Globalization", in R.J. Johnston et al. (eds.) *The Dictionary of Human Geography*, Oxford: Blackwell Publishers Ltd., pp. 315-16.

Dirlik, Arif (1994), "The postcolonial aura: third world criticism in the age of global capitalism", *Critical Inquiry*, 20 (Winter): 328-356.

Escobar, Arturo (1995), *Encountering Development: The Making and Unmaking of the Third World*, Princeton, NJ: Princeton University Press.

Escobar, Arturo (1984), "Discourse and power in development: Michel Foucault and the relevance of his work to the Third World", *Alternatives*, 10 (3): 377-400.

Fagan, G.H. (1999), "Cultural politics and (post) development paradigm(s)", in Ronaldo Munch and Denis O'Hearn (eds.), *Critical Development Theory: Contributions to a New Paradigm*, London and New York: Zed Books, pp. 178-95.

Gidwani, Vinay and Sivaramakrishnam, K. (2003), "Circular migration and the spaces of cultural assertion", *Annals of the Association of American Geographers*, 93 (1): 186-213.

Glyn, Andrew and Sutcliffe, Bob (1992), "Global but leaderless? the new capitalist order", in Ralph Miliband and Leo Panitch (eds.) *The Socialist Register 1992*, London: Merlin, pp. 76-95.

Gramsci, Antonio (1971), *Selections from the Prison Notebook*, (edited and translated by Quintin Hoare and Geoffrey Nowell Smith), New York: International Publishers.

Habermas, Jurgen (1984), *Theory of Communicative Action*, vol. 1 (translated by Thomas McCarthy), Boston, MA: Beacon Press.

Hirst, P. and Thompson, G. (1996), *Globalization in Question*, Cambridge: Polity Press.

Jackson, P. (1989), *Maps of Meanings: An Introduction to Cultural Geography*, Boston: Unwin Hyman.

Jameson, Fredric (2001), "Notes on globalization as a philosophical issue", in Fredric Jameson and Masao Miyoshi (eds.) *The Cultures of Globalization*, Durham, North Carolina: Duke University Press, pp. 54-77.

Jameson, Fredric (2001), "Preface", in Fredric Jameson and Masao Miyoshi (eds.) *The Cultures of Globalization*, (Durham, North Carolina: Duke University Press, pp. xi-xvii.

Jameson, Fredric (1981), *The Political Unconscious: Narrative as a Socially Symbolic Act*, New York: Cornell University Press.

Kang, Liu (2001), "Is There an Alternative to (Capitalist) Globalization? The Debate about Modernity in China", in Fredric Jameson and Masao Miyoshi (eds.) *The Cultures of Globalization*, Durham, North Carolina: Duke University Press.

Knox, Paul (1995), "Introduction", in Paul Knox and Peter Taylor (eds.) *World Cities in a World System*, Cambridge: Cambridge University Press, 1-20.

Knox, Paul and Agnew, John (1998), *The Geography of the World Economy: An Introduction to Economic Geography*, New York: John Wiley & Sons, Inc.

Knox, Paul and Marston, A. Sallie (2001), *Human Geography: Places and Regions in Global Context*, Upper Saddle River, NJ: Prentice Hall.

Lee, Roger (1986), "Development", in R.J. Johnson, Derek Gregory, and David M. Smith (eds.), *The Dictionary of Human Geography*, Oxford: Blackwell, pp. 103-104.

Leyshorn, A. (1995), "Missing words: whatever happened to the geography of poverty?, *Environment and Planning A.*, 27: 1021-1028.

Massey, D. (1994), *Space, Place and Gender*, Cambridge: Polity Press.

McGrew, A.G. (1992), "Conceptualizing global politics", in A.G. McGrew and P.G. Lewis (eds.) *Global Politics, Globalization and the Nation-State*, Cambridge: Polity Press, pp. 1-28.

McLuhan, Marshall, (1964), *Understanding Media*, Toronto: Signet Books.

Mitchell, Don (2001), *Cultural Geography: A Critical Introduction*, Malden, Massachusetts: Blackwell Publishers Ltd.

Nederveen Pieterse, Jan (1995), "The cultural turn in development: Questions of power", *The European Journal of Development Research*, 7 (1): pp. 176-192.

Norton, William, (2000), *Cultural Geography: Themes, Concepts, Analysis*, Don Mills, Ontario: Oxford University Press.

Perrons, Diane (1999), "Reintegrating production and consumption, or why political economy still matters", in Ronaldo Munch and Denis O'Hearn (eds.), *Critical Development Theory: Contributions to a New Paradigm*, London and New York: Zed Books, *pp.* 91-112.

Rahnema, Majid (1997), "Afterword: Towards post-development: searching for signposts, a new language, and a new paradigm", in Majid Rahnema and Victoria Bawtree (eds.), *The Post-Development Reader*, London: Zed Books, pp. 377-403.

Reich, Robert B. (1991), *The Work of Nations: Preparing Ourselves for 21st Century Capitalism*, New York: Simon and Schuster.

Relph, E. (1976), *Place and Placelessness,* London: Pion.

Rist, Gilbert (1990), "'Development' as part of the modern myth: The Western 'socio-cultural dimension' of 'development'", *The European Journal of Development Research*, 2 (1): 10-21.

Sachs, Wolfgang (ed.) (1992), *The Development Dictionary*, London: Zed Press.

Said, Edward W. (1994), *Orientalism*, New York: Vintage Books.

Sardar Ziauddin (1999), "Development and the Locations of Eurocentrism", in Ronaldo Munch and Denis O'Hearn (eds.), *Critical Development Theory: Contributions to a New Paradigm*, London and New York: Zed Books, pp. 44-62.

Sardar Ziauddin (1997), "Beyond development: an Islamic perspective", in Vincent Tucker (ed.), *Cultural Perspective on Development*, London: Frank Cass, pp. 36-55.

Sinha, J. (1999), *Indian Psychology*, Delhi: Motilal Banarsidass Publications.

Skelton, Tracey (1997), "Cultures of land in the Caribbean: a contribution to the debate on development and culture", in Vincent Tucker (ed.), *Cultural Perspective on Development*, London: Frank Cass, pp. 71-92.

Sklair, Leslie (1998), "Transcending the impasse: metatheory, theory and empirical research in the sociology of development and underdevelopment", *World Development*, 16 (6): pp. 697-709.

Stiglitz, Joseph, E. (2003), *Globalization and Its Discontents*, New York and London: W.W. Norton and Company.

Tai Peng, Wang (1994), *The Origins of Chinese Kongsi*, Selangor: Pelanduk.

Tomlinson, John (1997), "Cultural globalization: Placing and displacing the West", in Vincent Tucker (ed.), *Cultural Perspective on Development*, London: Frank Cass, pp. 22-35.

Tucker, Vincent (1999), "The myth of development: A critique of a Eurocentric discourse", in Ronaldo Munch and Denis O'Hearn (eds.), *Critical Development Theory: Contributions to a New Paradigm*, London and New York: Zed Books, pp. 1-26.

Tucker, Vincent (1997), "Introduction: A cultural perspective on development", in Vincent Tucker (ed.), *Cultural Perspective on Development*, London: Frank Cass, pp. 1-21.

Verhelst, Thierry G., (1990), *No Life without Roots: Culture and Development*, London: Zed Press.

Worsley, Peter (1984), *The Three Worlds: Culture and World Development*, London: Weidenfeld & Nicolson.

Chapter 4

African Culture and the Social Implications and Consequences of Globalization

Victor Ngonidzashe Muzvidziwa

Introduction

While accepting that globalization is a multi-faceted process, with economic, social, technological, political and cultural implications the thrust of this paper is on the social and cultural implications of globalization in Africa. Culture is a heritage from which a society draws its strength. Culture is a resource which enables any given individual, community or society to survive and cope with the demands of social life. It is that one resource Africans turn to in order to survive. For any given society, culture, through its shared and distinctive values, beliefs, forms of knowledge, symbols and language, expressiveness, and customs, charts life courses for its members. Yet, culture though dynamic marks people's way of life and gives each group its distinctiveness and humanity. Culture encompasses the symbolic, the non-material aspects as well as the material objects that society produces in order to guarantee individual and group survival. Through culture African communities are able to dig into the past in order to understand the present so as to come up with sound visions for the future. This chapter discusses African traditions and culture in the face of globalization processes.

The present is a time of change. It is also noteworthy that in times of rapid change culture and tradition play an important role in terms of whether individuals or groups make it or break. The post-modern condition with its emphasis on difference and rejection of globalizing and totalizing schemes undermines any attempts to privilege western knowledge as the only source of all valid knowledge. However, despite this recognition of the validity of non-western knowledge systems and claims, the social sciences in Africa continue to be dominated by western concepts and views. It then becomes clear and critical in the era of globalization to carry out an examination of traditional African cultures, values and authority structures and their implication for societal development.

The discussions on issues of culture, tradition and development takes place in the context of a supposedly post-modern globalizing world in which rules of the old with regards to power, authority and leadership have been or are being replaced by new ones. Yet it is argued in this chapter that globalization, which is supposedly an integrative and unifying factor in an increasingly fractured but co-operating but antagonistic global village, has failed to do away with local narratives and local issues. To the contrary, globalizing tendencies have produced contrasting forces: one set pulling towards greater Cupertino and the other towards diversity and difference. In the process, there has been greater space for local cultures and even an increasing valuing of these cultures as having a role to play in any theatre of social life. This chapter places much weight on the important role local cultures can play in changing environments.

The chapter is organized into five sections excluding the introduction and conclusion. The first section explores the meaning of globalization. This is followed by a discussion of African values, African culture, and globalization. The third section is devoted to a discussion of the consequences of globalization on African culture. The fourth section focuses on the link between globalization and the Human Factor (HF). HF decay as part of the negative consequences of globalization is examined. The section on African renaissance as one of the techniques for dealing with globalization precedes the conclusion.

What is Globalization?

Globalization is a complex, multi-faceted, multi-vocal and fluid term. Globalization provides a key to an understanding of the micro and macro socio-economic processes obtaining in Africa. Generally most of the discussions of globalization focus on financial or industrial flows or inputs. However, globalization has had far-reaching socio-cultural changes. It has resulted in the compression of distance and time, and the establishment of inter-connections across communities. Globalization is characterized by the diffusion of consumer goods, ideas and socio-cultural symbols in new settings. In a way globalization refers to the perceived shrinking of the world due to such things as the adoption of new technologies, the pervasiveness of internationalized business interests, the toppling of old regimes and weakening of long established borders between countries.

Kellner (1998, p. 23) observed that globalization is 'used in so many different contexts, by so many different people, for so many different purposes, that it is difficult to ascertain what is at stake in the globalization problematics, what function the term serves, and what effects it has for contemporary theory and politics'. According to Owolabi (2001) the seeming integration of world societies since the beginning of the 1990s has encouraged the interpenetration of ideas along former cultural and ideological divides. Globalization is seen as the homogenization of ideas, images and institutions leading to what has been termed the global village. For Owolabi (2001, p. 73) globalization 'refers to the interpenetrating and interdependency taking place among divergent peoples of the world'. It has resulted in the compression of distance and time and the establishment of inter-connections across communities. According to Yearley

(1996, p. 9) globalization refers to the 'growing awareness of the interrelations among people on the globe'. This is what Robertson (1992) sees as the compression of the world and growing awareness of humanity's interdependence. These definitions of globalization have implications to our understanding of African cultures and traditions.

Featherstone (1990) observed that the globalization process is an extension of global cultural interrelatedness leading to what Hannerz refers to as the 'global ecumene' a process characterized by intense cultural flows, interaction and exchange. Cultural homogeneity, disorder and transnational cultures co-exist. This image of unimagined cultural flows to a large extent depicts the situations prevailing in many parts of Africa today. Globalization has proved itself to be a double-edged sword to African communities.

Albrow (1990, p. 9) regards globalization as 'all those processes by which the people's of the world are incorporated into a single world society, [the] global society'. However, Long (2001, p. 214) observed that 'globalization should not be visualized as some kind of overarching hegemonic process that structures outcomes at the level of nations, cultures, economies and people's livelihoods, but rather as a convenient shorthand for depicting the on-going complexities, ambiguities and diversities of contemporary patterns of global/local relations'. Hence globalization defies logic but affects the patterning of social life within and between communities. This lends support to Hannerz's (1996, p. 102) observation that the global relates to the 'organization of diversity, a sort of interconnectedness of varied local cultures, as well as the development of cultures without a clear anchorage in any one territory. And to this interconnected diversity people can relate in different ways'. For Giddens (1990, p. 64) globalization entails the 'intensification of worldwide social relations which link distant localities'. It involves the organization and re-organization of various processes such as business activities, communication and ideologies governing for instance the role of women in the economy. Globalization is defined as 'the phenomenon of increasing close international integration of markets, both for goods and services, and for capital' (IMF, 1997, p. 112). However, globalization in content is not just about trade and investment but it also entails cultural reawakening. Globalization is also a product and reaction to modernization (Benoist, 1996).

Hannerz (1996, p. 24) observed that by and large globalization means 'a global homogenization in which particular ideas and practices spread throughout the world, mostly from the centres of the West, pushing other alternatives out of existence', as is happening in many parts of Africa in the fields of the arts, trade, commerce, science and technology. The theme of globalization as westernization is emphasized in many definitions of what constitute globalization. As Hannerz (1996, p. 111) noted 'there is one world culture, all the variously distributed structures of meaning and expression are becoming interrelated, somehow, somewhere'. What Hannerz did not take note of is that the one world culture is a euphemism for westernization of people's way of life on a global scale. To some, globalization entails the triumphant march of modernity but for others it involves a cultural take over and bastardization of non-western cultural forms. Globalization produces positive as well as negative outcomes at one and the same time.

To Pieterse (1995) globalization is a process of hybridization. Instead of speaking of homogenization and a single globalization we should talk of multiple globalizations. Globalization is multi-dimensional and unfolds in multiple realms. Globalization is characterized by varied organizational forms and increasing functional networks leading to a 'global melange'. Hybridization puts emphasis on the mixing of cultures and their ability to maintain their distinctiveness simultaneously. Pieterse (1995) noted differences in the language relating to whether people view globalization as homogenization or hybridization. Terms that go along with the homogenization view are cultural imperialism, cultural dependence, cultural hegemony, autonomy, modernization, westernization, cultural synchronization and world civilization. On the other hand for the hybridization side we have cultural planetarization, cultural interdependence, cultural interpenetration, syncretism, synthesis, hybridity, modernizations, global melange, creolization, crossover and global acumen. When examining globalization in the African context it is therefore important that the process be viewed as being fluid, diversified and multi-dimensional rather than uni-dimensional. What is important though is that irrespective of definitions used no part of the globe remains unaffected by globalization processes. Africa needs to learn how to survive in the face of multiple globalizations.

African Values, African Culture and Globalization

While globalization is a much talked about topic, discussions have tended to concentrate on financial or industrial flows or inputs. Globalization is a concept that is useful in our discussion of African values and traditions. There is a tendency for theories of human behaviour to be Euro-centric as they largely draw their examples from western experiences. In view of the interconnectedness and simultaneous disconnectedness of diverse cultures in today's world, an inclusive approach that would ensure the representation and strategic positioning of non-western values would be highly beneficial and would go a long way in creating a global value system.

African culture is defined broadly to include all aspects that have to do with group survival and continuity. It encompasses the material and non-material aspects of life. African culture like other cultures is dynamic, diverse and ever changing rather than static and monolithic. Culture spans the whole range of issues from the area of norms, values, beliefs and behavioural expectations to issues of technological competence and matters of trade and governance. What is clear today is that globalization has not spared Africa; every area of African social life has been affected.

Today's societies need to draw their strength from and focus on those aspects that contribute to unity in diversity. This is a call for human and social sciences studies to privilege every culture including African traditions. There is a tendency to view African traditions as archaic and therefore of no relevance to understanding modern society. Yet within each culture there are those qualities that are resilient and span over time to ensure group survival. Amongst these are aspects that relate to societal organization, its character, form and style. There are specific contributions that Africa has made to all humanity. In the area of the arts, music, architecture, medicine and basic moral principles, Africa's contribution to all humanity should be acknowledged. The recognition of African heritage as part of humanity's heritage is seen in the many sites of historical, cultural and archaeological significance that are on the World Heritage list for preservation and conservation. These sites are dotted all over the continent from South Africa to Egypt.

African traditional societies generally emphasized participatory values as a tool to be utilized by members of society in order to ensure group survival. For instance it was seen as highly imperative for leaders to carry their followers along with them, by involving them in decisions that concerned them. Practically in every settled African community the use of open-air informal gatherings as discussion fora and assemblies for reaching consensus on contentious and non-contentious issues is well documented and fairly widespread. In other words, the experiences of African societies show that there is no need to lecture modern day Africa on issues of democratic government and community involvement. The many sayings, proverbs and bedtime stories extolling the virtues of participatory leadership in Sotho society for instance do confirm this. For instance the saying *Letlaila le tlailela Morena* (let people say what they want even if it is not good). There is another saying amongst the Shona emphasizing the transient nature of leadership. *Vushe madzoro huno ravanwa* (Chieftanship comes in turns, people in leadership positions circulate). In the context of globalization the rich African heritage on organizational matters calls for the need to incorporate this knowledge in studies relating to leadership, organizational behaviour and other such related matters.

Wunsch (1990) stressed that traditional decision making institutions are being marginalized in postcolonial states and attempts to replace these institutions with centralized western models have invariably failed. We can learn a lot, improve our leadership skills and sharpen those values that make for effective leadership for instance by taking a leaf from African traditions and value systems. Mararike (1998) in a study in Zimbabwe argues that a major lesson Africans need to learn comes from the history of the Japanese and the Jewish people who embraced western technological achievements and yet remained firmly anchored in their cultural roots. The results have been a resounding success for these societies. Consequently it means that going back to African roots should, however, not be seen as return to antiquity. It is a question of refocusing one's values in such a way as to recognize and embrace those aspects that will make Africans more efficient in executing developmental and survival tasks in a world characterized by growing interdependence. In the global village Africans and those interested in the development of African approaches and studies focusing on human development need to be anchored in our rich traditions of past and present African societies as well as other non-African societies. Globalization calls for the need to accept the commonality of humanity but at the same time an acknowledgement of difference should be made.

Globalization demands that we deconstruct and discard notions that privilege western values and norms in the different spheres of social life. From each and every society we can draw our strength and come up with a rich source of data on human organizational forms. It makes great sense for African scholars to strive to put African values at the centre in their studies. The marketing of local cultural specificities is vital for success in human sciences. This is what globalization should entail rather than a swallowing up of local cultures, which is what has been happening.

The Consequences of Globalization on African Culture

The consequences of globalization flow from an understanding of the exact nature of this process. Globalization presents a paradox. On one hand is the seeming integration and on the other hand the apparent fragmentation and chaos characterizing the nation state in Africa and the Third World in general. This led Hobsbawm (1994) to conclude that the present age is an age of extremes. In the present divide we see the prosperous, peaceful advancing western nations co-exiting along side the instability and chaos of the Third World. In this context globalization is seen as a new project aimed at sustaining the age-old western hegemonic influences. Globalization is a force that engages and disengages all at the same time. Its many faces co-exist and operate simultaneously. This is a process that offers unlimited possibilities and opportunities and at the same time sets limits and is limiting in what societies can and should do.

While some writers have emphasized the argument that globalization is a process that integrates cultures and is thus responsible for moving humanity towards a global culture, unfortunately this movement has been equated to westernization instead of being truly global. The idea about the universal culture or civilization pervades much of the debate about globalization. Hannerz (1996) noted that 'as the civilization of modernity enters into contact with other cultures, changes and refractions result' leading to internally diverse civilizations. There is a tendency to equate civilization to modernity and westernization. Yet a hybrid notion of globalization requires that the humanity of Africans and the contribution of Africa to human progress be acknowledged in the globalization literature. Africa is replete with the rise of many great historical figures dating back to the pharaohs of Egypt, Tshaka Zulu, the Lewanikas, Meneleks and many others. Africa has also given the world philosophical ideas. African music, attire, menu, and a variety of languages have had an impact in the global theatre.

The impact of globalization has generated varied opinions. On one hand are the optimists those who see globalization as a solution to age-old problems of underdevelopment, and on the other hand are the pragmatists and pessimists who see globalization in negative terms. Instead of heralding a new international order characterized by declining poverty and social inequalities globalization has deepened the problems of underdevelopment. Akokpari (2001) observed that while economies across the globe have become globalized and unified contrary to expectations that globalization will hasten the eradication of poverty, the process has deepened the economic crisis being experienced in the third world. Africa has experienced an unprecedented increase in poverty, unemployment, social exclusion, social disintegration and environmental destruction. For instance New York City consumes more electricity than the whole of sub Saharan Africa (de Benoist (1996). Sub Saharan GNP is only 17% of that of the North, 85% of the world's wealth is in the industrial world representing only 25% of the world's population, 358 billionaires have annual revenue of half of humanity nearly three times Africa's population. Africa as a continent has also witnessed a systematic destruction of the middle class thereby generating instability and transborder migration movements. Diminishing human quality and marginalization of Africa continues unabated as globalization takes a firm root. The negative consequences of the market forces ushered in by globalization is well documented in the many writings of scholars who have highlighted the plight of Africans, especially women and children (Adepoju, 1993; Smith, 2001; Orr, 2001 and de Benoist 1996).

Globalization in Africa has witnessed an intensification of restructuring processes resulting in increased volumes of retrenched workers as seen in South African mines where emphasis on efficiency and profitability has seen millions of workers from within South Africa itself and the region being retrenched. The development of a social contract putting emphasis on workers' welfare never took root in Africa hence the reason for such negative impact on working people's well being when restructuring processes took place.

For Gilroy (1995) globalization entails the imposition and implosion of western values on a global scale. Globalization is a western orchestrated programme; it is the same old imperialism with new tools. Globalization contributed to the intensification of inequalities. Globalization has brought about traumas to those at the margin of society, the poor and Third World peoples (Owolabi, 2001). Non-governmental organizations (NGOs) and the new euphemism of civil society organizations are seen as part of the global western project of imposing a dominant value system across the world under guise of universal principles. The general failure of NGOs to make a significant headway as far as poverty reduction is concerned is not surprizing given the nature of globalization. Globalization is not about empowerment and liberation; its thrust is on domination. Globalization is not a neutral term; it is a smokescreen for repackaging imperialist domination in more acceptable ways. Uroh (2000) observed that globalization is a cover to neutralize the legacy of the horrors of colonialism and slavery.

In many ways globalization has produced far-reaching socio-economic changes. It is characterized by the diffusion of consumer goods, ideas and socio-cultural symbols. To some extent 'globalization refers to the perceived shrinking of the world due to the adoption of new technologies, the pervasiveness of internationalized business interests … and the weakening of long established borders between countries' (Muzvidziwa, 2001, p. 43). Hannerz also links up the concept of cosmopolitanism with globalization. The cosmopolitan develops skills to manage and survive under conditions of increasing diversity. And to a greater extent 'cosmopolitans are usually somewhat footloose, on the move in the world' (Hannerz, 1996, p. 104). Mobility is to an extent part of the survival strategies adopted by the cosmopolitans. At the same time it should be borne in mind that mobility is regulated by cultural norms or the lack thereof. The ruptures in family life and values that accompany migration are part of the resulting consequences of global flows of people a consequent of globalizing tendencies. Population movements and shifts have been greatest in sub Saharan African over the past century. Such movements have implications in terms of how local cultures cope with increasing diversity in a global world.

For developing countries and Africa in particular there is the expectation of building sustainable and thriving market economies due to improved trade linkages and interconnected markets. Globalization promises solutions to socio-economic problems of Third World countries and increased social and economic opportunities, but as Mlambo and Pangeti (2000) argue there are limited opportunities for the poor in the global market especially Africans.

There is a need therefore to revisit our African history so as to discover the strong cultural roots and traditions, principles and values that will enable Africans at any level in society to forge ahead successfully together with their communities. The rediscovery and drawing of lessons from African history, values and traditions is likely to be of significance to the growth of a global culture. With globalization this has not been the case. Taking note of the importance of history Malcolm X (1970, p. 53) observed that 'a race is like an individual man; until it uses its own talent, takes pride in its own history, expresses its own culture, affirms its own selfhood, it can never fulfil itself'. If a people are denied their own history it means the same people's contribution to a hybrid world culture is impossible. African people's heritage is a defining feature of their identity and everyday experiences. Malcolm X (1970, p. 56) went on to note 'armed with the knowledge of our past, we can with confidence chart a course for our future. Culture is an indispensable weapon in the freedom struggle. We must take hold of it and forge the future with the past'. This is a wake up call for Africa and those involved in the teaching of African values, to do something positive in terms of cultural reawakening. African heritage and traditions need to be discussed and valued as part of a rich culture that must be seen as part of growing integral global culture and value system. African heritage is capable of making an input in all areas of social life, be it in the medical, scientific, agricultural, arts and any other field of human endeavour. The neglect and exclusion of African heritage deprives the modern world of a potential for enrichment.

People working in any field in Africa must take stock of a rich African past in order to understand the demands of the present situations and the role Africa can play in a global world. The flow of information and values continues to be one way, from the West into Africa. A two-way flow of ideas would be quite enriching as Africa has a rich knowledge heritage. For instance, there is a growing acknowledgement in the field that indigenous knowledge systems are vital to scientific developments. Farmers, medical personnel, artists and philosophers stand to benefit if they can only draw from indigenous knowledge. With globalization this has not been the case as the assumption has been that the flow of information and knowledge is from the West into other parts of the world including Africa.

Despite the representation of Africa as a dark continent in history, literature, philosophy and classical anthropology there are many examples in history of African leaders who were inspired by positive human factor (HF) development qualities. Globalization seems to deny this rich history as an inspiration for growth and renewal of Africa and Africans. The result has been that in search of current problems of Africa there is no deliberate move to anchor solutions in Africa's past and knowledge system. There are historical figures Africans can draw an inspiration from, for instance leaders such as Moshoeshoe I, the Mwenemotapas who administered an empire spanning through the southern African sub continent for more than four hundred years, the Lewanikas in Zambia and the kings of Ethiopia. All these African leaders led effectively and possessed positive HF qualities, which were rooted in their respective cultures. These leaders had the courage and vision, were tacticians as well as strategists and had diplomatic skills, served as moral beacons in their societies and above everything else managed to run efficient and effective bureaucracies long before Weber's works came into being. There were those who were military geniuses and strategists, and people with a long vision like Tshaka Zulu who moulded a nation out of nothing. These examples of past African leaders mean that we should be able to benefit from such a history of successes rooted in and coming from African people themselves. Africa need not look up to Europe for basic leadership principles, theories and styles and values whatever our interests are. The tendency in the global village is to impose a western value system on other non-western peoples. The process could have been more enriching and global with an acknowledgement and mutual respect of the contribution each and every people's culture and heritage makes to humanity's progress.

For instance Mamimine (2001, p. 2) rightly observed 'modern institutions of governance are structures steeped in western tradition, invariably bureaucratic and inherited in part or wholly by post-colonial sub-Saharan African governments from their former colonial masters'. Modern institutions draw their inspiration from centrist, impersonal, elitist and absolutist systems of authority. This is in contrast to most traditional African systems of good governance and leadership, which invariably depended on decentralized, personalized and consultative structures. For Mamimine (2001, p. 2) traditional 'leadership derives much of its legitimacy from its embeddedness in the social and cultural life of rural communities, where the discourses of tradition and cultural identity remain persuasive for many of the residents'. It appears there is very little that globalization has done to integrate local knowledge systems in the various human endeavours. The unconditional acceptance that each and every culture has a rich heritage useful for human progress would go a long way in creating a mutual self-respecting global tradition that will not only empower all nations but will minimize the divisive and ethnocentric approaches to matters involving human life.

We all need to take heed of Malcolm X's warning against cultural laxity and abandonment of traditional values, something that seems to be on the increase as people tend to emphasize globalizing influences. Africans at all levels should heed Malcolm X's (1970, pp. 55-56) observation that

> History is a people's memory ... When you have no knowledge of your history, you are just another animal ... you don't know who you are, you don't know what you are, you don't know where you are, you don't know how you got here. But as soon as you wake up and find out ... you ... become somebody.

Stressing the significance of culture in organizing humans in any one-society Ousmane (1979, p. 8) noted:

> Yesterday's culture which some considered a manifestation of primitives, symbol of ineptitude, stirred up thousands ... of men and women. This ancient culture is leaven. It is the ember, which blazes in the heart and lungs. And ... those who shaped it, created it, sculpted, sang, wove, and thought it for themselves in their own time, in their own situations, snatched this generation as well as those to come from prostration.

Malcolm X (1970) made a strong plea for blacks to revisit the past in order to understand the present and the future. People who embrace their historical roots learn to avoid errors of the past. Effective leaders and successful communities are those that recognize the power and continuity of culture in any society and its capacity to outlive generations of individuals. Culture knows no age and today's Africans must draw strength from the rich past cultural heritage. In the words of Sekou Toure it is imperative that Africans see themselves and their traditions and culture as ' ... an element of that popular energy which is entirely called forth for the freeing, the progress, and happiness of Africa' (Fanon, 1963, p. 206). In other words, unless globalization becomes an all encompassing force it will continue to be an oppressive and limiting force rather than a liberating and enriching force. So far globalization has had negative consequences on Africa, as it tends to undermine and ignore the positive contributions African heritage can make to human progress. This tendency does not mean that globalization per se is out and out a bad thing. Yet in many ways globalization has had a negative impact on African cultures and traditions. The forces of globalization have tended to impose western values, tastes and cultural influences on Africa. A hybrid global culture truly global in its orientation emphasizes humanity's common destiny would go a long way in creating sustainable conditions for humanity's progress.

It can be said that globalization should not seek to privilege a single culture, but recognizes the potential in each and every culture, if development is to spread to all corners of the globe. Experience so far has been that globalization is driven by self-interest and forces that seek to privilege the western values and interests at the expense of non-western groupings, in particular Africa. The restructuring processes are driven by economic self-interest and profit and tend to ignore people's needs. The problem of this approach has been more pronounced in Africa as seen by a deepening socio-economic crisis. This has led to HF decay and collapse of African societies. In Africa, globalization, instead of being an integrating force ushering in rapid development, operates as a constraining force limiting and undermining the free development of Africa (Smith, 2001; Orr, 2001; de Benoist 1996). The argument presented by Benoist (1996, p. 131) is quite compelling as he points out that

> Globalization destroys sovereignties, cuts through territories, abuses established communities, challenges social contracts and renders obsolete earlier concepts of international security ... Democratic principles are also threatened. There is a direct link between the loss of national sovereignty and the weakening of democracy.

This is especially true in Africa where the nation-state has never been strong. The decline in the influence of state institutions in some cases the disappearing state such as what happened in Somalia, Sierra Leone the Democratic Republic of the Congo has worsened the conditions of the poor especially women. It has fuelled the immizeration of general population.

The point I am trying to argue is that globalization as such is not necessarily a positive force. It has so far impacted on social development in Africa negatively because of the manner and way it has been defined and implanted. However, globalization has the potential to stimulate and channel people's energies for their own development, if only it can harness that potential that lies from within any given group of people. Globalization should embrace rather than exclude the positive aspects in Africa including Africa's positive HF qualities. First, by putting an emphasis on people and setting up institutions founded on positive HF principles and values that include an emphasis on African renaissance, a break from the perennial tragedies confronting Africa might come to an end. Positive HF development of Africa will not simply occur. It is likely to be a slow educational process that will eventually guarantee success. The HF will ensure that feelings of being uprooted, powerless and western dominated will go and more assertive and forward-looking Africans will engage in successful development efforts. Globalization, divested of the tendency to be equated with western values, the market and a strengthening of state institutions, but rather on respect and dignity of persons is a necessary condition for successful developmental influences in Africa. In other words, positive change will not simply occur: there is a need for Africans to invest and work towards sustainable development goals within the global village.

The Human Factor (HF) and Globalization

In order to fully understand the role and consequences of globalization it is critical that people understand the meaning and significance of the HF. The HF puts people at the centre of everything and is critical to Africa's development in this day of increasing global connectedness. Adjibolosoo (1995, pp. 33-34) defines the HF as the 'spectrum of personality characteristics and other dimensions of human performance that enable social, economic and political institutions to function and remain functional over time'. The HF affects the quality of life of any given group of people. It is not a pre-given but something people acquire in the course of living. Culture is a reflection of the quality of the HF of any given group of people. Some of the dimensions of the HF include personality traits such as honesty, trust, truth, loyalty, commitment, integrity, respect, accountability, responsibility, and dedication. HF principles guide people's behaviour in the course of daily interactions. The HF approach argues that at every stage the focus should be on people, their welfare and life chances. Development is that which has a positive effect on people's lives. Unfortunately, globalization has seen people sidelined in the development discourse affecting most of Africa.

The debate on globalization raises key issues that are useful to any discussions on the consequence and impact of globalization on African peoples. The HF is liberating, empowering and deeply ingrained in people's psyche. It is against this background that globalization in the African context is discussed. An understanding of factors that contribute to the disorienting and marginalizing influences of globalization in Africa can be enhanced through the HF approach. The HF is a key determinant of the quality of people's life. Six key dimensions of the HF as noted by Adjibolosoo (1995) include spiritual capital, moral capital, aesthetic capital, human capital, human abilities and human potential. Possession of higher qualities of these forms of capital has a positive bearing on the quality of life.

The centrality of the HF to organizational success led Adjibolosoo (1998, p. 27) to conclude that, 'the HF is the kingpin of every human endeavour. No human program achieves its best results without it'. Similarly the HF can be seen as both a necessary and sufficient condition for human happiness and when it is underdeveloped or absent it is likely to lead to moral degeneracy, human decay and in extreme cases disoriented communities characterized by HF decay. Globalization consistently begs the question of what is happening to African people's HF competencies and its content. The point is that unless increasing global-local connections affecting Africa incorporates people's HF principles there can never be any talk of meaningful development. The inclusion of the HF would result in globalization processes that would produce meaningful development in Africa.

African Renaissance: A Response to Globalization

Flowing from the idea of incorporating the HF in the development discourse in Africa is the need to single out African renaissance as one of the key techniques for dealing with globalization. The above discussions have shown that there are two schools of thought as far as globalization is concerned. On one hand, globalization does not address issues of inequality and injustices inherent in the post-colonial African state. Globalization can reinforce human disparities. This school is pessimist about Africa's future in the global world. On the other hand, is the cultural optimistic school. African culture is treasured and seen as a creative force to boost Africa's chances for development. For cultural optimists and those focusing on hybridization globalization poses a problem in that it challenges the idea of homogenization and a closed system as far as culture is concerned. The idea of cultural renaissance seeks to bridge the gap between the two schools of thought, the optimists and pessimists. Africa renaissance is a force that cab be marshalled to counter the negative impacts of globalization. African renaissance focuses on processes that seek to raise people's consciousness of their condition. African renaissance is about human dignity, self worth, self-respect, responsibility and a host of other positive HF attributes. As stressed by Robertson (1992, p. 183) contemporary globalization refers to 'cultural and subjective matters', incorporating growing awareness and reflection on humanity's condition. It is precisely this focus on the humanity of all and a call to an end to marginalizing influences of globalization that African renaissance is striving for.

There are many who view the concept of African renaissance, as an attempt to empower African peoples, to rebuild and revitalize a people's identity including the recovery of African women's identity and dignity. Underpinning this cultural revival is the quest to situate African men and women in a position that ensures they are visible in programmes that seek to end the indignities of poverty and underdevelopment.

Khoza (1999) drawing on the discussions of those championing the notion of African renaissance points out that the concept entails a process of rebirth, renewal, revitalization, rededication, learning and value reorientation, positive transformation, taking charge of one's identity, an end to poverty and human deprivation. In short, African renaissance is about raising people's HF attributes and qualities and to minimize the negative influence of globalization as westernization. Africa can then rise to take its place in the global village. Renaissance seeks to put men and women at the centre of Africa's development. It is in this context that the discussions linking renaissance to globalization should be considered. There should be a recognition amongst cultural revivalists that cultures do influence each other consciously and unconsciously. Renaissance then implies a need for promoting regional integration on the African continent.

Renaissance also needs to be situated within the global socio-economic and political order. This means that for African renaissance to take root a moral renaissance should be an integral component of this new development. Critical to the implementation of a successful cultural reawakening programme in a global world are gender considerations. There is a need to privilege not only the voice of African men but also that of African women if African renaissance is to have meaning and a place in the debate regarding globalization and Africa. African renaissance can be seen as a countervailing force to globalization. African renaissance fits in very well with the debate of globalization as hybridization. It is not a total rejection of globalization per se but renaissance discards the notion of globalization as homogenous but accepts the enriching influence of African culture to globalization debates.

Concluding Remarks

It is the argument in this chapter that globalization is at once a liberating as well as a constraining factor. It produces negative as well as positive consequences. To a large extent though, unless deliberate steps are taken to reverse the trend, globalization is a euphemism for westernization of non-western societies. It is a process contributing greatly to the destruction of local African cultures. The undermining of local narratives, values and belief systems assumes a global perspective through globalization processes. Yet with the recognition of humanity's diversity and differences globalization can usher in an era of cultural enrichment and prosperity. It is also possible that cultural contact that result with globalization can contribute to the creation of an awareness of other cultures and consequently can result in greater tolerance of difference. The chapter made it clear that embracing globalization for African societies should not be equated to discarding and abandonment of African traditions and culture. To the contrary, globalization can result in a cultural revival process and cultural reawakening as seen with African renaissance. There is also a deliberate attempt to privilege African traditions and culture in the context of globalizing influences.

Globalization is also linked to issues of positionality and representation of Africans in the global domain. Consequent to global influences more and more Africans would be able to articulate and pursue their interests. Africans have reached a stage where they can speak for themselves. This has come about as a result of growing awareness and commitment to freedom by Africans. The ability to articulate African values and interests can be traced to the liberating influences of globalization. As a phenomenon it is impossible to ignore the way globalization is changing power relations. The chapter also tries to show that there are strong links between globalization and processes relating to the development discourse such as restructuring, retrenchments, informalization of the economy, the decline, destruction and masculinization of the state and the feminization of poverty. The chapter has examined the consequences of globalization in Africa and made suggestions as to what could be done to salvage the negative state of affairs in Africa in the context of a globalizing world.

References

Adepoju, A. (ed.) (1993), *The Impact of Structural Adjustment on the Population of Africa: The Implications for Education, Health and Employment*, London: James Currey.

Adjibolosoo, Senyo B.-S.K. (1995), *The Significance of the Human Factor in African Economic Development*, Westport, CT: Praeger.

Adjibolosoo, Senyo B.-S.K. (1998), "The Human Factor: Foundation for Development and Democracy", in V.G. Chivaura and C.G. Mararike, (eds.), *The Human Factor Approach to Development in Africa*, Harare: University of Zimbabwe Publications.

Akokpari, J.K. (2001), "The debt crisis, the global economy and the challenges of development: Sub Saharan Africa at the crossroads", *Journal of Social Development in Africa*, 16 (2): 147-169.

Albrow, M. (1990), "Introduction", in Albrow, M. and King, E. (eds.) *Globalization, Knowledge and Society*, London: Sage.

De Benoist, A. (1996), "Confronting Globalization", *Telos*, 108: 117-137.

Fanon, F. (1963), *The Wretched of the Earth*, New York: Grove Press.

Featherstone, M. (ed.) (1990), *Global Culture: Nationalism, Globalization and Modernity*, London: Sage Publications.

Giddens, A. (1990), *The Consequences of Modernity*, Cambridge: Polity Press.

Gilroy, P. (1995), *There Ain't No Black in the Union Jack: The Cultural Politics of Race and Nation*, Chicago: University of Chicago Press.

Hannerz, U. (1996), *Transnational Connections: Culture, People, Places*, London: Routledge.

Hobsbawm, E. (1994), *Age of Extremes: The Short Twentieth Century, 1914-1991*, London: Michael Joseph.

IMF (1997), *World Economic Outlook*, New York: IMF (May).

Kellner, D. (1998), "Globalization and the Postmodernist Turn" in Axtamann, R. (ed.), *Globalization and Europe: Theoretical and Empirical Investigations*, London: Pinter.

Khoza, R. (1999), "The institutional structures that should underpin the African renaissance", in Makgoba, W. (ed.), *African Renaissance*, Cape Town: Mafube and Tafelbert Publishers.

Long, N. (2001), *Development Sociology: Actor Perspectives*, London: Routledge.

Malcolm X. (1970), *By Any Means Necessary*, New York: Pathfinder.

Mamimine, P.W. (2001), *Traditional Authority and Modern Institutions of Governance in Community Based Natural Resource Management*, Harare: CASS/PLAAS. CBNRM Occasional Paper.

Mararike, C.G. (1998), "The Role of Culture and History in Human Factor Development: A Comparative Analysis", *Review of Human Factor Studies*, 4 (1): 21-35.

Mlambo, A.S. and Pangeti, E.S. (2000), *Globalization, Structural Adjustment and the Social Dimensions Dilemma in Zimbabwe: 1990 – 1999*, unpublished paper presented at OSSREA's Sixth Congress held in Dar Es Salaam, Tanzania from the 24th to 28th of April 2000.

Muzvidziwa, I. (1999), "Transformational Leadership and School Effectiveness in the Zimbabwe", *Bulletin of Teacher Education*, 2 (1): 58-73.

Ndhlovu, T. (2000), "Globalization and Transformation: An Investigation of Whole School Development in South Africa", *Journal of Education*, 25: 49-62.

Ousmane, S. (1979), *Man is Culture*, Indiana University: African Studies Programme.

Owolabi, K.A. (2001), "Globalization, Americanization and Western Imperialism". *Journal of Social Development in Africa*, 16 (2): 71-91.

Pieterse, J.N. (1995), "Globalization as Hybridization" in Featherstone, M.; Lash, S. and Robertson, R. (eds.) *Global Modernities*, London: Sage.

Robertson, R. (1992), *Globalization: Social Theory and Global Culture*, London: Sage.

Smith, G. (2001), "Cutting Threads: Retrenchments and Women Workers in the Western Cape Clothing Industry", *Agenda*, 48: 38-43.

Uroh, C.O. (2000), *Globalization and the Commoditization of Knowledge in Africa*, paper presented at the AISA 40th Anniversary Conference "A United States of Africa?" Pretoria: May 30 – June 2, 2000.

Wunch, J.S. (1990), "Centralization and Development in Post-Independence Africa", in Wunsch, J. S. and Olowu, D. (eds.) *The Failure of Centralized State: Institutions and Self-Governance in Africa*, San Francisco, Western Press.

Yearley, S. (1996), *Sociology, Environmentalism and Globalization: Reinventing the Globe*, London: Sage Publications.

Chapter 5

Globalization and Diversity in the Tourism Industry: A Human Factor Perspective

Francis Adu-Febiri

Introduction

At the interface of globalization and tourism is a natural diversity in the areas of demographic and cultural representations. However, the tourism industry tends to push this diversity to the margins with the assumption that cultural cloning at the core of the industry would maximize the bottom-line. This chapter agues that this assumption is faulty. It agrees with postmodernist thinking that tourism can optimize productivity/profit, enhance social justice, enrich cultures, and motivate environmental conservation when it facilitates rather than destroys cultural diversity. It also affirms the postmodernist position that diversity can be successfully facilitated in tourism in spite of the homogenizing tendencies of globalization. However, contrary to the perspective of postmodernism, this chapter does not problematize globalization. This is because globalization is not the problem; the problem is human factor decay and/or underdevelopment. Therefore, the key to successful facilitation of diversity in tourism is not the halting of globalization and/or multiculturalism policies and diversity management programs as many postmodernists believe, but rather the application of appropriate human factor. Adjibolosoo (1995, p. 33) refers to the human factor (HF), as 'a spectrum of personality characteristics that enables social, economic, and political institutions to function and remain functional over time'. In other words, the human factor is a complex interaction of knowledge, skills, abilities and principles that transform human capacity and control human conduct for the betterment or debasement of the individual and society (Adu-Febiri, 2000).

Tourism in a global society produces diversity and this diversity needs to be facilitated to increase productivity/profitability, enhance social interactions, enrich cultures, and conserve the physical environment. Yet tourism managers/entrepreneurs tend to control and destroy diversity in the areas of demographic representation, management style, and organizational culture. This managerial diversity paradigm solidifies the pre-modern and modern hierarchical organizational mold of the political economy of domination that works for the benefit of the few rather than unleashing the energy of diversity to produce greater wealth, organizational effectiveness, and social justice. 'From the postmodern vantage point, the homogenization of capitalist culture worldwide represents a hegemonic attempt to suppress cultural diversity and identity differences' (Peter Li, 1999, p. 9). It could be inferred from this postmodern notion of globalization that what explains this tourism managers/entrepreneurs' tendency to destroy diversity is the homogenizing force of globalization to maximize profit. That is, the tourism industry has no choice but to annihilate or marginalize diversity in the interest of the bottom-line. What postmodernists (McClellan and Richmond, 1994; Lyotard, 1984, 1992; Jameson, 1991; Bauman, 1992) fail to realize is that globalization or capitalist culture does not necessarily obliterate cultural diversity. It is human factor decay/underdevelopment that destroys diversity. With human factor competency tourism managers/entrepreneurs would realize that a more natural way to profit optimization is to facilitate rather than control diversity that globalization naturally produces.

Globalization is not a problem or a dominating force *per se*. It is merely the integration of existing social structures and interactions of the world through communication technology, trade, immigration, transportation, and tourism. However, in a situation of human factor decay/underdevelopment, globalization can be a homogenizing force that produces 'industrialized production, routinized procedures, standardized consumption, and monoculturalism' (Fleras and Elliott, 1999, p. 105). Put metaphorically, Nelson and Fleras (1998) likened globalization to the McDonald fast food system: 'In place of diversity is a growing trend toward 'McDonaldization' of societies into a single global loop where differences are dismissed or commodified' (cited in Fleras and Elliott, 1999, p. 105). The irony is that the very globalism that threatens cultural diversity bolsters demographic and cultural diversities by facilitating immigration and other population movements (that also imply cultural diversity). As well, globalism promotes a greater urge to be special or claim differences in the midst of mass consumerism and pressures of conformity and routinization (Behrens, 1994; Fukuyama, 1994). The most crucial question is whether or not the diversity resulting from globalization can be harnessed to the interest of all rather than few (Fleras and Elliott, 1999, p. 105). This paper resonates with postmodernist belief that diversity can be harnessed to the benefit of society. However, it parts company with postmodernists when it comes to the effective approaches to realize this noble dream. The multiculturalism model Fleras and Elliott (1999) suggest cannot unleash the positive energy of demographic and cultural diversity that emerges from globalization to work for tourism. The experiences of pioneering multicultural countries like Canada, Australia and Singapore reveal that multiculturalism policies fossilize cultural diversity and push it to the margins of communities, institutions, and organizations (Adu-Febiri, 2002). Neither could the managing diversity model adequately do the job of harnessing diversity for the benefit of all tourism stakeholders. The managerial approach adopted by these models tends to freeze diversity in the mold of political economy of domination (Adu-Febiri, 2001). It is in light of the track record of the failed attempts to make diversity work for all stakeholders of the tourism industry that this chapter proposes a new diversity model: Facilitating Diversity Model. This new model claims that the key to putting diversity to work for the tourism industry is the application of appropriate human factor in the form of human factor competency.

To substantiate this claim, section one of the chapter explores the diversity dynamics of tourism in the context of globalization. Section two looks at the multiculturalism model of diversity in the tourism industry while section three focuses on the managing diversity model. These two models are discussed under the umbrella of the concept managerial paradigm. In section four, the facilitating diversity model is introduced. It is used to show why and how globalization-induced diversity in the tourism industry could be harnessed to boost tourism's bottom-line, enhance tourists-host interaction, and enrich the economies, cultures, and physical environments of destination communities. The concluding section reiterates the linkages among globalization, diversity in the tourism industry, and the human factor. It highlights that human factor competency is the key for unleashing the energy of diversity to work for all stakeholders of the tourism industry.

The Global Implosion and Diversity Dynamics of Tourism

Before globalization drew nation-states into a single world economy and community, tourism was largely monolithic. That is, it involved mainly elite (aristocratic and bourgeois) males of Greece, the Roman Empire, Western Europe, and the Western Sudanese Empires of Africa (English, 1986; West Africa, November 23, 1987). With the global implosion all that has changed, especially since World War II. Rapid modernization and post-modernization, particularly economic growth, technological advancement, and cultural/social liberation, has produced a large number of tourists from the Americas, Europe, Australia, Asia, and Africa. This new development has added social class, gender, able-ness, racial, and ethnic dimensions to tourism guests in tourism destinations. Labor and capital migrations have also increased the demographic, cultural, and organizational diversity of tourism hosts.

Analyzing the demographic variations in international travel, Pearce (1983, p. 51) correctly observed that

> Comparative analysis of different groups of international travelers has been hampered by the limited availability of comparable data. Age and sex statistics, however, exist for a number of countries and have been utilized by Weiss (1971) and Pearce (1978a) to examine the demographic variations in international travel. Both these studies, while being far from comprehensive, suggest that significant variations do occur in the demographic characteristics of international travelers from different countries.

These different countries include the United Kingdom, West Germany, USA, Japan, Australia, and New Zealand (Ibid.). Because globalization has made these countries multiracial and multicultural, tourists from these countries include a proportion of non-Whites and non-Westerners. In fact, although the proportion is small, African, South American, and other Asian countries also produce international tourists. This dimension of the data shows that there is racial/ethnic aspect of the demographic variation of international tourists. Despite this racial/ethnic diversity of postmodern tourists in the global village, travel and tourism brochures feature monolithic tourists (Adu-Febiri, 1998). Tourists are portrayed mainly as white and western.

The composition of demographic characteristics of the tourism labor force is not different from that of the tourists described above. The tourism labor force is very diverse in the areas of gender, age, ability, sexuality, social class, race and ethnicity. However, white males dominate the skilled and managerial positions in the tourism industry. According to English (1986, p. 42), 'Some transnational hotel corporations have shown considerable reluctance to hire or train [non-western/white] nationals for positions of responsibility'. Kenya is a typical illustration: 'The ILO study (1987) on the structure of hotel employment corroborates earlier studies such as those of Mitchell (1968), and Tourist Consult (1979), and Migot-Adholla et al. (1982). These studies point to the native Kenyan-expatriate hotel employee imbalance, especially for key positions' (Dieke, 1991, p. 285). Even in countries like Ghana (Adu-Febiri, 1994), Mauritius and Zimbabwe (Christie and Crompton, 2001) where the tourism 'industry has been heavily locally or regionally owned and managed from the outset' (Christie and Crompton, 2001, p. 22), it is very male dominated at the top. The fact is, demographically diversity in the tourism industry, like other organizations in the global village, is pushed from the core to the margins. Even the diversity occurring at the margins of tourism is only demographic. Culturally, these employees are compelled to conform to western cultural and/or masculine travel and hospitality norms and values. The managerial paradigm of diversity, that is, the multiculturalism model and the managing diversity model, discussed below lends credence to this claim. The managerial paradigm organizes diversity for profit/productivity, if even at the cost of some stakeholders. It lacks the vision and commitment to foster a diversity environment in which all individuals and groups can work together harmoniously and to their full potential to enrich themselves, the organization, and their communities.

Multicultural Model of Diversity in Tourism

Globalization has transformed many countries into demographically multiracial and multicultural societies. Until about the 1970s this demographic mixtures was managed with explicit assimilationist model. The contestation between those who endorse this exclusionary system and those fighting for inclusiveness has produced the need to multiculturalize race/ethnic relations management agenda (Giroux,

1994, cited in Fleras and Elliott, 1999, p. 349). Multiculturalism policies and programs are thus formulated to manage the conflictual interface of the multiracial/multicultural interactions. The multiculturalism model declares to relativize cultural difference. However, its operation has tended to focus on symbolic multiculturalism or celebration of multicultural events and employment equity at the margins of communities, institutions, and organizations. The practice of diversity, mainly by default, in the tourism industry reflects this multiculturalism model of diversity. This falls short of the postmodern vision of multiculturalism that questions 'the idea of cultural homogenization through the global transformation of industrial capitalism and mass-market consumerism' (McClellan and Richmond, 1994, p. 665). The postmodern vision portrays multiculturalism as

> A process of engaging diversity as different yet equal, With multiculturalism a framework is established for full and equal participation of minority women and men through removal of discriminatory institutional barriers (both cultural and structural). Cultural space is created that confirms a minority right to be different yet the same ('equal'), depending on the circumstances. Under multiculturalism, a social and political climate is fostered in which diversity initiatives can be introduced without inciting a backlash or social turmoil (Fleras and Elliott, 1999, p. 296).

An examination of publicity and employment practices of the tourism industry would show that this vision of multiculturalism does not exist. Demographic diversity is extended to the middle levels of the industry as a reaction to 1) accusations of exploitation and imperialism from radical groups, and 2) employment equity legislation. There may be few token minorities, usually women from the dominant groups, in top management. Management and employees attend few workshops on cultural competency that would suppose to make them culturally sensitive to minority members and issues. The organizational culture and structure, however, remain monolithic.

In effect, the multiculturalism globalization engenders in the tourism industry is controlled as cultural, racial, and gender vertical mosaic rather than unleashing its energy to work for the industry through the facilitation of productive diversity. The Managing diversity model emerged to fix this reactive approach to diversity the multiculturalism model adopts. However, although the managing diversity model is a proactive approach to diversity, it is bound to fail to truly multiculturalize the tourism industry because of its neglect of human factor competency.

The Managing Diversity Model of Tourism

Unlike the multiculturalism model of diversity, the managing diversity model adopts a proactive approach to the globalization-induced diversity. That is, it voluntarily chooses to organize cultural diversity for increased productivity or profit. In tourism this model accounts for the commoditization of minorities and their cultures. This model extends the conception of diversity from racial, ethnic, and gender differences to cover other pertinent differences such as ability, sexual orientation, age, class, family status, and individual idiosyncrasies (Jackson, 1992; Cox and Beale, 1997; Poole, 1997; Carr-Ruffino, 2000; Carrell et al.). It focuses on managing the various forms of cultural diversity for increased organizational effectiveness and/or profit. For example, a recent article from DiversityInc.com (2001, p. 1) emphasizes that

> In the 21st century, companies and universities alike are shifting from diversity strategies focused on race to knowledge- and skills-based initiatives that stress ways in which a workforce's cultural insights can be integrated into its business model and used to boost the bottom line (Emphasis original).

Organizations that adopt this model concentrate on educating and training managers to acquire and apply diversity competency and cultural competency (diversity knowledge and skills) to primarily advance the productivity goals of the organization, and secondarily to meet the management-constructed needs of employees.

The orientation of the managing diversity 'model' is a response mainly to the business necessities created by workforce diversity and marketplace diversity emerging from globalization. Thus in the tourism industry this diversity is defined primarily as a business asset to the organization that needs to be utilized to maximize productivity/profit. Diversity is organized as cultural artifacts and events for the enjoyment of tourists. The focus is on packaging cultural artifacts and events such as arts, crafts, foods, clothing, performances, and minority people themselves as part of the tourism product for profit. The organizational culture and structure remain mainstream. In tourism the managing diversity model, like its predecessor the multiculturalism model, continues to favor the hiring of women and minorities. In fact, the tourism industry is praised for employing more women and local people than other sectors (Christie and Crompton, 2001). However, these women and minorities are usually absorbed at the margins or lower levels of the industry.

The managing diversity model reflects the sociological paradigm of structural-functionalism postulating that the efficient management of diversity in the workplace, even if it maintains status quo inequalities, is good for the organizational bottom line. It argues that diversity policies, programs, and projects are initiated and implemented only when there is a consensus that they will reinforce societal values, increase productivity/profit, and benefit deserving employees. Furthermore, this model claims to aim at developing diversity programs that facilitate organizational transformation by using socialization techniques to alter 'organization members' beliefs, values, and ideologies in dealing with difference in the workplace' (Prasad et al., 1997, p. 8). Diversity competency is the specific tool identified to accomplish this transformation (Cox and Beale, 1997). It is the stance of this chapter that diversity competency is inadequate.

The point is, diversity competency, although contributes to the workplace diversification process, is not enough to succeed in eliminating the monolithic workplace structure and culture that frustrate non-mainstream employees of organizations. Diversity competency can only tinker with diversity because it is a heartless managerial tool or an add-on of the managing diversity 'model'. No wonder, organizations operating in the managerial diversity mode tend to package diversity for public consumption while leaving the monolithic value, belief, normative, and symbolic systems and work assignments in the organization virtually intact. In effect, these organizations do not develop an adequate competency that will help them facilitate diversity to experience its full benefits. Organizations identified as diversity showcases (see Jackson, 1992 and Canadian Heritage, 1993 for examples) exhibit this inadequacy.

It is important to note that organizations adopting the managing diversity 'model' and its 'cultural competency' and 'diversity competency' tools are unable to go beyond human capital (knowledge and skills) development and catering to the interests of the mainstream. They pursue diversity by organizing activities and controlling resources in such a way as pleases the owners and mainstream employees of the organizations. That is, workplace diversity is considered seriously only when it dovetails with the managerial mode of operation, namely, upholding mainstream normative system, maximizing profit, and favoring mainstream employees. The benefits of diversification using the managing diversity 'model', if any, to racial and cultural minorities are only incidental.

Cultural competency and diversity competency are great tools for workplace diversification. However, they will not work well in situations of human factor decay/underdevelopment. Adjibolosoo (1995) observed that human factor decay/underdevelopment is a situation where there is lack of not only knowledge and skills, but also lack of honesty, integrity, trust, accountability, responsibility, commitment, acceptance, loving-kindness, and the like due to overemphasis on personal wealth and self-gratification. Because of human factor decay/underdevelopment, some organizations see the negative impact of racial, ethnic, and gender conflict on their operations, but they lack the capacity to eliminate the conflict. In the absence of human factor competency all that organizations can do is to *manage* conflict. That is, they control such conflict by pretending to value diversity. This is done through the promotion of some cultural events like folk festivals and religious holidays. Many organizations at this diversity stage do not go beyond 'dress, diet, and dance' dimensions of culture. That is, the heroes, logos, legends, stories, time use pattern, dress code, diet code, and other aspects of workplace culture remain monolithic and logocentric. In a sense, the substantive values and needs of racial/ethnic minorities, women, and other marginalized groups are excluded from the organization, hence the tension continues but in a suppressed form ready to explode. This is not an accident. The gatekeepers of the organization use this management tactic to maintain the ivory tower and the glass ceiling to perpetuate the interests of the dominant groups.

The multiculturalism and managing diversity models make the diversity generated at the interface of globalization and diversity a terrain of tensions, conflicts, and inequities. These problems limit the benefits of diversity not only for gender, racial and cultural minorities, but also for organizations, institutions, and industries. Yet diversity is a powerful energy that can be unleashed to develop organizational effectiveness, optimize productivity/profit, and enhance social justice. The cultural and diversity competencies that the managerial paradigm of diversity advocates are necessary but insufficient to unleash the positive energy of globalization-produced diversity in tourism because of human factor decay/underdevelopment. The neglect of human factor competency underlies the inability of the managing diversity model to fully include gender, racial, ethnic and other minorities into the core of organizations and institutions.

In sum, underlying the façade of the managerial diversity model are organizational structure and corporate culture that reproduce prejudice and stereotype that devalue the 'other' and rationalize discrimination and segregation in the workplace. This is a major source of conflict and complaint in the workplace (BC Human Rights Commission Report, 2001). In short, existing organizational structure and culture in both the public and private sectors do not place adequate value on non-mainstream people, welcome their differences, and integrate them into the workplace. This lends credence to the superficiality critique of many of the workplace diversity success stories. The superficiality of diversity showcases is the outcome of diversity programs operating exclusively in the managerial model with parochial competencies. That is, competencies like diversity competency and cultural competency that focus primarily on knowledge and skills.

Given the track record of the managerial diversity models shown above, for the tourism industry to achieve diversity that is sustainable and beneficial to all stakeholders, diversity modeling must transcend the managerial paradigm of diversity to focus on diversity facilitation that emphasizes human factor competency development and application.

Human factor competency (HFC) involves the acquisition and application of appropriate knowledge and understanding, relevant skills and strategies, respectful attitude and behavior, useful abilities, and essential human qualities of integrity, vision, accountability, responsibility, loving-kindness, tolerance, acceptance, etc. HFC is at the core of Facilitating Diversity Model introduced in the next section of this chapter.

Facilitating Diversity Model of Tourism

The managerial paradigm of diversity presents a discrete, mechanical view of diversity. Yet the reality is that workplace diversity is a process consisting of integrated dimensions and dynamics that needs to be facilitated to benefit all stakeholders. A new model needs to be formulated to capture this reality of workplace diversity. Since this reality has more to do with the human factor than mechanical managerial efficiency, the new model must transcend the managerial paradigm and introduce human factor competency into diversity programs. It requires a diversity leadership that is not only able to value, create, and manage diversity, but also provide the nurturing environment and the vision and passion to facilitate diversity to ensure sustainability as well as utility for all constituents. This new model, Facilitating Diversity Model, produces diversity programs characterized by holism, passion, vision, and strategy guided by human factor competency (HFC). HFC is the ability to apply appropriate knowledge, skills, and normative principles to effectively identify and solve problems that work against productivity, profitability, social justice, cultural development, and environmental preservation (Adu-Febiri, 2001). According to the Human Factor Competency Model, in addition to appropriate knowledge, skills and attitude, there is the need for other essential human qualities such as determination, commitment, responsibility, accountability, tolerance, loving-kindness, care, and integrity with regard to the human community, to produce competent leadership.

Diversity programs without human factor competency, particularly leadership without caring, sharing and integrity, can be oppressive and exploitative. Leadership with caring, sharing and integrity is one of the crucial missing links in the existing diversity programs. Short of caring, sharing and integrity diversity directors, facilitators and committees cannot act justly and responsibly, value selflessness and humility, and act honestly and accountably to the human community as a whole. Where caring, sharing and integrity are lacking external coercion such as legislation (Canada's Employment Equity Act and America's Affirmative Action legislation) has to be applied to elicit expected behavior. However, external social control cannot take the place of competent leadership. This is because the influence of such a control, if any, is superficial and short-lived as revealed in the dismal impact of Canada's Multiculturalism and Employment Equity programs (see Deeby, 2001; BC Human Rights Commission, 2001; and Purewal, 1999 for detailed discussion on this issue). This is in addition to the fact that it is too expensive to operate coercive systems. With human factor competency built into it, the facilitating diversity model effectively utilizes non-coercive socialization strategies to help management and employees to develop and apply diversity competent leadership.

Since the Facilitating Diversity Model functions with competent people, human factor competency is its linchpin. Unlike the managerial diversity paradigm, embedded in this new diversity model is the conviction that managers and employees of organizations have to be qualitatively transformed, that is, experience paradigm shift both in mind-set and behavior, in order to transform the monolithically organized workplace into a truly diversified workplace. The pertinent challenge is how to develop human factor competency. Throughout history society has most of the time succeeded in using socialization agencies (the family, religious institution, peer group, school, criminal justice system, the media) and techniques (persuasion, training, rewards, punishments, rituals, and mentoring) to produce the competencies it deemed necessary. The facilitating diversity model uses these same socialization agencies and techniques to cultivate and foster human factor competency in the managers and workers of organizations. The tourism industry could benefit from this new diversity model.

Human factor competency seems to be the only real solution to under-/miss-representation, alienation, frustration, and rage problems of workplace diversity. As such this competency should be acquired and applied throughout all dimensions of the tourism industry. The human factor competency development involves a five-stage cyclical process – assessment, awareness, understanding, valuing, and action – of socialization that develops not only the intellectual and technical dimensions of people, but also their moral, social, cultural, spiritual, aesthetic and other domains. It is these processes that need to be effectively applied to develop human factor competency among tourism entrepreneurs, tourism managers, and tourism employees.

In effect, HFC development in tourism is necessary for the industry's diversity programs to create and maintain high employee morale, quality service/product, customer satisfaction, and profitability/productivity. In other words, these benefits of diversity can only be realized through the total commitment of tourists to HFC development and application. Since the process of HFC development is cyclical rather than linear, there will always be new challenges at the various stages of the cycles as HFC programs are designed and implemented. It is imperative, therefore, for tourisiers to know that HFC development 'is a journey, not a destination' (Ellis, 1998, p. 211). Continuous evaluation and revision of the proposed HFC model is the key to successful development of HFC that will effectively facilitate diversity in the tourism industry in a global world.

Conclusion

Tourism as an integral aspect of globalization does not necessarily produce homogenization, domination, and inequality. The main culprit of these problems which postmodernists falsely associate with globalization is human factor deficiency. It is this deficiency that Adjibolosoo (1995) terms human factor decay/underdevelopment. The postmodernist approach to maintain cultural diversity through the halting of globalization, official multiculturalism, and managerial diversity programs are therefore flawed. The global integration of societies and communities is so powerful that it is unlikely to be stopped. It is not even necessary to halt the process because globalization is not the problem, globalization merely reinforces existing domination systems and inequalities resulting from human factor deficiencies. Moreover, postmodernist evocation of official multiculturalism and managing diversity programs as guides to a transformative diversity practice will not work because they ignore the root cause of lack of true diversity. As the discussion of this chapter reveals, multiculturalism and managerial approach to workplace diversity without human factor competency perpetuate the status quo wittingly or unwittingly. However, given the dynamics of diversity in postmodern society 'the status quo is no longer an option' (Soto, 2000,

p. 1). It is in this light that the facilitating diversity model is imperative. The facilitating diversity model offers hope for a more effective direction to productive diversity in the tourism industry. This is not only because the facilitating diversity model is holistic and operates on a strong passion, a more inclusive vision, and a comprehensive strategy, but mainly because its focal point is human factor competency. Since the existing identified barriers to productive diversity in tourism are symptomatic of human factor deficiencies, neither diversity competency nor cultural competency endorsed by postmodernists could fundamentally change the tourism industry. Therefore if the tourism industry is serious about diversification that works for the benefit of all its stakeholders, it needs to channel adequate resources to the development and application of human factor competency among tourism entrepreneurs, managers, and employees.

References

Adjibolosoo, Senyo. B-S.K. (1995), *The Human Factor in Developing Africa*, Westport, Connecticut: Praeger.

Adu-Febiri, Francis (2002), "Workplace Diversity: Going Beyond the Managerial Model of Diversity", www.pacificcoast.net/~diversity.articles.

Adu-Febiri, Francis (2001), "Human Factor Competence and the Performance Effectiveness of Hospitality Professionals", in Senyo Adjibolosoo (ed.) *Portraits of Behavior: The Human Factor in Action*, Lanham: University Press of America, Inc.

Adu-Febiri, Francis (2000), "Putting the Human Factor to Work in African Tourism: A Human Factor Competency Model", a paper presented at the 4th Bi-Annual Conference of the International Institute for Human Factor Development (IIHFD), July 17-18, 2000. Harare: University of Zimbabwe.

Adu-Febiri, Francis (1998), "Tourists Welcome in the Great White North", *Voices*, Victoria, B.C. Canada, pp. 18-19.

Adu-Febiri, Francis (1994), *Tourism and Ghana's Development Process: Problems of and Prospects for Creating a Viable "Post-Industrial" Service Industry in a Non-Industrial Society*, Unpublished Ph.D. Dissertation, Department of Anthropology and Sociology, University of British Columbia.

Bauman, Z. (1992), *Intimations of Postmodernity*, London: Routledge.

Behrens, Gerd, (1994), "Love, Hate, and Nationalism", *Time Magazine*, March 21.

British Columbia Human Rights Commission (2001), *Not Good Enough! Representation of Aboriginal People, People with Disabilities, and Visible Minorities in the British Columbia Public Service*, Vancouver, BC: BC Human Rights Commission.

Canadian Heritage (1993), "Diversity Success Stories: Case Studies", in *Toward Full Inclusion: Gaining the Diversity Advantage*, Quebec City: Department of Canadian Heritage.

Carrell, Michael R., Norbert, Elbert F., and Robert D. Hatfield (2000), *Human Resource Management: Strategies for Managing a Diverse and Global Workforce*, Sixth Edition, New York: The Dryden Press.

Carr-Ruffino, Norma, (2000), *Managing Diversity: People Skills for a Multicultural Workplace*, Needham Heights: Pearson Custom Publishing.

Chan, Janet (1996), "Police Racism: Experiences and Reforms", in E. Vasta and S. Castles (eds.) *The Teeth are Smiling: The Persistence of Racism in Multicultural Australia*, Sydney: Allen and Unwin.

Christie, Iain T. and Crompton, Doreen E. (2001), Tourism in Africa: World Bank Working Paper Series No. 2. www.worldbank.org/afr/wps/wp12.pdf.

Cox Jr., Taylor and Beale, Ruby L. (1997), *Developing Competency to Manage Diversity*, San Francisco: Berrett-Koehler.

Deeby, Dean (2001), "Equity Program Bombs", *The Canadian Press*, Halifax, July 12, 2001.

Desroches, F.J. (1998), "The Occupational Subculture of the Police", in Brian Cryderman, Chris O'Toole and Augie Fleras (eds.) *Policing, Race, and Ethnicity: A Guidebook for the Policing Services*, 3rd Edition. Toronto: Butterworths.

Dieke, Peter U.C. (1991), "Policies for Tourism Development in Kenya", *Annals of Tourism Research*, 18 (2): 269-294.

DiversityInc.com. (2001), "Culture: A Corporate Asset That Keeps Growing, Even in a Downturn", Retrieved July 12, 2001 www.diversityinc.com/insidearticlepg.cfm.

Eagly, A.H. and B.T. Johnson (1990), "Gender and Leadership Style", *Psychological Bulletin,* 108: 233-256.

Ellis, Taylor (1998), "Quality Service in the Hospitality Industry", in Robert A. Brymer (ed.) *Hospitality and Tourism: An Introduction to the Industry*, Eighth Edition. Dubuque, Iowa: Kendall/Hunt Publishing Company.

English, Philip E. (1986), *The Great Escape: An Examination of North-South Tourism*, Ottawa: The North-South Institute.

Fleras, Augie and Elliott, Jean L. (1999), *Unequal Relations: An Introduction to Race, Ethnic, and Aboriginal Dynamics in Canada*, Third Edition. Scarborough: Prentice Hall.

Fukuyama, Frances (1994), "The War of All Against All", *New York Times Book Review*, New York: New York Times Co.

Gates, T. (1993), "White Male Paranoia", *Newsweek* (March 29): 48-53.

Gordon, J.R. (1993), *A Diagnostic Approach to Organizational Behavior*, Boston: Allyn & Bacon.

Gowing, Marilyn K. and Payne, Sandra S. (1992), "Assessing the Quality of the Federal Workforce: A Program to Meet Diverse Needs", in Susan E. Jackson and Associates, *Diversity in the Workplace. Human Resources Initiatives*, New York: The Guilford Press.

Gupta, Tania Das (1996), *Racism and Paid Work*, Toronto: Garamond Press.

Jackson, Susan E. and Associates (1992), *Diversity in the Workplace. Human Resources Initiatives*, New York: The Guilford Press.

Jameson, F. (1991), *Postmodernism, or The Cultural Logic of Late Capitalism*, London: Verso.

Li, Peter S. (1999), *Race and Ethnic Relations in Canada*, Second Edition, Toronto: Oxford University Press.

Lyotard, J.-F. (1992), *The Postmodern Explained*, Minneapolis: Minnesota University Press.

Lyotard, J.-F. (1984), *The Postmodern Condition: A Report of Knowledge*, Manchester: Manchester University Press.

McClellan, Janet and Anthony H. Richmond, (1994), "Multiculturalism in Crisis: A Postmodern Perspective on Canada", *Ethnic and Racial Studies*, 17: 662-683.

Mighty, Joy E. (1997), "Triple Jeopardy: Immigrant Women of Color in the Labor Force", in Pushkala Prasad, Albert J. Mills, Michael Elmes and Anshuman Prasad (eds.)

Managing the Organizational Melting Pot: Dilemmas of Workplace Diversity, Thousand Oaks: Sage Publications.

Miller, Earl A. (2001), "Equitable Leadership at Scotiabank", Presentation to Government of British Columbia Senior Managers, Victoria, B.C., June 27, 2001.

Nelson, Adie and Fleras, Augie (1998), *Social Problems in Canada: Conditions and Consequences*, 2nd Edition, Scarborough: Prentice-Hall.

O'Mara, Julie (1984), *Diversity: Activities and Training Designs*, San Diego: Pfeiffer & Company.

Pearce, Douglas (1983) *Tourism Today: A Geographical Analysis*, London: Longman.

Poole, Phebe-Jane (1997), *Diversity: A Business Advantage: A practical Guide*, Ajax, Ontario: Poole Publishing Company.

Prasad, Pushkala (1997), "The Protestant Ethic and the Myths of the Frontier: Cultural Imprints, Organizational Structuring, and Workplace Diversity", in Pushkala Prasad, Albert J. Mills, Michael Elmes and Anshuman Prasad (eds.), *Managing the Organizational Melting Pot: Dilemmas of Workplace Diversity*, Thousand Oaks: Sage Publications.

Prasad, Pushkala and Mills, Albert J. (1997), "From Showcase to Shadow: Understanding the Dilemmas of Managing Workplace Diversity", in Pushkala Prasad, Albert J. Mills, Michael Elmes and Anshuman Prasad (eds.) *Managing the Organizational Melting Pot: Dilemmas of Workplace Diversity*, Thousand Oaks: Sage Publications.

Purewal, Shinder (1999), "Visible Minorities Badly Under-represented", *The Indo-Canadian Voice*, January 16, 9 (3): 1 and 6.

Soto, Jose J. (2000), "The Status Quo is no Longer an Option: Diversity is about Change and Leadership", Retrieved January 14, 2001, www.immotionmagazine.com/soto3.html.

Towers Perrin and Hudson Institute (1990), *Workforce 2000: Competing in a Seller's Market: Is Corporate America Prepared?*, Valhalla, NY: Towers Perrin.

Vancouver Ethnocultural Advisory Committee of the Ministry for Children and Families (1997), *Cultural Competency: Assessment Tool*, Vancouver: Ministry for Children and Families.

West Africa (1987), "City in the Sands", November 23, London: West Africa Publishing Company Limited: 2288-2289.

PART III:
GLOBALIZATION, THE HUMAN
FACTOR AND SCIENCE AND
TECHNOLOGY

Chapter 6

National Agricultural Research Systems, the Biotechnology Revolution and Agricultural Development

Korbla P. Puplampu

Introduction

The recent strides in technology have revolutionized agricultural, marketing and consumption systems worldwide. Biotechnological innovations, in particular, have changed the nature of agricultural production, and have significant implications for the marketing and consumption of agricultural goods and services. Underlining the technological innovations is the fact that agricultural systems are no longer likely to be slow and laborious (Sherwood, 1989). These changes, especially in agricultural research, no doubt, have immense possibilities and implications for global agriculture. However, it is equally important to subject the possibilities and implications of technological changes in agriculture to a reality check, given the significant differences in agricultural research systems worldwide, differences that, in turn, mirror global inequalities.

Agricultural research systems in the developed industrialized and capitalist societies, to a very large extent, have undertaken innovative measures, are up to the potential of biotechnology and, indeed, are already utilizing it to improve upon their production, marketing and consumption systems (Janssen, 2002; UNDP, 2001; Tzotzos, 2000). For one thing, the gigantic multinational corporations (for example, Monsanto) at the helm of the research and development in biotechnology, have their targets on the temperate crops consumed in wealthy societies (DaSilva, 2001; Paarlberg, 2000).

To be sure, the role of biotechnology in advanced capitalist industrial countries has not been problem-free. Long before the French activist, José Bové, became popular in 1999 after leading a campaign against McDonald's, the global fast-food chain, and the destruction of genetically altered rice fields, prominent Europeans like Prince Charles and the musical icon Paul McCartney had made remarks critical about biotechnology. From the latter part of the 1990s, Western Europeans, particularly the British and the French, have been ambiguous about genetically modified food (Hodgson, 1999). Public resentments through organizations like Green Peace and some farmers' associations in the United States and Canada have also been growing against and, are sometimes, ambivalent with respect to genetically modified foods (Eichenwald, Kolata and Petersen, 2001, Einsiedel, 2000; Priest, 2000). The grounds for the ambivalence, in both Europe and North America, range from the safety of genetically modified food for human consumption, the implications of biotechnology for the environment, to the regulative framework being proposed by governments and the industry (*The Economist*, 1999). Such ambivalence continues even though various bodies have stressed the importance and potential of biotechnology, provided effective safeguards are introduced and enforced (see Nuffield Council on Bioethics, 1999).

Thus, it is not surprising that the role of biotechnology in global agricultural systems has been mixed and tapered with considerable caution and, at times, controversy (Gaskell and Durant, 2002; Gaskell and Bauer, 2001; Pinstrup-Andersen and Schiøler, 2001; Persley and Lantin, 2000; AgBioForum, 1999; Panos, 1999; Ruttan, 1999). With specific reference to Africa, there are analysts who demonstrate that biotechnology is the missing link that would bring about increases in agricultural production (Thirtle et al., 2003; Omiti, Chacha and Andama, 2002; Cherry, 2002; UNDP, 2001; Wambugu, 1999; Woodward, Brink, and Berger, 1999). The argument here is that there is a positive and demonstrated effect of the impact of biotechnology from agricultural systems in industrial societies. References are also made to the dramatic improvements in agricultural production in India, Pakistan, Phillipines, Thailand and Indonesia as a result of an earlier technological innovation in agriculture – the Green Revolution (Lee and Tank, 1992). If Africa, because of, for example, the limited use of high-yielding varieties of maize and rice, missed the Green Revolution, the contention is that the region should not miss the biotechnology one (Brink, Woodward, DaSilva, 1998). Analysts in this group can be labeled as the optimists in terms of the role of biotechnology in African agriculture and development.

On the other hand, are the analysts who analyze the extent to which biotechnology should be seen as the magic bullet for Africa's agricultural development (ETC, 1999a; Maathai, 1998; Shiva and Holla-Bahr, 1996; Mihevc, 1995). These analysts do not deny the technical efficiency of biotechnology. Rather, they highlight the political and socio-cultural contexts of biotechnology and agricultural policy. For example, they draw our attention, again, with reference to the Green Revolution, to the fact that the success of any technology depends on broader political and socio-cultural forces.

Multinational corporations (MNCs) are at the helm of the biotechnology revolution and some of their research initiatives are being carried out in partnership with universities. Thus, industry-academia relations have attracted considerable attention in the relationship between biotechnology and agricultural development (Vallance, 2001; Clark, 2000; Press and Washburn, 2000; Argyres and Liebeskind, 1998). The question then is whether the profit orientation of biotechnology MNCs would enhance or restrict the use of biotechnology in Africa. Analysts in this group can be labeled as the pessimists, they stress the other variables that need to be factored into any analysis if we are to understand how and if biotechnology can contribute to African agricultural development.

This study acknowledges the contributions of the optimists and the pessimists of the role of biotechnology in African agriculture. However, it argues that the debate needs to be placed within the broader context of globalization. Underpinning globalization are the dramatic technological innovations in communication technologies. These innovations have led to 'the intensification of worldwide social relations which link distant localities in such a way that local happenings are shaped by events occurring many miles away and vice versa' (Giddens, 1990, p. 64). The result has been new forms of economic, political, and socio-cultural relationships (Hoogvelt, 2001; Held et al., 1999; Mittelman, 1996; Schuurman, 1993; Giddens, 1990).

The economic manifestations of globalization include the spatial reorganization of production, the interpenetration of industries across borders, the spread of financial markets, the diffusion of identical consumer goods to distant countries, massive transfers of population within the South as well as from the South and the East to the West ... (Mittelman, 1996, p. 2). The political aspects of globalization have seen a steady assault on the role of the state in society, with calls on it to disengage from the economic sector. With that disengagement, the economic sphere is supposed to be guided by free market forces. The socio-cultural aspects of globalization are expressed in terms of the harmonization of standards and the homogenization of tastes associated with the emergence of a global culture. The highly contentious assumption here is that the whole world would be exposed to or be consuming one universal set of cultural goods and services.

The significant aspects of globalization for this study include the withdrawal of the state from productive economic activities and the resultant privatization and deregulation of the economic space. Governments would restructure their role in crown corporations and considerably scale back their financial contribution to public institutions such as those in agricultural research. Implicit in this argument is the renewed emphasis on a political and legal regime that will honour the rights of corporations, relative to those of labour. New investment regimes (for example, the North American Free Trade Agreement and World Trade Organization) also encourage high levels of trade flows (Tabb, 2000). The restructuring of state bureaucracy would permit the private sector, under the direction of the market, to run hitherto state functions more successfully because of the assumption that the market would ensure greater efficiency than statist orientations.

Globalization has affected all sectors of the social and political economy, and agriculture is not immune from it. Thus, any analysis of the role of biotechnology in African agriculture needs to pay some attention to the broader context of globalization, since that context will define outcomes for agricultural policies on biotechnology and research.

In view of the foregoing remarks, this study examines the relationship between agricultural development and biotechnology in Africa by focusing on two related issues. First, the institutional capability of national agricultural research systems in Africa to harness, exploit or utilize or engage the technology, and second, the ownership and transfer of biotechnology. The study finds problems with the institutional capacity of agricultural research systems in Africa and the global biotechnology regime, and argues from a human factor perspective that these barriers would undermine the extent to which African countries could benefit from it.

In what follows, I first offer a brief review of the nature of the national agricultural research systems in Africa. This is followed by a discussion of globalization of agriculture, biotechnology and African agriculture. A subsequent section examines the institutional capabilities of public agricultural research systems in Africa and the ownership and transfer of biotechnology. The section also examines whether biotechnology offers real possibilities or is another false start in transforming African agriculture. The study ends with some thoughts about how biotechnology can be harnessed to benefit agricultural development in Africa.

The National Agricultural Research System in Africa: A Brief Overview

The National Agricultural Research System (NARS) in Africa is made of several institutions, from policy-setting units within the national ministry of agriculture, relevant units in ministries of science and technology, institutions of higher education to private-sector agricultural institutions (See CSIR/ISNAR, 1991; ISNAR, 1981). A key feature of the NARS is that many of the participating institutions are publicly owned. The few private-sector organizations in the NARS collaborate with the public ones in order to enhance various aspects of their operations, some of which could then have multiplier effects for the public sector.

The NARS in Africa, like many aspects of the region's institutional framework, has to be examined with reference to its colonial past. That examination will reveal four major features. First, the research activities were largely in response to the commercial interests of the settlers, hence an external orientation of agricultural research. Second, colonial botanical gardens, as early incubators of NARS, were more interested in the 'de facto transfer of plant resources' (Deo and Swanson, 1991, p. 190) to metropolitan research centres. Third, there is a heavy reliance on expatriate staff; and finally, research activities focused more on technical considerations than on political and socio-cultural considerations (Puplampu, 1996; George, 1986; Nweke, 1979).

Many African states, in the immediate post-colonial era, set out to address some of the above features of the NARS. Several of them now have a critical mass of their own nationals, as is the case in Nigeria, Kenya and Ghana (Eicher, 1989, p. 13). However, the economic crisis the region faced in the last three decades has led to a declining capacity of the state in funding agricultural research and this has resulted in a mass exodus of qualified staff (Tettey, 2002). Consequently, the quality of human resources within the NARS and the policy capacity of the various institutions have been undermined. The system continues to rely on the state for funding and the nature and form of agricultural research has not changed dramatically since the colonial era (Puplampu and Tettey, 2000).

The African economic crisis of the 1980s reiterated the importance of the agricultural sector and the need to address institutional capacity, especially in agricultural research, since many agricultural research institutions were unable 'to provide answers to the problems which confront African agriculture' (World Bank, 1981, p. 69). Thus, restructuring of agricultural research institutions was high on the agenda of the international financial institutions in their policy framework for African development. Among other things, the restructuring called for the delegation of research to the private sector and the integration of the national agricultural research system into the international (public or private) agricultural research system, especially the network of the Consultative Group on International Agricultural Research (CGIAR). This move, as Deo and Swanson (1991, p. 94) argue, would make possible the '[g]lobal transfer of new varieties, pesticides, fertilizers, and machinery as a 'package of technology'. This is the backdrop to the activities of the International Service of National Agricultural Research's (ISNAR), part of the CGIAR network, in several African countries (for example, Ethiopia, Ghana, Kenya, and Zimbabwe).

The restructuring of agricultural research in Africa was taking place within the context of global forces. Therefore, the World Bank in its 1989 study, *Sub-Saharan Africa: From Crisis to Sustainable Growth*, made what is, arguably, the initial case for biotechnology in African agriculture. The study identified biotechnology as holding out promise and potential for raising agricultural production in Africa by producing drought and disease resistant crops (World Bank, 1989, p. 30). Specifically, the 'direct use of biotechnology for plant propagation and breeding could dramatically raise crop productivity and overall food production in developing countries' (World Bank, 1989, p. 31). Crops mentioned included cassava, oil palms, and groundnuts.

However, the World Bank has also acknowledged that a 'flexible African response to these competitive dynamics must be based on a close monitoring of biotechnological trends, more joint research and development partnerships with Western companies, and the development of substitute products' (World Bank, 1989, p. 31). It is worth noting the unstated assumption that the biotechnological advances are external to Africa. More recently, UNDP (2001) noted the 'controversial' nature of genetically modified organisms (GMOs), but argued that they 'could be [the] breakthrough technology for developing countries'. Thus, it is fair to argue that much of the optimism for biotechnology in African agriculture springs from the analysis offered by the World Bank and other international institutions.

While there is no doubt that African agriculture can benefit from biotechnology, that optimism should not be taken as an inevitable outcome. Technology, as the Green Revolution demonstrated years ago, functions within a political and socio-cultural context and, therefore, is not neutral. The extent to which biotechnology can contribute to African agriculture and for that matter African development is contingent on several factors, two of which form the basis for this study – institutional capacity; ownership and transfer of biotechnology. Before examining these issues, the next section, against the broader context of globalization, will discuss some aspects of the debate about biotechnology and agricultural development in Africa.

Globalization of Agriculture, Biotechnology and African Agriculture

Globalization of agriculture can be seen in the three areas of agriculture production, marketing and consumption. In the area of production, globalization of agriculture has seen the internationalization of agricultural production and the emergence of the New Agricultural Countries or NACs (Friedman, 1993, p. 45-47). Most of the NACs are in the least industrialized countries of the South and specialize in the export of labour-intensive and off-season exotic fruits (bananas, pineapples), vegetables (tomatoes, cucumbers), agro-based industrial inputs (oil palm) and fresh-cut flowers (roses, lilies). The new production arrangements involve contract farming and biotechnology.

Contract farming is the production system in which 'plants and animals are produced on land in relation to the complex and changing profit conditions of global capitalism' (Watts, 1990:149). As a production system, it relies heavily on technology, and farmers work under conditions similar to industrial labourers. Transnational agro-based corporations (e.g., British American Tobacco and Del Monte in Kenya; Unilever in both Ghana and Cameroun and Pamol in Cameroun) are at the helm of contract farming. Such farms emphasize the production of exportable high-end or agro-based crops (Puplampu and Tettey, 2000; Raikes and Gibbon, 2000; Konings, 1998; Jaffe, 1994). Even though contract farming resembles the historical plantation system in colonial Africa, it is, however, different. Perhaps, the major difference between the plantation system and contract farming is that an elaborate transnational legal framework supports the latter. There is also considerable consensus among national governments, lending agencies, transnational agri-businesses and export-processors that contract farming is an integral part of globalization of agriculture (Puplampu and Tettey, 2000; Little and Watts, 1994).

Biotechnology involves the application of natural sciences and engineering techniques in direct and indirect ways to living organisms. Spurned by technological breakthroughs in bio-research (for example, genomics, transformation, molecular breeding and diagnostic) biotechnology is innovative (gene extraction and sequencing, recombinant DNA and genetically altered seeds) in the production of agricultural goods (Australia, 2001; Egwang, 2001; ETC, 1999a; Buttel, 1990). At the core of the technological breakthroughs are large private research institutes in the North with enormous resources to sustain various research programs and obviously seek to benefit from the research findings. Examples of these organizations are Monsanto, DuPont/-Pioneer Hi-Bred International, AgriBiotech, Norvatis and Advanta or what the ETC (1999a) calls the 'gene giants'.

As far as agricultural marketing and consumption under globalization are concerned, the former involves the activities of agro-based multinational corporations like Unilever and Del Monte (Dinham and Hines, 1983). With long histories in agriculture, some of the same corporations are also involved in contract farming. As a result, they are able to manage not only the production, but also the patterns of marketing agricultural goods, and can use that control to maximize their profit. Agricultural consumption can best be seen in the global distribution network of agricultural goods – fresh produce, designer plants and flowers – which are destined for markets in the North (Lappé and Bailey, 1998). As stated earlier, this paper stresses the need to place the role of biotechnology in African agriculture in a broader context.

The case for and against biotechnology in African crop agriculture involves economic, socio-cultural (including moral/ethical) and political considerations. The major economic argument for advocating biotechnology for crop production in African agriculture is that it can contribute to increases in agricultural production. A key aspect of biotechnology is the fact that genetic traits can be altered, and with that the possibility of withstanding certain viruses. For example, the genetic control of the rice yellow mottle virus is a clear indication that transgenics can outperform conventional approaches (UNDP, 2001, p. 34). With the global increases in transgenic food production, while conven-tional approaches to food production in African continue to perform poorly, '[t]here is the potential to double African production if viral diseases are controlled using transgenic technology' (Wambugu,1999, p. 15). When viruses and other diseases are controlled, all other things being equal, increases in the production of 'designer foods' can be attained and with that, the argument continues, there would be improvements in production, nutrition and the welfare of citizens. For example, the introduction of high-yield, drought resistant and early ripening varieties of maize have led to impressive gains in maize production in Burkina Faso, Ghana, Guinea, Mali, Nigeria and Zaire (DaSilva, 2001).

The improvements in seed technology suggest that farmers would be able to create better products that meet specific needs, and within a shorter period of time. Biotechnology in agriculture would therefore create tissue cultures that would be critical in the 'production of new varieties of plants' (Sherwood, 1989, p. 60). The multiplier effects of such a process are enormous. For example, plants could serve as factories and provide valuable materials through cell culture. Several analysts have stressed the value-added potential of biotechnology in African agriculture, especially because of the abundance of a diverse germplasm (See Wambugu, 1999). Flowing directly from the diverse germplasm base is the importance of focusing biotechnology in Africa on a needs-based basis. In other words, the biotechnology can be harnessed to address the specific needs of specific localities. For example, the Kenya Agricultural Research Institute (KARI), in collaboration with the US Agency of International Development and Monsanto, has been playing a dominant role in developing a variety of sweet-potato that is resistant to feathery mottle virus (Omiti, Chacha and Andama, 2002; Hassanali, 2000).

The critiques of biotechnology, on the economic front, do not dispute the productive capabilities of transgenic crops. Rather, they maintain that an economic logic would inform what types of crops are selected for transgenic transformation. Put differently, crops that make up the food basket in various African countries would likely not be transformed because the economic benefits from such a transformation would be considered minimal and thus not worth the investment. The critiques also point to the issue of how African farmers would 'obtain access to a technology that is being developed, patented and tightly controlled by researchers and corporations in wealthy countries' (Nature, 1999, p. 341 See also Nature Biotechnology, 2001). The argument here is the role of profit-driven agro-based corporations in biotechnology.

According to the critiques, the planting of genetically altered seeds bought from these giant corporations and the associated questions of patents and intellectual property rights constitute the ultimate technological threats to the economies of many African countries that depend heavily on agricultural exports for national revenue. For instance, genetically-produced cocoa and vanilla flavours are reducing the export market in Côte d'Ivoire, Ghana, and Madasgacar (Syngenta Foundation for Sustainable Agriculture, 2002; DaSilva, 2001; Mihevc, 1995, p. 214). The result is declining opportunities for income and employment for farmers, in particular, and the society at large.

The socio-cultural arguments for biotechnology in African agriculture are an eclectic mix of moral and ethical reasoning (McDowell, 2002; Nature, 1999). The proponents contend that it is morally wrong to turn a blind eye to the starving masses of the world, especially in the case of Africa, when transgenic technologies can give rise to increases in food production. The ethical reasoning, therefore, is that the scientists who have knowledge about transgenic technology cannot afford not to make the technology available to African farmers. Furthermore, since scientists are the experts, they should be allowed the chance to use the technology (Rampton and Stanber, 2000).

Agriculture is the mainstay of the African economy. Changes in the agricultural sector have political implications. These implications include food insecurity due to or as a response to food shortage, high food prices and political instability (Oliver, 2002; Weiss, 2002; Puplampu, 1999; Chazan and Shaw, 1988). It is therefore economically and politically expedient for African governments to embrace biotechnology, so as to improve food production and create a stable political environment.

The opponents charge that researchers, morally speaking, are playing God by attempting to manipulate nature's creation while focusing on a cost-benefit analysis of the process. It is an analysis, as the economic critique above indicates, that would not favour African agriculture. Ethically, the critiques contend that the impression that transgenetic crops are the missing link in African agriculture, and could therefore be the magic bullet for the region's search for food security, is disingenuous. The world, as George (1986, p. 23) reminded us several years ago, is capable of producing enough food to feed the planet. To the critiques, the world food problem is not one of production, but rather of distribution. While the proponents and opponents try to put their views across, it is also important to pay attention to the role of the human factor in agricultural development.

Several analysts have examined the role of the human factor in agricultural development in Africa (see Anyanwu, 2000; Puplampu, 1996; Abaka, 1995). Beyond Adjibolosoo's (1999, 1998) classical definition of the concept of human factor, it is clear that the overall essence of the concept is the role of human beings and their relationship to their environment in a manner that would bring about genuine human development. Human factor development therefore undertakes a critical analysis of how culture and development institutions interact, analyzing the interaction as both a means and an end. Significant aspects of the human factor concept for the current study include critical thinking, inventiveness and innovativeness of institutions. Institutions, it must be stressed though necessary, are not sufficient by themselves to ensure the success of development policies and programs. The performance of an institution is closely related to the nature and character of the human beings whose activities would define its success or failure. For human factor development, institutions can make a positive contribution to the development process only when it has a critical mass of individuals who have a sense of integrity, accountability, dedication, a vision and a sense of mission (Adjibolosoo, 1999, p. 102). In addition, human factor-inspired institutions must have an in-built preventive maintenance strategy, foster continuities in the sense of reinforcing the positive aspects of their activities and operate within a political environment that guarantees a high level of stability. The nature of the larger socio-political political environment therefore has significance for the successful performance of development institutions. The human factor perspective on biotechnology would raise the following questions that are not making the headlines in the current debate on biotechnology. Is the science behind the technology sufficient to guarantee the quality of the food we eat. Can GMO realistically benefit African farmers and thus promote agricultural development in Africa? Underlying these questions and many others are the nature of institutional capacity and access to the technology.

Biotechnology and Agricultural Research in Africa: The Policy Framework

Several African governments, either through national institutions or regional and international collaborations, have acknowledged the need for a policy regime to address agricultural development, and biotechnology has featured in that regard (Tzotzos and Skryabin, 2000). A review of plant biotechnology research indicated that several African countries are involved in different aspects of biotechnology research – production of quality controlled bio-fertilizers, cloning of *in vitro* plants (mainly export crops) of ornamental and economic, and bio-prospecting of new nitrogen fixing species of bacteria (Brink, Woodward and DaSilva, 1998). However, if biotechnology is to live up to its role in agricultural development, then the focus should also be on whether the dominant public agricultural research institutions, in addition to export crops, pay the same level of attention to research on food crops.

The issue of critical importance in this study is whether the restructuring of agricultural research institutions would lead to the emergence of capable or sustainable institutions (Eicher, 1989; World Bank, 1989). Underlying the notion of a sustainable agricultural research institution is how 'domestic political support is mobilized to provide adequate domestic financing of all core salaries and operating expenses of the national agricultural research system' (Eicher, 1989, p. 1). A sustainable NARS also amounts to what the World Bank (1989) calls capacity building. Capacity building seeks 'not just less government but better government' (World Bank, 1989, p. 5). Two aspects of capacity building of significance to this study are the 'restructuring of many public [agricultural] and private institutions to create a context in which skilled workers can function effectively, [and a] [p]olitical leadership that understands that institutions are fragile entities, painstakingly built up, easily destroyed, and therefore requiring sustained nurturing' (World Bank, 1989, p. 54).

Studies by ISNAR, Intermediate Biotechnology Service (IBS) and other entities in Kenya and Zimbabwe provide the material to address the relationship between agricultural research institutions and biotechnology in Africa (Hassanali, 2000; Gopo, 2000; Komen and Persley, 1993; Hobbs and Taylor, 1987; ISNAR, 1981). Kenya and Zimbabwe exhibit significant similarities in the evolution of their agricultural research systems. Both former colonies of Britain, they have a sizeable population of British settler farmers. Also significant is the fact that both Kenya and Zimbabwe are at 'an intermediate-low level of biotechnology' (Falconi, 1999, p. 2).

The policy framework for biotechnology in Kenya was the National Advisory Committee on Biotechnology and its Adaptations report of 1990 (Hassanali, 2000, p. 92; Komen and Persely, 1993, p. 11). The report, among other things, identified priority areas for biotechnology, and made several recommendations for a successful implementation of biotechnology. There are several institutions involved in biotechnology in Kenya. They include the Kenya Agricultural Research Institute (KARI), which started its biotech activities in 1982, and is the country's leading biotechnology institution (Hassanali, 2000, p. 95; Falconi, 1999, p. 3). Others are the Kenyan Medical Research Institute (KEMRI) and external institutions like the International Livestock Research Institute, and the International Centre of Insect Physiology and Ecology. The University of Nairobi and the Jomo Kenyatta University of Agriculture and Technology are also important in Kenya's biotechnology program, because they offer postgraduate courses in biotechnology. It is also important to stress that there are private institutions like Wellcome Kenya and Dawa Pharmaceuticals, but their activities in Kenya's biotechnology program are 'very limited and confined mainly to the manufacture of livestock products and pharmaceutical products for human use' (Hassanali, 2000, pp. 95-96; see also Hobbs and Taylor, 1987).

In Zimbabwe, the Research Council of Zimbabwe is the agency charged with the formulation of science and technology policy. The Research Council, working alongside other institutions such as the University of Zimbabwe and the National University of Science and Technology, established, in 1992, the Scientific and Industrial Research and Development Centre (SIRDC) and the Biotechnology Research Institute (BRI). The BRI is Zimbabwe's major biotechnology institution (Gopo, 2000, pp. 187-188; Falconi, 1999, p. 3; Komen and Persley, 1993, p. 12). Zimbabwe, as in the case of Kenya, also experiences an awful lack of private sector investments in biotechnology. The few multinational companies prefer to invest in research and development in their home countries. In any case, it is important to account for the areas of biotechnology in Kenya and Zimbabwe.

The technique of choice by researchers at both KARI and BRI is basic technical research in tissue culture. About 70 per cent of the researchers in the two counties used the less-advanced tissue culture, while 30 per cent used more advanced techniques like genetic engineering (Falconi, 1999, p. 7). In Kenya, KARI has been employing tissue culture to eliminate virus in crops like Irish potato, banana, cassava and sweet potato (Hassanali, 2000, p. 94). Even though the extent of collaboration between KARI and private biotech companies has been sporadic, as stated earlier, the work among KARI, Monsanto and the USAID led to the development of a variety of sweet potato resistant to the feathery mottle virus.

Biotechnology research in the two countries is donor-driven. In fact, the Dutch Government's Special Program on Biotechnology provided the initial impetus for biotechnology in Kenya, Zimbabwe and other developing societies. Donor support for research was 67 per cent and 50 per cent for Kenya and Zimbabwe respectively in 1996 and 1998. For the same years, government funding of research was 28 per cent and 34 percent for Kenya and Zimbabwe (Falconi, 1999, p. 6). In terms of personnel, there has been a gradual increase in the number of personnel with terminal degrees in both countries. The number of agricultural biotechnology research personnel in Kenya with PhDs was 14 and 41 in 1989 and 1996 respectively, while in the case of Zimbabwe, the number jumped from 5 to 27 in 1989 and 1998 respectively (Falconi, 1999, p. 5).

In an environment where many African countries are operating at the low-end of biotechnology, and where the role of donors is paramount in the research strategies, the ownership of and the thorny issue of intellectual property rights assume great significance. The low-end nature of the biotechnology technique in Africa suggests that advanced methods would be learned from advanced societies. In a global era, such learning is supposed to be efficient and, indeed, encouraged. However, there are the problems of the issue of suitability of international research for local conditions, as well as the cost of patents and complications resulting from intellectual property rights.

The United Nations Industrial Development Organization (UNIDO) has sponsored the establishment of the International Center for Genetic Engineering and Biotechnology (ICGEB) to conduct research and make its results available to all countries (including developed and developing). It, however, faced stiff opposition from the United States, United Kingdom, France, Germany, Canada and Japan, who refused to support it financially, largely because of strong domestic pressure from already established domestic biotechnology companies (Deo and

Swanson, 1991, pp. 200-201). As the next section would show, the involvement of multi-national companies in biotechnology is premised on a strong patent and intellectual property regime. The question is the extent to which they should be compensated under patent laws, and whether such laws would be consistent with access to agricultural knowledge, especially, since in some cases, they also want to patent traditional knowledge that is already available in the public domain.

Institutional Capacity, Ownership and Transfer of Biotechnology

It is certainly redundant to state that the effectiveness of any social institution depends on the policy regime, the availability and conditions of access to resources, and the quality and quantity of human capital. These variables are not only important, but critical if the NARS in Africa is to live up to its expected role in agricultural development; more so, in the context of globalization. The ensuing analysis, drawing from the human factor perspective, will address the extent to which the existing or restructured agricultural research institutions can engage biotechnology for agricultural and national development in Africa. The underlying human factor considerations are how the relationship between human beings (e.g. policy makers, researchers, farmers) and social institutions (public and private) affect policy (nature and form of research) and program outcomes.

Komen, Mignouna and Webber (2000) analyzed six major crops (banana/plantain, cassava, cowpea, maize, sorghum, and yams) at the centre of biotechnology research in nine African countries, including Kenya and Zimbabwe. Banana, maize and potato are the three main crops in biotechnology research in Kenya and Zimbabwe (Falconi, 1999, p. 4). Maize, cassava, and banana feature prominently in Africa's biotechnology research because they are also the focus of international research collaborations. That fact, itself, springs from the huge export potential of those crops, especially in the case of maize and banana. Since biotechnology research is donor-driven, it is clear that the NARS in Africa does not have sufficient control in forging a biotechnology research agenda. That also suggests a lack of ownership by African governments of the agenda of their research institutions, because of the lack of, in the main, resources. Obviously, reliance on external donors can only further distort the nature of the NARS in Africa.

The question then is whether the restructuring would re-orient the focus of agricultural research in Africa. Tabor, Quartey-Papafio and Haizel (1993, p. 4) did not find evidence to suggest a shift from the historical pattern, and argued that '[r]esearch activities of low priority for donor agencies, but which may have been of high priority nationally, were neglected due to the lack of sufficient and secure funding'. The concern here is the kind of research questions that could be raised and the type of crops under research. Puplampu and Tettey (2000, p. 263), for example, argue that in view of the market-driven thrust underlying the restructuring of agricultural research in Africa, the types of crops under research would be those that have an export potential. In the process, not much attention would be paid to crops that are critical to national food needs. The nature and priorities of research remain a big issue in agricultural research in Africa. Consequently, without addressing this issue, the potential of biotechnology in African agriculture would simply remain that – a potential.

With a skewed and donor-driven research agenda, the NARS in Africa also suffers from the lack of a critical mass of human capital. Since no human institution can perform effectively without the requisite human resources, the need for specialized forms of human capital to undertake biotechnology research is a critical problem for Africa. Despite the increases in biotechnology personnel noted for both Kenya and Zimbabwe, the overall picture in many African countries is not encouraging. For example, the Council of Scientific and Industrial Research, a pivotal anchor in Ghana's agricultural research system lost, through resignation, about forty-three top level scientists in 2002 alone (Ghana Web, 2002a). The reasons for the resignation include the lack of funds to support their research activities and the availability of greener pastures outside the country. It is the inability of African governments to fund agricultural research that underscores the donor-driven nature of biotechnology research in the region.

Human resource development requires the availability of training institutions. The success of agricultural research calls for specialized knowledge and institutions. It is no wonder universities, by default, occupy a pivotal role in biotechnology, and those in Africa cannot escape from that reality (see Kenny, 1986). Higher education or tertiary educational institutions, specifically universities, colleges and polytechnics play a major role in the training of minds and generating knowledge that could be utilized in addressing societal needs. Universities, in generating knowledge that could be of use in the policy making process, are major players in the knowledge industry and deeply involved in the business of generating knowledge for development (World Bank, 2002; Robinson-Pant, 2001; Tettey and Puplampu, 2000).

However, the state of knowledge production and the role of African universities and other institutions of higher education has been the subject of critical reviews (Zeleza, 2003; ASA, 2002). The fall-out has been the inability of African universities to play an active role in the training of graduate and post-graduate students in biotechnology. The existing programs (for example, at the University of Nairobi in Kenya) or emerging ones, are all donor-driven (Wafula and Falconi, 1998). CGIAR, a long-time partner in NARS in Africa, has been working with universities in the sub-region. ISNAR/WARDA (2001) has acknowledged that despite the benefits of the collaboration between CGIAR and universities, the focus has been too narrow and hence the need to broaden the partnership and involve other institutions in the NARS. Michelson and Shapiro (1998) also call for the strengthening of African universities to enable them to perform an effective role in agricultural research (See also FAO, 1993).

The state of knowledge production in African universities and the region's economic crisis have contributed to a constraining environment for academic labourers in African universities to research into biotechnology. Institutions of biotechnology in Africa are in a state of flux, and therefore the potential of biotechnology is confronted by institutional and human resource difficulties. What the preceding discussion shows is that the debate about biotechnology in Africa should not only focus on the presence or absence of risks inherent in the technology. Rather, considerable attention must be paid to the institutional and organizational mechanisms that would enable the technology to bring about the expected political, economic and social benefits (Tzotzos, 1999, p. 214).

While institutions of higher education continue their role in the NARS, even though not under ideal conditions, farmers – the supposed beneficiaries of biotechnology and an important constituency in the agricultural community – do not have or occupy an identifiable role in the NARS. The omission of farmers is an effect of the technical orientation of the NARS and the premise that technical fixes are what they need. Since the NARS addresses technical concerns, there is no need for farmers' input into the agricultural research agenda. More so, when majority of the farmers live in rural communities, and are not literate in the language of the researchers.

However, the success of agricultural research depends upon an adequate understanding of both technical and socio-cultural factors (Biggs and Farrington, 1991). Though some farmers might be illiterate, they do possess indigenous knowledge that could play a crucial role in developing technologies for crop production. In view of the structure of the NARS, farmers' indigenous knowledge have remained relatively untapped (Omiti, Chacha and Andama, 2002). Flowing from this neglect, farmers' indigenous knowledge, in many cases, has not been documented. While the NARS continues to neglect the indigenous knowledge of farmers, some agro-biotechnology companies have been quick to document such knowledge and claim intellectual property rights (illustrations would be provided later in the chapter).

Under globalization, public institutions are supposed to play a minimal role in the development agenda. Against the background of minimal state institutions, private institutions are expected to take over the role of public institutions. Agricultural research is an expensive undertaking, and the private sector's involvement would be predicated on a perceived profitability, and not necessarily because there is a social good to be derived from it. Indeed, private sector involvement in many African countries is collaborative in nature and concentrated in those areas (for example, plant breeding) that offer the best possibilities for securing patents and other forms of intellectual property rights (Rausser, Simon and Ameden, 2000; Pray and Umali-Deininger, 1998).

Collaboration needs not be invoked as the magic wand that would cure all the ills of biotechnology research in Africa. Institutional arrangements and synergies, the issue of ownership of technology, and the relevance of adapted technology to the local context are compelling difficulties. Even if public agricultural research institutions in Africa can collaborate with the international public or private ones, the basis of that partnership has to be carefully specified and monitored. This is because of the complications of ownership of technology and intellectual property rights (IPRs) brought about by the World Trade

Organization's Trade Related Intellectual Property Rights (TRIPs) (Shrybman, 2001; Wallach and Sforza, 1999).

TRIPs grant ownership and proprietary legal rights to novel ideas and technological innovations, and the WTO sets the parameters for the enforcement of such rights by calling on its member-states to enact such domestic legislation that would enforce IPRs. In other words, the type of biotechnology research that an African country can undertake, although dependent on availability of resources (capital and human), also depends on the global patent regime. As Acharya (cited in van Wijk, Cohen and Komen, 1993, p. 22) noted, tissue culture techniques have never been patented and are widely used today in many countries to develop new products and technologies. Thus, the source of the tissue-culture or the low-end of biotechnology research in many African countries can be situated in the global patent regime.

Some African countries (e.g. South Africa, Kenya and Zimbabwe) have established patent offices, but the enforcement of such laws in the agricultural sector is proving to be a monumental challenge. The institutional constrains aside, the major challenge is the documentation of indigenous agricultural knowledge, which is considered as part of the public good in several African countries. While the search for ways to document and file patents for indigenous agricultural knowledge in Africa continues, various external actors have made patent claims on some indigenous agricultural goods (ETC, 1999b; Shiva and Holla-Bhar, 1996).

ETC (1999b) has documented several instances of the patent wars in Africa. The International Rice Research Institute (IRRI) in the Philippines identified an important disease resistant in a well-protected rice in Mali, but allowed researchers from the University of California at Davis to patent the gene in the United States of America, leaving the Malians with only scholarships for further training. The University of Toledo (USA), has two patents on an endod (soapberry) found in Ethiopia. The patents are being claimed while the compound was bred and nurtured by Ethiopians – women farmers and scientists. In addition to institutions, individuals also seek to patent agricultural material from Africa. An Idaho researcher has claimed a variety of Ethiopian teff and a California scientist who crossed a cowpea in Kenya while working for the International Institute for Tropical Agriculture in Nigeria has patented 'Kunde Zulu'. Both crops are being marketed in the United States of America. In each of the cases, indigenous agricultural groups contributed the initial 'something'. However, without the research and development work of external actors, that 'something' could not have gone far, just as without the initial 'something' research and development would have nothing to start with (See Syngenta Foundation for Sustainable Agriculture, 2002). The persistent nature of patent claims on agricultural material from Africa, obviously, underscores the need to have a framework on ownership anchored in equity. Such considerations, in addition to others, need to be at the centre of any discussions of policy options for African governments and their NARS with respect to the global biotechnology regime.

114   *Globalization and the Human Factor: Critical Insights*

Policy Options and Conclusion

In our contemporary globalized world, policy makers often tend to give an impression of inevitability about their options. However, there is nothing inevitable about policy option, because the choices are made within a certain context and with respect to specific consequences. The preceding discussion suggests several policy options for African countries. First, the state, either in Africa or in any part of the world, continues to shape the development agenda. Indeed, the state's role in development is more urgent in an era of globalization. Even though the rallying cry in globalization is for a minimal role of the state in the economic sphere, it is the state that would set up the parameters for development to take place. Thus, the issue is not if the publicly owned NARS became private overnight, it would be efficient and capable of advanced biotechnology research. It is also not the case of whether or not the NARS in Africa is capable of undertaking advanced forms of biotechnology research. Rather, it is what kind of state would be able to oversee the nature of the NARS (Puplampu, 2003).

The continuing relevance of the state contradicts the argument of a minimal state. Perhaps a crucial distinction needs to be made between a minimal and an effective state. The former does not necessarily lead to the latter. What is needed is an effective state that can offer policy guidance, and more importantly, contest the growing power of agro-biotechnology companies. With respect to the nature of NARS, Eicher (1989) observed years ago that the restructuring of agricultural research in Africa did not pay particular attention to the establishment of sustainable institutions. How to build a NARS that would be able to engage biotechnology in an era of globalization should engage the attention of policy makers. This is in light of the changing perceptions about the public good nature of agricultural research, changes that are due to the increasing importance of for-profit non-state actors and their primary focus, understandably so, on securing patents for their work (Cohen and Pinstrup-Andersen, 2002; Pinstrup-Andersen, 2000).

Second, it is also necessary to reconceptualize the role of farmers in the NARS. Forming a genuine relationship between researchers and the various farmers' and crop growers' associations should be a policy option. Farmers, the end-users of biotechnology should begin to have an identifiable and consistent role in the NARS. Since farmers possess indigenous knowledge, and that knowledge can prove to be valuable to the specific farming communities, it is incumbent on policy makers to offer a framework that would encourage dialogue between farmers and agricultural researchers. Perhaps the need to acknowledge and incorporate farmers' indigenous knowledge is the increasing moves by agro-biotechnology companies to document such knowledge and claim patents and intellectual property rights. Underlying such policy measures is the need to craft agricultural policies, including those on biotechnology, that are consistent with the national interest (Ghana Web, 2002b).

Third, since the NARs in Africa cannot do it alone, it is incumbent for them to continue to forge multiple lines of alliances – within the national, the regional and the international (public or private) contexts (Puplampu and Tettey, 2000, p. 266). Within the national context, for instance, the overall framework for agricultural research should ensure the elimination of duplication and aim at deepening the synergies that the various institutions could bring to bear on their respective activities. At the regional level, the respective national agricultural institutions should be aware of the strengths of other institutions. That way, they could better collaborate on research activities that would address their specific needs. However, because of their collective institutional difficulties, the role of international agricultural research institutions cannot be underestimated.

The Consultative Group on International Agricultural Research (CGIAR) and affiliated institutions continue to play a strategic role in agricultural research in Africa. The affiliated institutions include the International Agricultural Research Centres (IARC), the International Services for National Agricultural Research (ISNAR), the International Service for the Acquisition of Agri-Biotech Applications (ISAAA), and Africa-based international institutions like the one for tropical agriculture in Nigeria, rice research in Sierra Leone. However, CGIAR's ability to continue to serve as a fulcrum for international agricultural research has been handicapped by the activities of some agro-biotechnology companies and their demands for intellectual property rights (Meldolesi, 2002; ETC, 2002a and b).

At the same time, development assistance is increasingly being channeled through either non-profit or for-profit non-governmental organizations. International development agencies present non-governmental organizations as replacements or preferred agents for the ineffective state in Africa (Edwards and Hulme, 1996, p. 3). Thus, the extent to which the NARS in Africa can collaborate with similar institutions within a regional perspective or international (public or private) context is contingent on several factors. The result is uncertainty in the activities of the NARS in Africa and its attempts to utilize biotechnology for agricultural development.

The NARS in many African countries depends on donor assistance. Governments would have to take their support for research through the allocation of more resources seriously if they want to have a better grasp on the national agricultural research effort. Donor support will continue to skew research priorities, and it will not continue forever. Policy makers must assist research institutions with funds and infrastructure for the purposes of research and development, which will, in turn, offer the results to the agricultural community. That is a sure way in which agricultural research and biotechnology can make the expected contribution to agricultural and national development in Africa.

References

Abakah, E.M. (1995), "The Relevance of Human Resource Development: The Case of Ghana's Experience in the Agricultural Sector", in Adjibolosoo, Senyo B.-S.K. (ed.) *The Significance of the Human Factor in African Economic Development*, Westport, CT.: Praeger, pp. 149-161.

Adjibolosoo, Senyo B.-S.K. (1999), *Rethinking Development Theory and Policy: A Human Factor Critique*, Westport, CT.: Praeger.

Adjibolosoo, Senyo B.-S.K. (1998), *Global Development: The Human Factor Way*, Westport, CT.: Praeger.

African Studies Association (ASA) (2002), "Special Issue – African Universities in Crisis and the Promotion of a Democratic Culture", *African Studies Review*, 45 (2).

AgbioForum, (1999), "The Economics of Biotechnology in Developing Countries", *AgbioForum*, 2 (3 and 4).

Anyanwu, S.S.O. (2000), "Towards a Strategy for Sustainable Agricultural and Rural Development in Nigeria", *Review of Human Factor Studies*, 6 (1): 93-109.

Argyres, N.S. and Leibeskind, J.P. (1998), "Privatizing the intellectual commons: Universities and the commercialization of biotechnology", *Journal of Economic Behaviour and Organization*, 32, 427-454.

Australia, (2001), *Australian Biotechnology Report 2001*, Commonwealth of Australia: Ernest, Young and Freehills.

Biggs, S. and Farrington, J. (1991), *Agricultural Research and the Rural Poor: A Review of Social Science Analysis*, Ottawa: International Development and Research Council.

Brink, J.A., Woodward, B.R. and DaSilva, E.J. (1998), "Plant Biotechnology: A Tool of Development in Africa", *Electronic Journal of Biotechnology* [online] 1 (3), December 15 http://www.ejbiotechnology.info/ .

Buttel, F.H. (1990), "Biotechnology and Agricultural Development in the Third World", in Bernstein, H. et al. (eds.), *The Food Question*, London: Earthscan, 163-180.

Chazan, N. and Chazan, T.M. (eds.) *Coping Africa's Food Crisis*, Boulder and London: Lynne Riemmer.

Cherry, M. (2002), "African Scientists Urge MG Acceptance", *SciDev.Net* http://www.scidev.net/articles2.asp?id=040920021301367&t=N& .

Clark, E.A. (2000), "Academia in the Service of Industry: The Ag Biotech Model", in Turk, J. (ed.) *The Corporate Campus: Commercialization and the Dangers to Canada's Colleges and Universities*, Toronto: James Lorimer, pp. 69-86.

Cohen, J.I and Pinstrup-Andersen, P. (2002), "Biotechnology and the Public Good", *SciDev. Net* http://www.scidev.net/frame3.asp?id=2708200210362353&t=C& .

CSIR/ISNAR (1991), *A Review of the Ghana Agricultural Research System*, The Hague: International Service for National Agricultural Research.

DaSilva, E.J. (2001), "GMOs and Development", *Electronic Journal of Biotechnology*, [online] 4 (2). http://www.ejbiotechnology.info/ .

Deo, S.D. and Swanson, L.E. (1991), "The Political Economy of Agricultural Research in the Third World", in Friedland, W.H. et al. (eds.), *Towards a New Political Economy of Agriculture*, Boulder: Westview Press, pp. 189-212.

Edwards, M. and Hulme, D. (1996), "NGO Performance and Accountability: Introduction and Overview", in Edwards, M. and D. Hulme (eds.) *Non-Governmental Organisations – Performance and Accountability: Beyond the Magic Bullet*, London: Earthscan Publications, pp. 3-16.

Egwang, T.G. (2001), "Biotechnology Issues in Africa", *Electronic Journal of Biotechnology* [online] 4 (3), http://www.ejbiotechnology.info/ .

Eichenwald, K., Kolata, G. and Petersen, M. (2001), "Biotechnology Food: From the Lab to a Debacle", *New York Times* – Jan 25, A1.

Eicher, C.K. (1989), *Sustainable Institutions for African Agricultural Development*, The Hague: ISNAR (Working Paper, No. 19).

Einsiedel, E.F. (2000), "Cloning and its discontents – a Canadian Perspective", *Nature Biotechnology*, 18 (September): 943-944.

Erosion Technology and Concentration Group (ETC) (2002a), *Neither Early Warning nor Early Listening – What the CGIAR is Not Doing*, Winnipeg, MB: ETC (February).

Erosion Technology and Concentration Group (ETC) (20002b), *Trouble in Paradise: Civil Society Denounces CGIAR for Denial of GM Contamination in Mexican Centre of Genetic Diversity*, Winnipeg, MB: ETC (October).

Erosion Technology and Concentration Group (ETC) (1999a), *The Gene Giants – Masters of the Universe?*, Winnipeg, MB: ETC (ETC Communique - March/April).

Erosion Technology and Concentration Group (ETC) (1999b), *TRIPS Traps Small Farmers*, Winnipeg, MB: ETC (May).

Falconi, C.A. (1999), *Agricultural Biotechnology Research in Four Developing Countries*, The Hague, ISNAR (Briefing Paper No. 42, December).

Food and Agricultural Organization (FAO) (1993), *The Role of Universities in National Agricultural Research Systems*, Rome: FAO (Research and Technology Paper, No. 5).

Friedman, H. (1993), "The Political Economy of Food: A Global Crisis", *New Left Review*, 197 (January/February): 29-57.

Gaskell G. and M. Bauer (eds.) (2001), *Biotechnology 1996-2000: The Years of Controversy*, London: Science Museums.

Gaskell, G. and Durant, J. (eds.) (2002), *Biotechnology: the making of a global Controversy*, New York: Cambridge University Press.

George, S. (1986), *How the Other Half Dies*, Harmondsworth, Penguin Books.

Ghana Web (2002a), "43 Top Scientists Quit CSIR", http://www.ghanaweb.com, General News, Saturday, 26 October 2002.

Ghana Web (2002b), "Ghana Must Chart Own Course in Biotech – Researcher", http://www.ghanaweb.com/GhanaHomePage/NewsArchive/artikel.php?ID=28096

Giddens, A. (1990), *The Consequences of Modernity*, Stanford, California: Stanford University Press.

Gopo, J. (2000), "Zimbabwe", in Tzotzos, G.T. and K.G. Skryabin (eds.) *Biotechnology in the Developing World and Countries in Economic Transition*, Wallingford: CABI Publishing, pp. 187-193.

Hassanali, A. (2000), "Kenya", in Tzotzos and Skryabin (eds.), pp. 91-131.

Held D. et al., (1999), *Global Transformations: Politics, Economics and Culture*, Stanford, California: Stanford University Press.

Hobbs, S.H. and Taylor, T.A. (1987), *Agricultural Research in the Private Sector in Africa: The Case of Kenya*, The Hague: ISNAR (Working Paper, No. 8).

Hodgson, J. (1999), "UK interest groups take all sides of GM issue", *Nature Biotechnology*, 17 (July): 630-631.

Hoogvelt, A.M.M. (2001), *Globalization and the Postcolonial World The New Political Economy of Development*, Baltimore, Maryland: The Johns Hopkins University Press, 2nd Edition.

ISNAR (1981), *Kenya's National Agricultural Research System*, The Hague: International Service for National Agricultural Research.

ISNAR/WARDA (2001), *Workshop on a Collaborative Platform for Agricultural Research in Sub-Saharan Africa*, Bouaké: ISNAR/WARDA (Report of Meeting No. 14).

Jaffe, S.M. (1994), "Contract Farming in the Shadow of Competitive Markets: The Experiences of Kenyan Horticulture", in Little, P.D. and W.J. Watts (eds.) *Living Under Contract – Contract Farming and Agrarian Transformation in Sub-Saharan Africa*, Madison: The University of Wisconsin Press, pp. 97-139.

Janssen, W. (2002), *Institutional Innovations in Public Agricultural Research in Five Developed Countries*, Hague: ISNAR (Briefing Paper No. 52), July.

Lappé, M. and Bailey, B. (1998), *Against the Grain: Biotechnology and the Corporate Take-over of Your Food*, Monroe, ME: Common Courage Press.

Little, P.D. and Watts, M.J. (1994), *Introduction*, in Little, P.D. and W.J. Watts (eds.) pp. 3-17.

Komen J. and Persley, G.J. (1993), *Agricultural Biotechnology in Developing Countries: A Cross-Country Review*, ISNAR Research Report No. 2 (Intermediary Biotechnology Service), The Hague: International Service for National Agricultural Research.

Kenny, M. (1986), *Biotechnology: The University-Industrial Complex*, New Haven: Yale University Press.

Komen, J., Mignouna, J. and Webber, H. (2000), *Biotechnology in African Agricultural Research: Opportunities for Donor Organizations*, The Hague: ISNAR (Briefing Paper No. 43, February).

Konings, P. (1998), "Unilever, Contract Farmers and Co-operatives in Cameroon: Crisis and Response", *Journal of Peasant Studies*, 26 (1): 112-138.

Lee H.H. and Tank, F.E. (1992), "A Conceptual Framework of Biotechnology", in Ahmed, I (ed.) *Biotechnology A Hope or a Threat*? New York: St. Martin's Press, pp. 17-42.

Maathai, W. (1998), "The Link Between Patenting of Life Forms, Genetic Engineering and Food Insecurity. Let Nature's Harvest Continue: African Counter-Statement to Monsanto", *Review of African Political Economy*, 25 (77): 526-530.

McDowell, N. (2002), "Africa hungry for conventional food as biotech row drags on", *Nature*, 418 (August): 571-572.

Meldolesi, A. (2002), "CGIAR Under Pressure to Support Seed Treaty", *Nature Biotechnology*, 20 (February): 103-105.

Michelsen, H. and Shapiro, D. (eds.) *Strengthening the Role of Universities in the National Agricultural Research Systems in Sub-Saharan Africa. Highlights of a Workshop*, The Hague: International Service for National Agricultural Research.

Mihevc, J. (1995), *The Market Tells Them So – The World Bank and Economic Fundamentalism in Africa*, London: Zed Books.

Mittelman, J.H. (ed.) (1996), *Globalization: Critical Reflections*, Boulder: Lynne Rienner Publishers.

Nature, (1999), "Access issues may determine whether agri-biotech will help the world's poor", *Nature*, 402 (25, November): 341-344.

Nature Biotechnology, (2001), "Rights of Access", *Nature Biotechnology*, 19 (August): 693.

Nuffield Council on Bioethics, (1999), *Genetically Modified Crops: The Ethnical and Social Issues*, London: Nuffield Foundation.

Nweke, F.I. (1979), "The Organization of Agricultural Research in Ghana: Priorities, Problems. Implications for Domestic Food Production and Policy Issues", *Agricultural Administration*, 6 (1): 19-29.

Oliver, M. (2002), "Famine in Southern Africa", *The Guardian*, July 25, http://www.guardian.co.uk/Print/0,3858,4468641,00.html.

Omiti, J.M., Chacha, R.N. and Andama, M.S. (2001), "Biotechnology Can Improve Food Security in Africa", *African Journal of Food and Nutritional Science – Online Version*, 2 (2) July http://www.ajfns.net/volume2no2/omiti.html.

Paarlberg, R. (2000), "The Global Food Fight", *Foreign Affairs*, May/June, pp. 24-38.

Panos, (1999), "Greed or Need? Genetically Modified Crops", *Panos Media Briefing*, No. 30A (Re-Issue).

Persley G.J. and Lantin, M.M. (eds.) (2000), *Agricultural Biotechnology and the Poor*. Washington D.C.: Consultative Group on International Agricultural Research.

Pinstrup-Andersen, P. (2000), *Is Research a Global Public Good?*, Washington, D.C.: International Food Policy Research Institute.

Pinstrup-Andersen, P. and Schiøler, E. (2001), *Seeds of Contention World Hunger and the Global Controversy over GM Crops*, Baltimore: The Johns Hopkins University Press.

Pray, C.E. and Umali-Deininger, D. (1998), "The Private Sector in Agricultural Research Systems: Will it Fill the Gap?", *World Development*, 26 (6): 1127-1148.

Press, E. and Washbrun, J. (2000), "The Kept University", *The Atlantic Monthly*, 285 (3): 39-54 (Online version http://www.theatlantic.com/issues/2000/03/press.htm).

Priest, S.H. (2000), "US public opinion divided over biotechnology?", *Nature Biotechnology*, 18 (September): 939-942.

Puplampu, K.P. (2003), "State-NGO Relations and Agricultural Sector Development", in Tettey, W.J. Puplampu, K.P. and Berman, B.J. (eds.) *Critical Perspectives on Politics and Socio-Economic Development in Ghana*, Leiden and Boston: Brill Publishing, pp. 135-151.

Puplampu, K.P (1999), "The State, Agricultural Policies and Food Security in Ghana (1983-1994)", *Canadian Journal of Development Studies*, 20 (2): 337-359.

Puplampu, K.P. (1996), "A Social Science Analysis of the Agricultural Research System in Ghana", *Review of Human Factor Studies*, 2 (2): 73-91.

Puplampu, K.P. and Tettey, W.J. (2000), "State-NGO Relations in an Era of Globalisation: The Implications for Agricultural Development in Africa", *Review of African Political Economy*, 27 (84): 251-272.

Raikes, P. and Gibbon, P. (2000), "'Globalisation' and African Export Crop Agriculture", *Journal of Peasant Studies*, 27 (2): 50-93.

Rampton S. and Stanber, J. (2000), *Trust Us, We're Experts: How Industry Manipulates Science and Gambles with Your Future*, New York: Jeremy P. Tarcker/Putnam.

Rausser, G., Simon, L. and Ameden, H. (2000), "Public-Private Alliances in Biotechnology: Can They Narrow the Knowledge Gaps Between Rich and Poor?", *Food Policy*, 25 (4): 499-513.

Robinson-Pant, A. (2001), "Development as Discourse: what relevance to education? *Compare*, 313 (3): 311-328.

Ruttan, V.W. (1999), "Biotechnology and Agriculture: A Skeptical Perspective", *AgBioForum*, 2 (1): 54-60.

Schuurman, F. (ed.). (2001), *Globalization and Development Studies – Challenges for the 21st Century*, London: SAGE Publications.

Sherwood, M. (1989), "Tomorrow's Agriculture", in Yanchinski, S. (ed.) *Biotechnology: A Brave New World?*, Cambridge: Lutterworth Press, pp. 57-63.

Shiva V. and R. Holla-Bahr (1996), "Piracy by Patent: The Case of the Neem Tree", in Mander, J. and E. Goldsmith (eds.) *The Case Against the Global Economy and for a Turn Toward the Local*. San Francisco: Sierra Club Books, pp. 146-159.

Shrybman, S. (2001), *The World Trade Organization – A Citizen's Guide*, Toronto: The Canadian Centre for Policy Alternatives and James Lorimer and Co.

Syngenta Foundation for Sustainable Agriculture (2002), The Socio-Political Impact of Biotechnology in Developing Countries, http://www.syngentafoundation.com /biotechnology_developing_countries.htm .

Tabb, W.K. (2000), "The World Trade Organization? Stop World Take Over?", *Monthly Review*, 15 (8 January): 1-12.

Tabor, S., Quartey-Papafio, H.K. and Haizel, K.A. (1993), *Structural Adjustment and Its Impact on Agricultural Research*, The Hague: International Service for National Agricultural Research (Working Paper No. 3).

The Economist (1999), "Genetically Modified Food – Food for Thought", June 19, 351 (8124): 19-21.

Thirtle, C. et al. (2003), "Can GM-Technologies Help the Poor? The Impact of Bt Cotton in Makhathini Flats, KwaZulu-Natal", *World Development*, 31 (4): 717-732.

Tettey, W.J. (2002), "Africa's Brain Drain: Exploring Possibilities for its Positive Utilization Through Networked Communities", *Mots Pluriels*, no. 20. February, http://www.arts.uwa.edu.au/MotsPluriels/MP2002wjt.html .

Tettey, W.J. and Puplampu, K.P. (2000), "Social Science Research and the Africanist: The Need for Intellectual and Attitudinal Reconfiguration", *African Studies Review*, 43 (3): 81-102.

Tzotzos, G.T. and Skryabin, K.G. (eds.) (2000), *Biotechnology in the Developing World and Countries in Economic Transition*, Wallingford: CABI Publishing.

Tzotzos, G.T. (2000), "Industrial Biotechnology: Challenges and Opportunities", in Tzotzos and Skryabin (eds.), pp. 1-13.

Tzotzos, G.T. (1999), "Regulation of Biotechnology in LDCs: Implications for Technology Development and Transfer", *AgBioForum*, 2 (3 and 4): 212-214.

United Nations Development Program (UNDP) (2001), *Human Development Report 2001*, New York: Oxford University Press for UNDP.

Vallance, P. (2001), "Biotechnology and New Companies Arising from Academia", *Lancet*, 358 (November 24): 1804-1805.

van Wijk J., Cohen, J.I. and Komen, L. (1993), *Intellectual Property Rights for Agricultural Biotechnology: Options and Implications for Developing Countries*, a Biotechnology Research Management Study. ISNAR Research Report No. 3, The Hague: International Service of National Agricultural Research.

Wafula J. and Falconi, C. (1998), *Agricultural Biotechnology Research Indicators: Kenya*, ISNAR Discussion Paper No. 98-9. The Hague: International Service for National Agricultural Research.

Wallach, L. and Sforza, M.(1999), *The WTO: Five Years of Reasons to Resist Corporate Globalization*, New York: Seven Stories Press.

Wambugu, F. (1999), "Why Africa Needs Agricultural Biotech", *Nature*, 400 (July): 15-16.

Watts, M. (1990), "Peasants Under Contract: Agro-Food Complexes in the Third World", in Bernstein, H. et al. (eds.), pp. 149-162.

Weiss, R. (2002), "Zimbabwe Ends Altered-Corn Dispute", *Washington Post*, August 10, A14.

Woodward, B., Brink, J. and Berger, D. (1999), "Can Agricultural Biotechnology Make a Difference in Africa?", *AgBioForum*, 2, (3 and 4): 175-181.

World Bank (2002), *Constructing Knowledge Societies: New Challenges for Tertiary Education*, Washington,D.C.: The World Bank.

World Bank (1989), *Sub-Saharan Africa: From Crisis to Sustainable Growth A Long Term Perspective Study*, Washington, D.C.: World Bank.

World Bank (1981), *Accelerated Development in Sub-Saharan Africa: An Agenda for Action*, Washington, D.C.: World Bank.

Zeleza, P.A. (2003), *Rethinking Africa's Globalization – Volume 1: The Intellectual Challenges*, Trenton, New Jersey: Africa World Press.

Chapter 7

Globalization, Diasporization and Cyber-Communities: Exploring African Transnationalism

Wisdom J. Tettey

Introduction

Globalization has been highly touted as the 'fundamental dynamic of our time – an epoch-defining set of changes that is radically transforming social and economic relations and institutions in the 21st century', (Petras and Veltmeyer, 2001, p. 11). McGrew (2000, p. 348) defines it as

> A process (or set of processes) which embodies a transformation in the spatial organization of social relations and transactions – assessed in terms of their extensity, intensity, velocity and impact – generating transcontinental or interregional flows and networks of activity, interaction, and the exercise of power.

He outlines four dimensions of the phenomenon, encompassing economic shifts that result from capitalism's tendency to expand; technology shifts which facilitate other dimensions of the process; political shifts that see the lessening of state influence in the world; and cultural shifts that result from redefinitions of community and nation that are a consequence of their inextricable link to developments within the other dimensions.

In spite of the multifaceted nature of globalization, there has been a tendency among analysts to accentuate its economic dimension. As an economic concept, it has both descriptive and prescriptive elements. The former refers to the reality of a world that is becoming increasingly inter-linked and integrated as a result of intersecting networks of trade as well as capital, technological, and information flows. The prescriptive element is at the base of the preponderant neo-liberal ethos that suffuses contemporary policy discourse at different levels of resolution – from state institutions to multilateral organizations. It outlines a set of policy suggestions that, its proponents argue, will create efficiencies in global and national economies. At a broad level, the economic facet of globalization evokes a clash of interpretations in terms of its implications for humanity. While some observers see it as an inexorable and intrinsic outcome of the processes of capitalist development, others have a less sanguine interpretation of the phenomenon, suggesting that it is the product of conscious manipulation by transnational capitalist elites who stand to gain from it (Petras and Velmeyer, 2001).

I do not propose to get into this debate. To the extent that this debate is relevant to the focus of this chapter, it has to do with how processes of economic globalization have led to economic distress in African countries, which has contributed to spawning a population exodus (see Tettey, 2001a; 2002). This exodus has led to a huge expansion in the African diaspora, with implications for the (re)definition of community and nation, and varied processes that result thereby.

Transnational migration has assumed unprecedented global proportions over the last few years. At the same time as this process of global migration gathers momentum, the world has also seen a significant increase in the development of information technologies. This has allowed disaporic communities to emerge in cyberspace and to interact beyond the confines of geographical space. These developments are not captured, or are downplayed, by critiques of globalization which tend to emphasize the economic dimensions of developments in information technology. The economic centered perspective is outlined by Petras and Veltmeyer (2001, p. 50) who argue that:

> Contrary to what many globalist ideologues say, [technology] has an important but secondary role. These innovations themselves are based on a state-sponsored or – subsidized research, later transferred to the private sector. Pre-existing economic forces largely determine the application of the technology ... High tech is the handmaiden of globalist financial engineering ... The emphasis on quality of data and the rapidity of processing reflects the need to make rapid investment decisions based on short-term shifts in the paper or real economy. Hence, high technology is reinforcing the most volatile and unproductive of economic activities, paper exchanges in the financial field.

Khor (2001, p.12) also argues that some technological developments, such as satellite television, e-mail, and the internet, constrain the ability of states to devise cultural and communication policy and to determine the flow of information and cultural products. This constrain is, however, just one dimension of the Globalization – Information and Communications Technology (ICT) – Culture matrix. What critics do not seem to adequately appreciate is the significance of these technologies as conduits for the expression of subaltern voices and the construction of communities of affinity that are not controlled by the state. In fact, implicit in Khor's argument is the assumption that the state's ability to control cultural policy and communication flows will necessarily be beneficial to all groups within the imaginary polity. It also loses sight of the fact that the state does not have the prerogative, and indeed may not be counted on, to serve as the only legitimate actor for transnational cultural flows, particularly for groups whose cultures may be the target of state annihilation. Arguments such as Khor's seem premised on a traditional anthropological perspective in which 'the nexus between identity and place was a central tenet' (Rabinowitz, 2000, p. 766). However,

> In a world increasingly deterritorialized by migration, mediatization, and capital flows, modernist nationalisms with their tendency to connect cultures and identities to specific places have become an ever more retrograde ideology, even as they retain ever greater power to produce history (Pollock et al., 2000, p. 579).

Contemporary developments that have resulted from processes related to globalization and migration, therefore, require a deconstruction of the traditional anthropological orientation if we are to adequately understand the multiple manifestations of transnational communities and discourses, as they are shaped by developments in information technology. What we see is a new media ecology emerging in tandem with a new physical ecology which is represented by world wide migrations over international borders, and the formation of diaspora groups (Carey, 1998). The convergence of these dual processes has created a situation that merits designation as the diaspora of the internet. This refers to the organization of social groups outside their countries of origin as communities of action, not primarily according to the necessities of physical propinquity, but rather by the possibilities presented by the boundlessness of the new technological architecture of the internet.

Two distinct models of the on-line world have emerged since the mid-1980s when networking spread beyond a narrow user base. These are labeled the 'consumption model' and the 'community model'. According to Barkadjieva and Feenberg (2002, p. 182), the former model emphasizes the potentials for information accessibility and product marketing, while the latter is characterized by how 'communities form and ways of life are elaborated'. The promise articulated by the 'community model' has led ardent proponents of the internet to speculate that it can provide solutions to many of our social problems. Giddens (1991) opines that this model's idea about the emptying of time and space gave vent to the view that we could move towards the creation of a single world where there is no 'otherness' and where the collective 'we' shares problems and opportunities together. Other assessments of the community-building potentials of the internet, however, highlight the fragmented and unharmonious consequences that developments in information technology portend. What is not in doubt is the acceptance, by both proponents and critiques of the community model, of what the new technology of the internet allows us to explore. That is, the invisible and spatially unrestricted conceptions of cultural and non-material expression, such as discourse and identity, which have crucial consequences for national and world politics. Despite this agreement, 'little attention has been paid to the less institutionalized and more episodic transnational discourse communities made possible by the combination of two conditions: new information technologies and diaspora population' (Yang, n.d.).

Conceptual Framework and Methodology

To address this deficit, I will focus on the various manifestations of the community model vis-à-vis Africans in the Diaspora. The goal is to 'unpack the unproblematized connection between territory, ethnos, and state' (Rabinowitz, 2000, p. 758) and its (re)configuration in the context of globalization and the Internet. This chapter, thus, focuses on how globalization intersects with particular human variables to shape the phenomenon of a virtual and transnational civil society.

I adopt a concept of the human factor that extends beyond the normative and prescriptive understanding that is reflected in trait theory. This and related frameworks (eg. Adjibolosoo, 1995; Adjibolosoo and Soberg, 2000) tend not to focus on a critical analysis of the socio-economic and political dynamics that define and shape human actions, attitudes and behavior. Rather, they formulate a narrow view of the human factor as a synthesis of particular virtues. This formulation, with its 'exclusive emphasis on normative prescriptions of behavior, [results in a focus on 'positive' traits, and] do not provide the tools for assessing the socio-political dynamics of everyday life within organizations and society as a whole' (Tettey, 2000, p. 17).

In contrast to the preceding approach, the following discussion is based on a framework that emphasizes the contingencies underlying human interactions. Such a framework, which draws from the social systems and social constructivist approaches to analyzing human-technology interfaces (see Tettey, 2002a), enables us to explore not only what is ideal and desirable. It also 'encompasses relationships of power, resistance, and negotiation' that occur at different levels of resolution from the personal to the transnational (Tettey, 2001b, p. 111). From this perspective, we are able to appreciate the dialectical manifestations of individual and group action, and the discursive spaces within which ideas of community are constructed.

The discussion is based largely on analyses of African discussion forums, chat rooms and web sites over the last year. It explores how Africans, living abroad, are using the internet as a vehicle for the construction of ethnic, cultural, and national identities; the advancement of home-Diaspora linkages for the purposes of socio-economic development at home; and engagement in political discourse relating to their country of origin. It also examines issues of community building and intra-African zones of contestation in cyberspace.

The specific objectives of the chapter include delving into the nature of the various African communities that are emerging on the internet, in order to understand the mechanisms, if any, that sojourners have devised to provide mutual support for each other, sustain their cultural heritage, and maintain linkages with their societies of origin. It also addresses some of the tensions and clashes that characterize what are by no means homogeneous aggregations of people. Finally, I evaluate the extent to which the technologies have allowed these cyber-communities to engage in civic discourses about Africa, their countries of origin, and/or their 'home communities', in order to bring a diasporic flavor to the processes taking place in their homeland. The chapter draws on

> Dynamics that are industrial (the pathways by which these media travel to their multifarous destinations), textual and audience-related (types of diasporic style and practice where popular culture debates and moral panics are played out in culturally divergent circumstances among communities marked by internal difference and external 'othering'), ... [It also] interrogates ... the nature of the public sphericules formed around diaspora media (Cunninghan, 2001, p. 131).

ICTs, Communities Without Propinquity, and Social Capital

The appropriate starting point for this section is a critical interrogation of the debate regarding the appropriateness of the concept of 'community' in describing groups of interactants in cyberspace who are brought together and sustained by a common cause, ideal or shared backgrounds. Some have argued that the designation of these groups as communities is inaccurate because they lack the key prerequisites of togetherness and a sense of obligation (see Postman, 1992). The basis for this position is the fact that these spaces of group interaction are 'completely open [and] the acceptance of common rules, mutual respect, stable identity, and authentic communication are not easily assured' (Bakardjieva and Feenberg, 2002, p. 183). Other reasons for this view include the contention that cyber networks are populated by unidentifiable lurkers and that the exchanges that take place are so disarticulated that it is difficult to make thematic linkages among them.

The views expressed above by critiques of the 'community' metaphor on the internet appear to have very narrow definitions of the concept that do not reflect the real-life representations of what we refer to as communities. When we talk about 'the African community' or the 'Islamic community', for example, it will be naïve to assume that they are characterized by all the ingredients that the critics outline above. There is, in fact no unquestioned acceptance of common rules, no ossified notion of identity, and of course, mutual respect, though desired, is not assured. As Werbner (1997, p. 228) aptly suggests, the kind of essentialism suggested by these critics 'obscures the relational aspects of group culture or identity and valorise[s] instead, the subject itself ... as if such subject can be demarcated out of context, unrelated to an external other or discursive purpose .... It is simply to imply an internal sameness'. It is crucial that we do not get trapped in dominant discourses of community, but that we appreciate its demotic dimensions as well (see Baumann, 1997, p. 214).

It is within this framework that we have to look at the impact that the development of digitally based ICTs has had on the reconceptualization of what it means to be a community and its relationship to globalization, particularly in the context of what Falk (1993) calls 'globalization from below'. What binds people together in virtual communities are not necessarily the sharing of proximate circumstances, but rather their common purpose of accessing, co-producing, and sharing information, which purpose is not limited by physical proximity. In effect, there is the emergence of 'community even in the midst of anonymity' (Raha and Rudolph, 2001, p. 455). It is in this context that Jacobsen (1997) argues that 'developments, including the use of global communications ... have desacralized national boundaries, making them mundane demarcations rather than borders that inspire devotion and connection'. In fact,

> It is over thirty years since the concept of community without propinquity was first proposed. According to this concept, communities might be spatially far-flung, but nevertheless close-knit, intimate and held together by shared interests and values, rather than geographical proximity. Although the idea of community without propinquity has been heavily criticised, the advent of advanced telecommunications and the emergence of cyberspace mean that a reappraisal of the concept, and of the changing nature of community, generally, is warranted. ... place and local community are, and will continue to be, fundamental to the functioning of society. Cyberspace may have annihilated distance but not place (Walmsley, 2000, p. 5).

Guidry et al. (2000, p. 6) see the transnational public sphere as 'a space in which both residents of distinct places (states or localities) and members of transnational entities (organizations and firms) elaborate discourse and practices whose consumption moves beyond national boundaries'. The online public sphere is, however, unique because it is less visible and less bound to physical location, even though it may reflect it and all what it represents – i.e., it is deterritorialized.

Katz (1986) argues that the trends in television programming and mass marketing contribute to the fragmentation of national cultures whereas in earlier generations, media and marketing contributed to national cohesion. Bennett (1998) contends further that these technological changes not only weaken national commitments, but collective identities of all kinds, creating what he calls 'identity disorders'. The validity of these views are questionable for a couple of reasons, particularly in the context of Africa. First, the earlier generations of media did not necessarily contribute to national cohesion. They were used to foster a coerced sense of national unity, which translated into subjugation of certain voices, thereby creating feelings of resentment, alienation, and dissent. Bennet's idea of 'identity disorders' reflects only part of what the Janus-faced new technologies are creating. A more contextually-based analysis, that focuses on contingent specificities, will show that the results of the connection between technology and identity is not always unidirectional and inevitably centrifugal, but that the outcomes could either reflect a solidification of national identity or its diminishment, depending on the issues at stake. The nature of the issues is, therefore, more important than the technology per se.

The relationships among diasporization, community, and ICTs are also closely tied to issues of social capital. Wellman et al. (2001) identify three dimensions of social capital in the context of these relationships. These are: 1) network capital; 2) community commitment; and 3) participatory. Network capital refers to relationships with friends and work mates for companionship, emotional aid, information, and belonging. Community commitment, exists when people have a strong attitude to community. This dimension suggests that when people have a responsible sense of belonging they will mobilize their social capital more willingly and effectively toward the pursuit of common objectives. The last type of social capital, participatory capital, on its part, has to do with interest aggregation and articulation among people that lead to the creation of joint accomplishments.

In the ensuing discussion the chapter explores the 'public sphericules' (Cunningham, 2001) that the Internet provides for diaspora communities to engage in various cultural and political debates as well as to display cultural identifiers in environments of 'internal difference and external 'othering'. These issues are very important to examine because

> African discussions of these concepts [modernity, globalization, and cosmopolitanism] tend to privilege unilateral assimilation of the civilizing mission of colonialism and the modernization necessarily defined by the West. ... postcolonial subjects continue to pursue their ambivalent and ambiguous projects of constructing autonomous or subordinate identities while also struggling to reconcile native temporalities and forms of spirituality with the temporality of the world at large. ... The issue that continues to defy analysis is how to elaborate a single explanation of both the process of globalization and the multiplicity of individual temporalities and local rationalities that are inserted into it (Diouf, 2000, p. 679).

To get at these manifestations of the dual processes of globalization and multiple temporalities in the diaspora-internet connection, I will employ Wellman et al.'s analytical framework referred to above.

Network Capital

As noted in the preceding section, network capital is manifested in information provision and sharing, companionship, and the generation of emotional support among members of the group or network (see Mandaville, 2001). In order to critically examine the extent to which these variables are present within the African cyber communities, I analyzed various listserves, chatrooms, and newspaper sites. These sites provide insights into the following: exchanges that range from discussions about socio-economic and political events and issues at home; peddling of rumors; postings that elicit nostalgic feelings about the past and about home; solicitations for romantic adventures and discussions of issues relating to them; and avenues for news about Africa.

The Ghana National Council of Metropolitan Chicago (GNCMC), for example, has a site that provides an opportunity for reflecting on the state of the African community in the Diaspora. Part of the September 2002 issues of the *African Spectrum*, a Ghanaian internet publication based in Chicago, focused on the challenges facing Ghanaians in the area as a group and proffered ways of dealing with these. The GNCMC site provides information on community services such as Ghanaian food markets/stores and has a calendar of social events such as dances, dinners, and funerals.

The geographical fluidity of the internet means that the information exchange that takes place in cyberspace manages to incorporate participants located in Africa, albeit in relatively small numbers. This is symbolic of the fact that while people might be geographically dispersed, they are still able to assemble in cyberspace as an embodiment of their country of origin and so manifest the same kinds of interaction that could be seen within the spatially defined conceptualization of the African state or community. This is exemplified by a letter purported to have been written by a 16-year old Ghanaian boy, based in Ghana, who was looking for his father whom he suspects to be domiciled in Canada. The letter was published on the *GhanaianNews* website, a publication operating out of Toronto. The significance of this letter is that it is based on the premise of a Ghanaian community that reflects the village concept of primary social relations rather than the anomie that would normally characterize life in an urban setting like Toronto or a vast entity such as Canada. Whilst the thousands of Ghanaians in the Toronto area may not know one another personally, there is the perception that there are significant webs of interaction that could enable one to find someone they may not have contiguous relationships with. The community, whilst numerically large, is small enough as a micro world of interaction although with varying levels and scopes of mutual contact. By providing detailed information about his father, the boy in Ghana was hopeful that he would be able to trace his father, because the news would travel through the webs of interaction in a way that will eventually get to his father or to someone who knew the father. Services such as Nigeriannet's 'Alumni Locater' allow Nigerians to find, and link up with, their classmates and to post announcements about year-group events.

Some of the sites provide opportunities for second generation diaspora youth to engage with one another in order to reinforce and mutually support one another in their efforts to maintain their ethnic/national identity and build a community of peers. The youth forum on the Ewe-Canadian Cultural Organization of Ontario web site is being used to exchange messages and greetings. It is also being employed to solicit ideas for the next meeting of the Council of Ewe Associations of North America (CEANA), an umbrella organization for Ewe ethnic associations in various US and Canadian cities. These interactions are not unique to diasporic Africans, but reflect a similar situation among other diasporas. Among the Indian-American community, "the Global Hindu Electronic Network ... turn[s] the resilience of the South Asian cultural practices into a hidebound heritage that appeals to the parents (since it promotes order) and ... to the children (since it offers distinct and easy ways to be 'Indian' in the face of the condescension of liberalism and the violence of racism' (Mathew and Prashad, 2000, p. 521; see also Thompson, 2002, p. 410).

Through a variety of news sites and newsgroups, Africans in the diaspora are able to keep up with what is going on in their countries of origin and to share information about developments there. The Buganda Home Page (www.buganda.com) for example, provides news of interest to Baganda in the diaspora. What is unique about this news service is the fact that all the stories are in the indigenous language, Luganda. Its sister service, Bugandanet, provides a forum for citizens of the Kingdom to discuss issues related to their ethnic group (see bugandanet@listserv.tamu.edu). Some of the African websites provide access to live radio and television programs that either originate from the continent (e.g., http://www.cbsfmbuganda.com/) or in the diaspora (e.g., http://www.gfmradio.com/radio_popup.html). The Buganda radio station, referred to above, has, as its objective, the provision of 'an efficient, professional, cost effective broadcasting service aimed at bringing about social cultural and economic advancement of the people of Buganda and beyond'. As a result of access to such a variety of sources, it is not surprising that some diasporic Africans are far more abreast with goings on in their home countries that their compatriots who are domiciled there.

Network capital also manifests itself in the various opportunities provided by the technology of the internet to allow sharing of emotions. Walmsley (2000, p. 9) discusses how telecommunications allow rites of passage, such as funerals, to be conducted among relatives without the constraints of travel and the limitations of distance. Kissaghanaian.com, for example, is a site that claims to be the premium Ghanaian dating service online. It states that 'our goal is to help Ghanaians and non-Ghanaians around the world find that special Ghanaian for a penpal, friendship, dating, romance and marriage'. Such avenues for developing partnerships are attractive to some residents of the diaspora who may want to have relationships with people from the same ethnic or national background but have difficulties doing so, because of the lower probability of meeting such people in their communities abroad. Kadende-Kaiser (1998, p. 127) also points out that Brurundinet served not only as 'a cultural space ... [but also as] a tool for maintaining personal relationships'. There are similar services for other countries as well (eg., http://www.nigeriannet.com/personals/).

Community Commitment

'Place' is at once a physical construct and a mental imaginary. Thus, while people may be separated from the physical construct of 'home', as a result of immigration and other forms of geographical mobility, they tend to retain their attachment to that space through mental connections and outward practices that invoke that geographical location. This is the case even though signifiers of their cultures of origin are adapted to their new settings, new cultures, and by new generations. Williams (2002) examines how the intersection of physical and social space affects the sense of identity among immigrants and their daily practices. He debunks those perspectives of contemporary culture that conceive of the internet as representing a novel, disembodied cultural awakening. He argues, rather, that diaspora life is characterized by a definitive and situated culture. Consequently, immigrants practice familiar rites in new settings and give new meanings to familiar practices and rituals, which are then exhibited in cyberspace during interactions among compatriots. Liu (1998), in his examination of Chinese voluntary associations in the diaspora, also concludes that globalization has enabled them to engage in new transnational functions that allow them to link up with their home country at the level of the locality, lineage and dialect. These include the construction of business networks. In a similar vein, Hassanpour (1998) shows how media are used by Kurds in the diaspora to mobilize support for causes in their homeland.

These manifestations of mediated connections to places of origin are reflected in the activities of African ethnic associations on the internet. Whilst they are located outside their countries of origin, it is clear that the projection of what the membership represents is informed by their attachment to a distant physical and cultural space. The sites tend to have information on the history of the particular group, its traditions, and various activities that show the group members' collective pride in their association with their home culture, even as they claim identification with their host communities. This is especially so among first generation migrants, whose ties to their home countries are relatively intense, but does not exclude subsequent generations.

The Buganda.com website, for example, is linked to an elaborate wealth of information on the Luganda language (www.buganda.com/language.htm). This electronic language source is useful for second generation Baganda in the diaspora whose parents want them to learn their 'mother tongue'. At the 2000 Covention of the Baganda Diaspora, delegates requested that the Kabaka's Government award certificates to children born in the diaspora who are able to read and write Luganda, and perform traditional dancing, drumming (http://www.buganda .com/bug20res.htm). The Ghana National Council of Metro Chicago has a scholarship scheme for students of Ghanaian descent currently attending a public or private school in Illinois. Its web site has information on application procedures which include writing an essay that demonstrates students' aspirations for Ghana; their contributions to Ghana and the US; how to educate people about Ghana; and how their education can support their community.

The Council of Ewe Associations of North America has a website which states the following as its main objective: 'to establish and maintain a community of people of Ewe ethnic background, who are eager to advance the cultural heritage of Ewes in North America'. It is obvious from the preceding objectives that the representation of this group on the internet is far from a disembodied aggregation of disparate individuals who come together in cyberspace to pursue certain goals that have no grounding in their antecedents of cyber contact. Rather, the very essence of who they are on the internet, and all the interactions that are spawned as a result, are rooted in a distinct cultural ethos that is outside, and yet determinant, of their cyber location. It is obvious from the discussion above that we need to revise

> The classic sociological picture of assimilation as a zero sum model of acculturation, in which the acculturation of immigrants and their children involves the gradual replacement of their ethnic culture by that of the culture of the host nation (Thompson, 2002, p. 409).

Groups see their identities and their obligations not only in relation to their host societies but to their communities of origin and ethnic groups as well. As Hall (1999) observes, the process of globalization has intensified commitments to the local. The local, as far as the African diaspora is concerned, is not only the physical here and now, but also an imaginary or 'distant' local. This imaginary local is defined by cultural affinity and shared origin, and though groups or individuals may be physically removed from their communities or ethnic groups, they nevertheless maintain ethical, cultural, and pecuniary obligations and linkages. They exhibit these through mobilization of their social capital towards specific projects to benefit their compatriots.

The Ghana Nurses Association of the Mid-West is an organization that coordinates the expertise of a group of Ghanaian medical professionals in this US region. Its members occasionally provide free medical services to their compatriots and other residents of the region. But a big part of their internet presence is devoted to the provision of medical information about various medical conditions and ailments as well as advice about how to deal with them. Their site also serves as a portal for information about common diseases in the US as well as in Africa.

The Council of Ewe Associations of North America recently sent hospital equipment to a children's hospital in its home region. It collected donations worth US$37, 278 to send the equipment home. Contributions were, and continue to be, solicited online. The Council's web page tells people to 'please make your donations/contributions electronically using the 'Click to Donate' button'. At its September 2002 meeting in Dallas, USA, the group decided to award scholarships to students in the Volta region, renew the existing five scholarships, and extend the scholarship program to Togo. It is interesting that the web site projects a pan-Ewe orientation that goes beyond Ghana. This suggests that the group's identity is not constrained by the boundaries of the geographical construct of Ghana, but rather flows from an imagined concept of ethnicity that is based on a sense of common heritage, shared values and historical experience. The forgoing supports Appadurai's assertion that the electronic media 'offer new resources and new disciplines for the construction of imagined selves and imagined worlds' (1994, p. 3).

Community commitment has also been demonstrated on the internet through the operation of a different kind of organization – the old students' association. Graduates of various secondary schools in Ghana are making efforts to link up with one another for social purposes and to mobilize support for various developments in their alma mater. The technology allows such students to come together in one place to share information about their schools, discuss matters relating to the schools, and coordinate the mobilization of resources to help improve conditions in the schools. The role of the Diaspora graduates in the last area is made even more critical by the fact that the state is unable to support infrastructural developments in many schools. Furthermore, the local corpus of alumni does not have the capacity to generate the resources needed to keep their schools functioning at the required levels of performance.

There are other manifestations of community commitment via the web-based African community, which are a response to the brain drain and attendant discussions about the Diaspora option (see Tettey, 2002b). This involves a drive towards building online communities for specific efforts that will enable Diaspora Africans to contribute toward macro-level development initiatives in their countries. It takes forms such as entrepreneurial collaboration and resource mobilization based on trust networks that have been developed on the internet as well as off it. They are aimed at bringing together like-minded individuals whose association is not based on a coincidence of physical vicinity but by clearly defined macro-level interests whose coordination is enhanced by technological proximity, and directed at a common imaginary – the nation.

An example of such an initiative is the Ghana Cyber Group whose members are strewn all over the globe. It defines itself as 'a non-partisan and pro-democracy organization that will leverage economic, political and social resources to create and sustain viable institutions for the development of Ghana'. It aims at collaborative investment in a number of areas, proceeds from which will not only benefit members individually, but will be channeled towards development programs in their home country. The initiative seems to be paying off. Recently, the Kapland Fund offered to match every $50,000 that the group raises for a specific project, because it is impressed by what the network seeks to do for their country. In early 2003, the Group organized a series of conferences aimed at improving the health care system in Ghana, and used the internet to mobilize support for the cause.

Some of the processes of community commitment are demonstrated by the activities of pan-African groups that engage in deliberative discussions for the purpose of achieving goals related to curbing the continent's socio-economic ills. AIDS Africa (http://www.groups.yahoo.com/group/aids-africa), for example, dubs itself an African HIV/AIDS working group, and is a discussion forum with hundreds of members. Its purpose is to bring 'together a multisectional community of Africans and other countries to raise and jointly address health-related issues, particularly HIV/AIDS in Africa'. The focus underscores the severity of this health problem across the continent as a whole, as well as the perception that Africans as a single community have to respond to it. The use of the internet to elicit discussions about remedial measures is an indication of how the technology has made it possible for discourse communities to be created with relative ease, and without spatio-temporal encumbrances.

The protean and intersecting patterns of association do not support the following observation:

Communities based upon interests and not localities might well reduce diversity and narrow spheres of influence, as like will only communicate with like. As such, rather than providing a better alternative to real-world communities cyberspace leads to dysfunctional online communities while simultaneously weakening communities in real space (Kitchen, 1998, p. 90).

Any centrifugal forces operating in cyberspace cannot be blamed on the technology, but are rather the transfer of concrete societal fissures into virtual interactions where the technology allows them to spread faster, intensify, and incorporate widely dispersed interactants. Furthermore, what the discussion shows is the fact that '[d]iasporic collectivities are constituted in relationship to nation-state systems as well as other groups with whom they share histories and compete to establish claims to the homeland. The collective 'we' emerges as a shifting formation as the identity of the diaspora, its borders, and who counts as its members is constantly contested and repositioned' (Drzewiecka, 2002, p. 1).

Participatory Capital

This involves interest aggregation and articulation and efforts at creating joint accomplishments. In this section I explore the processes that go toward the realization of these dimensions of the internet-social capital nexus. I examine the discursive construction of socio-political and economic events in Africa within cyberspace. The focus is to distill the discourse of Africans, domiciled abroad, who are committed to different struggles in their homeland, using the concept of long-distance nationalism. Most of these interactions take place in forums such as UgandaNet, RwandaNet, Zimnet (Zimbabwe) and KCI-Net (Kenya), which are representative of the phenomenon called 'NationaNets'. It is worth noting that while some continental Africans do engage in these discussions, the overwhelming number of interactants are located outside the continent. For example, In 1997, the virtual community of UgandaNet had only ten percent of its 3000 members resident in Uganda (Tindimubora, 1997).

Findings from this analysis of civic engagements show that there is a significant amount of political discourse among those Africans in the Diaspora who choose to avail themselves of the opportunities provided by the internet to discuss various issues. 'Brundinet serves as a multiethnic forum of internet communication which enables Burundians in the diaspora to create a virtual community with the diverse visions and agendas regarding the strategies that would facilitate peaceful cohabitation of [Tsutis and Hutus] in the country' (Kadende-Kaiser, 1998, p. 142). Not all those who participate in the discursive spaces provided by these forums are active, however. There are certainly many lurkers who adopt a passive orientation to the discussions. They therefore do not directly contribute to the generation of participatory capital, even though they are able to derive some networking capital out of the experience.

The internet also provides a forum for the transposition of ethnic politics which are articulated in ways that are sometimes more strident than they are in overt real space. In the mid-1990s, UgandaNetters engaged in a significant amount of exchanges that highlighted the politicized ethnicity and ethnicized politics that was shaping the political situation in the country. Acholis, Baganda, Langis, and Itesots blamed one another for one political problem, or another, in the country. In their investigation of one form of long-distance nationalism, i.e. resurgent

Abyssinian fundamentalism, Sorenson and Matsuoka (2001) turn to sites of its discursive reproduction, including the internet. According to them, theorists of transnationalism have considered the internet as a site for new forms of communication and community and argue that internet discourse among diaspora professionals and academics embodies creolized discourse produced by a distinct type, the cybernaut. In the case of the Abyssinian cybernauts, however, they detected not a new creolized discourse but a ghostly repetition of old views. They contend that

> Contrary to suggestions that diasporic cybernauts create new, oppositional and critical discourse, long-distance Ethiopian nationalists who logged onto the Internet reiterated and reinforced themes of Abyssinian fundamentalism ... Exiled Ethiopian cybernauts were jubilant at destruction in Eritrea and urged the Ethiopian government to recapture it and to inflict revenge. ... Indeed, the cybernauts considered death, displacement and starvation to be appropriate punishments for the arrogance Eritreans had shown by rejecting Ethiopian identity. As they cheered reports of slaughter and devastation, it became clear that fantasies of national identity were central to the conflict (Sorenson and Matsuoka 2001, pp. 55-56).

In a similar vein, the Islamist conflict in Algeria has become deterritorialized and disembedded from its original geographical settings, taking on a regional dimension in diaspora discourses and eliciting alternative political identities and all kinds of support from citizens resident abroad.

The politicization of diaspora discourse on the Internet finds resonance on the Ghanaian web sites and discussion forums. In the period leading up to, and during, the December 2000 presidential and parliamentary elections, web sites were created to champion the cause of particular parties or candidates, and also to articulate the same positions that were being expounded in the real world. One site that provided a forum for political discourse to take place was 'Say it Loud' (http://www.ghanaweb.com/GhanaHomePage/sil2/1.php). It provides a platform for people to discuss and express their opinions on matters of national concern to Ghanaians.

An analysis of the polemical discussions on many of the African discussion forums shows that the language has a tendency to be caustic in a way that is significantly different from exchanges that take place in face-to-face encounters on terra firma. For instance, in a discussion on Somalinet, one poster solicited the views of members, especially non-Isaaq Somalis, regarding the idea of UN recognition for Somaliland. His/her request generated a lot of flaming directed at the Isaaq Somalis. The poster was called a 'separatis [sic] ass hole!!' while his supporters called his critics 'idiotic ignorant Somalis' (http://somalinet.com/forum/viewtopic.php?topic=24700&forum=44&13). The nature of some discussions on the forum provides support for the following observation:

> Traditionally emblematic of the standardized lore of CMC, that is, 'high tech' without 'high touch', flaming becomes the primary symptom of CMC's

pathology. The traditional theoretic discourse that CMC does not adequately provide a sense of another person's social presence or the non-verbal information richness of face-to-face communication, is summarized by Lea as the 'clueless' model (Vrooman, 2002).

This situation can be accounted for largely by the confluence of anonymity, deindividuation and deregulation that characterize these forums. These features of the technology, when conflated with the discursive politics that surround the articulations by various sub-communities, generate an inclination toward the kind of behavior noted above. The incendiary nature of some diaspora discourses gives credence to Benedict Anderson's characterization of diaspora nationalists as

> Unaccountable and irresponsible: while technically a citizen of the state in which he comfortably lives, but to which he may feel little attachment, he finds it tempting to play identity politics by participating (via propaganda, money, weapons, any means but voting) in the conflicts of his imagined Heimat – now only fax time away. But this citizenless participation is inevitably non-responsible – our hero will not have power to answer for, or pay the price of the long-distance politics he undertakes (cited in Lyons, 2003, p. 5; see also Werbner, 2002).

In fact, in the Uganda exchanges referred to earlier, one contributor's posting mirrored Anderson's view when he/she lashed out at his/her virtual compatriots and admonished them thus:

> I challenge all of you, 'Ugandans' on the net, who think they are worth the time they spend expressing convoluted opinion on Ugandan politics from the safety and anonymity of the net and in the comfort of foreign capitals far removed from the grind of realities at home, to have so called 'testicular' fortitude to stand up and show our (their?) aversion to violence and violation of human rights (http://www.cco.caltech.edu/~ootim/acoli/coment.html#Toronto).

Onliness is developing into an embodiment of real life phenomena. It reflects the complexities that attend struggles for power and control over public and political spheres of everyday life. Franklin echoes this observation, from a gender perspective, when she states that 'one way of seeing these dynamics at work in everyday life online is when women from non-western diasporas talk about their personal-public lives and changing sociocultural obligations on Internet discussion forums. Such discussions provide newer, electronically mediated (re)articulations of the 'public-private' problematic and a (re)articulation of how the 'personal is political'' (Franklin, 2001, p. 387). Thus while cyberlibertarians see the internet as a site of liberation, the experience of many users shows that it could, in fact, be a site that stifles certain voices and allow certain perspectives to hold sway. This is exemplified by different patterns of behavior and attitudes in these cyberspaces that stratify participants in a way that privileges certain groups/individuals and denigrates or subjugates others. Interestingly, the criteria for this delineation reveal another significant impact of the internet in relation to social stratification in the real world.

Not all those in the diaspora can participate in discussions. Status differences that are premised on standards in the real world, and that are exclusionary in terms of participation in political discourse, get attenuated. A significant number of diasporan Africans cannot participate in internet discussions between of socio-economic barriers – inability to afford computers; non-familiarity with the operation of the navigational architecture of the technology; and or defects in the language of the forums. Thus, while traditional centers of political control seem to disappear, there are still manifestations of power imbalance in the sphericles of cyberspace. In the midst of this imbalance, subalterns have neither the epistemic capital nor the political position to have a strong and influential voice in discussions that pertain to their places of origin (see Mitra, 2001, p. 30).

In spite of the lack of a strong subaltern voice within the diasporan community itself, it is important to note that, from a relational position vis-à-vis hegemonic groups, African diasporic voices, as a collective, are being articulated in significant measure. This is particularly so with regard to discourses about Africa in general. While admitting that the counter-hegemonic discourses about Africa, particularly by Africans, are still on the fringes of policy and perceptual representations of Africa, it needs to be acknowledged that the Internet has allowed those communities of discourse to emerge, mobilize, and give vent to their positions. The majority of the members of these communities are located in the diaspora because of the relatively better opportunities that they have to access the technology. They are exemplified by the various online coalitions of Africans who are making a case for reparations against slavery (see for eg., http://www.the.arc .co.uk/arm/home.html). As Karim (n.d.) observes:

> Although some diasporic web sites do carry scholarly and archival material, their particular strength is functioning as repositories and as means of disseminating cultural knowledge. In the light of the enormous production and export levels by the cultural industries of developed countries, on-line networks facilitate a global accessibility to Asian, Latin American African views of the world. This becomes an important means to counter the effects of cultural imperialism and to foster a world-wide cultural diversity.

These developments are a veritable indication that there is an emergent sub-politics on, and made possible by, the Internet. Sub-politics, defined by Beck (1997) as the articulation, and shaping, of socio-political events by agents outside the state and corporate systems, thus allow peripheral representations of issues. The Internet enables those at the margins to, at least, find an outlet for expression and nurture hopes of being accessed by audiences located far and wide, with potentials for political mobilization. As Mitra (2001, p. 43) observes, 'for the marginal, this gain of capital, to have a voice in cyberspace, makes it possible to be heard, not only as a singular voice but a hyperlinked heteroglossic voice of a cyber community that often tells the same alternative story'.

Conclusion

Through the processes of globalization, that enhance migration, as well as the time and space compression that has resulted from information technologies, we see the internet providing opportunities that reinforce the building of hybrid cultures among Diaspora communities. What the analysis in this chapter makes clear is the need to move away from the zero-sum model of acculturation that has engulfed a lot of scholarly work, and recognize the fact that geographical mobility does not translate into an inevitable replacement of home cultures by host cultures. The internet has made it even easier for diaspora communities to maintain attachments to, and retain, their cultures and communities of origin.

Furthermore, as Lyons (2003) argues, 'increasingly, the location where key political, economic, and social developments take place with regard to a specific state is not within the sovereign territory of that state'. Clearly, interactions in cyberspace are not disembodied. People bring their antecedent collection of values, affiliations, etc. to the engagements that take place in the virtual world as shown by the activities of ethnic associations and political discourses. Rheingold (1993) has applied the notion of 'tribe' to interactions on the internet, while Appadurai (1993) has suggested that 'there is an increasing emergence of the trope of the tribe as the internet is being mobilized to rediscover fundamental affiliations and allegiances' (Thompson, 2002, p. 412). Unlike the bourgeois public space conceptualized by Habermas in the context of eighteenth century Europe, which suggests rational debates among a unitary public with a consensual opinion, the discursive spaces of the Internet indicate otherwise. There are various groups located outside the bourgeois realm which articulate different, and in some cases conflicting, positions and directions on issues of national and local concern.

There is fluidity across various cyber groups, in terms of membership and objectives. Individuals may simultaneously engage in national-, ethnic-, and alma mater-based expressions of social capital, which may be both contradictory and complementary. What this demonstrates is that there are multiple sites of identity and community construction/articulation among Africans in the Diaspora. We therefore need to apply the same tools of dialectical analysis in cyberspace as is necessary in discussions of real life situations that it tries to replicate. It is important not to essentialize community, but to see it as a sociopolitical process involving negotiation of 'who we are' and what it means to be 'who we are' during particular performative moments. As Stubbs (2001) opines, the intersection of nationalism and diasporas produces complex outcomes that are not necessarily represented by the antagonisms and ethnic provincialism of the Abyssinian cybernauts for example, but encompass overarching notions of identity and community as well. What we see in the preceding discussions is that while the reality of civic engagement on the internet and the politics of cyberspace do not necessarily bear out Dertouzos' (1997) idea of a 'computer-aided peace', they do not portend the kind of pathological 'identity disorders' suggested by Bennet (1998) either.

While this chapter has highlighted the role of the internet in fostering social capital formation among the African diaspora in the face of globalization, it is important to note that internet interactions, by themselves, do not generate that capital. For social capital, in all the forms discussed above, to be generated it has to be nurtured by, and anchored in, real life situations and associations. The translation into cyberspace of activities that facilitate social capital formation flows from the work of human agents whose need for affiliation, commitment and sharing, based on defined parameters, allow particular interactions to happen. The technology facilitates, but does not give birth to, these objectives. This is particularly so with regard to some aspects of community commitment where financial contributions have to be made. Internet interactions are largely unable to elicit the social trust that is necessary to mobilize people in a way that allow the transposition of ideals from the ether of cyberspace to the concreteness of particular communities. For this to happen, people still tend to rely on traditional forms of interaction. They prefer to engage each other on a face-to-face basis and thus get the opportunity to assess each other in concrete settings that allow cyber claims to be tested and for non-verbal indicators of comfort to be evaluated.

There is no doubt that diaspora Africans are building communities without propinquity in cyberspace in response to a confluence of factors that define the phenomenon of globalization. The pressures of economic globalization have, in part, compelled them to leave their countries of origin, while their geographical mobility, as a result of these and other factors, have been made possible by transformations in technologies and institutions that are products of globalization. These transformations have also allowed them to maintain contacts with their home communities and nations. But globalization also poses threats to the traditional cultures of these diaspora Africans as they immerse themselves in a hegemonic Western culture where their 'otherness' gets accentuated and their cultures are threatened with significant erosion at best. They therefore make assiduous efforts to resist this onslaught in whatever way they can. These include retaining attachments to their places of origin and sharing, with their compatriots at home and abroad, the benefits that their insertion into the global center has generated. The internet has allowed them to do these things in news ways, with more 'extensity, intensity, velocity, and impact' (McGrew, 2000, p. 248). The internet is thus not a 'new' site of social interaction but rather a new space that replicates, even if it complicates or simplifies, real life relational dynamics.

Acknowledgement

Support from the Social Science and Humanities Research Council of Canada (SSHRCC) is gratefully acknowledged.

References

Adjibolosoo, Senyo B.-S.K. (1995), "The Significance of the Human Factor in African Economic Development", in Senyo B.-S.K. Adjibolosoo (ed.), *The Significance of the Human Factor in African Economic Development*, Westport, CT: Praeger, pp. 3-14.

Adjibolosoo, Senyo B.-S.K. and Sodberg, A. (2000), "A Human Factor Approach to Human Resource Management and Organization Development", *Review of Human Factor Studies*, 6 (2): 1-12.

Appadurai, A. (1996), *Modernity at Large: Cultural Dimensions of Globalization*, Minneapolis, Minn.: University of Minnesota Press.

Appadurai, S. (1993), "Patriotism and Its Futures", *Public Culture*, 5: 411-429.

Bakardjieva, M. and A. Feenberg (2002), "Community Technology and Democratic Rationalization", *The Information Society*, 18: 181-192.

Baker, P. and Ward, A. (2002), "Bridging Temporal and Spatial 'Gaps': The Role of Information and Communications Technologies in Defining Countries", *Information, Communication and Society*, 5(2): 207-224.

Baumann, G. (1997), "Dominant and Demotic Discourses of Culture: Their Relevance to Multi-Ethnic Alliances", in P. Werbner and T. Madood (eds.), *Debating Cultural Hybridity: Multi-Cultural Identities and the Politics of Racism*, London: Zed Books.

Beck, U. (1997), *The Reinvention of Politics*, London: Blackwell Publishers.

Bennett, L. (1998), "The Uncivic Culture: Communication, Identity, and the Rise of Lifestyle Politics", *PS: Political Science and Politics*, 31(4): 740-741.

Carey, J. (1998), "The Internet and the End of the National Communication System: Uncertain Predictions of an Uncertain Future", *Journalism and Mass Communication Quarterly*, 75(1): 28-34.

Cunningham, S. (2001), "Popular Media as Public "Sphericules" for Diaspora Communities", *International Journal of Cultural Studies*, 4(2): 131-147.

Dertouzos, M. (1997), *What Will Be: How the New World of Information Will Change Our Lives*, San Francisco, CA: HarperEdge.

Diouf, M. (2000), "The Senegalese Murid Trade Diaspora and the Making of a Vernacular Cosmopolitanism", *Public Culture*, 12 (3): 679-702.

Drzewiecka, J. (2002), "Reinventing and Contesting Identities in Constitutive Discourses: Between Diaspora and its Others", *Communication Quarterly*, 50(1): 1-23.

Falk, R. (1993), "The Making of Global Citizenship", in J. Brecher, J. Childs and J. Cutler (eds.), *Global Visions: Beyond the New World Order*, Boston: South End Press.

Franklin, M. (2001), "Quality of Life – Computer Network Resources", *International Feminist Journal of Politics*, 3(3): 387-414.

Giddens, A. (1991), *Modernity and Self-Identity: Self and Society in the Late Modern Age*, Stanford, CA: Stanford University Press.

Guirdy, J., Kennedy, D. and Zald, M. (2000), "Globalization and Social Movements", in J. Guirdy, D. Kennedy and M. Zald (eds.), *Globalization and Social Movements: Culture, Power, and the Transnational Public Sphere*, Ann Arbor: The University of Michigan Press, pp. 1-34.

Hall, S. (1999), "A Conversation with Stuart Hall", *Journal of the International Institute* (University of Michigan, Ann Arbor), Fall, p. 15.

Hassanpour, A. (1998), "Satellite Footprints as National Borders: MED-TV and the Extraterritoriality of State Sovereignty", *Journal of Muslim Minority Affairs*, 18 (1): 53-72.

Jacobsen, D. (1997), *Rights Cross Borders: Immigration and the Decline of Citizenship*, Baltimore, MD: Johns Hopkins University Press.

Karim, K. (n.d.), "Diasporas and Their Communication Networks: Exploring the Broader Context of Transnational Narrowcasting", http://www.nautilaus.org/virtual-diasporas/paper/Karim.html, Retrieved March 17, 2003.

Katz, E. (1996), "And Deliver Us from Segmentation", *Annals of the American Academy of Political and Social Science*, 546: 22-33.

Khor, M. (2001), *Rethinking Globalization: Critical Issues and Policy Choices*, London and New York: Zed Books.

Kitchin, R. (1998), *Cyberspace: The World in the Wires*, Chichester: Wiley.

Liu, H. (1998), "Old Linkages, New Networks: The Globalization of Overseas Chinese Voluntary Associations and its Implications", *The China Quarterly*, 155 (Sept.): 582-609.

Lyons, T. (2003), "Note on Globalization, Diasporas, and Conflict", http://www.intlstudies.ucsd.edu/iicas/pdf/lyons.pdf. Retrieved March 17, 2003.

Mandaville, O. (2001), "Reimagining Islam in Diaspora: The Politics of Mediated Community", *Gazette*, 63(2-3): 169-186.

Mathew, B. and Prashad, V. (2000), "The Protean Forms of Yankee Hidutva", *Ethnic and Racial Studies*, 23(3): 516-534.

McGrew, A. (2000), "Sustainable Globalization?: The Global Politics of Development ande Exclusion in the New World Order", in T. Allen and A. Thomas (eds.), *Poverty and Development Into the 21st Century*, Oxford: Oxford University Press, pp. 345-364.

Mitra A. (2001), "Marginal Voices in Cyberspace", *New Media and Society*, 13(1): 29-48.

NIDO. (n.d.), "Mission Statement" http://www.nidoamericas.org/missionstatement.htm, Retrieved March 17, 2003.

Petras, J. and Veltmeyer, H. (2001), *Globalization Unmasked: Imperialism in the 21st Century*, Halifax; London: Fernwood Publishing; Zed Books.

Pollock, S., Bhabha, H., Breckenridge, C. and Chakrabarty, C. (2000), "Cosmopolitanisms", *Public Culture*, 12(3): 577-589.

Postman, N. (1992), *Technology: The Surrender of Culture to Technology*, New York: Knopf.

Rabinowitz, D. (2000), "Postnational Palestine/Israel? Globalization, Diaspora, Transnationalism and the Israeli-Palestinian Conflict", *Critical Inquiry*, 26 (Summer): 757-773.

Rahn, W. and Rudolph, T. (2001), "National Identities and the Future of Democracy", in W. Bennett and R. Entmara (eds.), *Mediated Politics: Communication in the Future of Democracy*. Cambridge: Cambridge University Press, pp. 453-467.

Rheingold, H. (1993), *The Virtual Community: Homesteading in the Electronic Frontier*. Reading, MA: Addision-Wesley.

Sorenson, J. and Matsuoka, A. (2001), "Phantom Wars and Cyberwars: Abyssinian Fundamentalism and Catastrophe in Eritrea", *Dialectical Anthropology*, 26(1): 37-63.

Stubbs, P. (2001), "Imagining Croatia? Exploring Computer-Mediated Diasporic Public Spheres", in M. Frykman (ed.), *Beyond Integration: Challenges of Belonging in Diaspora and Exile*, Lund: Nordic Academic Press.

Tettey, W. (2002a), "ICT, Local Government Capacity Building, and Civic Engagement: An Evaluation of the Sample Initiative in Ghana", *Perspectives on Global Development and Technology*, 1(2): 165-192.

Tettey, W. (2002b), "Africa's Brain Drain: Exploring Possibilities For Its Positive Utilization Through Networked Communities", *Mots Pluriels*, no. 20, February http://www.arts.uwa.edu.au/MotsPluriels/MP2002wjt.html.

Tettey, W. (2001b), "What Does it Mean to be African-Canadian?: Identity, Integration and Community", in David Taras and Beverly Rasporich (eds.), *A Passion for Identity: An Introduction to Canadian Studies*, 4th Edition., Toronto: ITP Nelson, pp. 161-182.

Tettey, W. (2001a), "Human Factor Analysis and Democratic Transitions in Africa", in Senyo B.-S.K. Adjibolosoo (ed.), *Portraits of Human Behavior and Performance*, Lanhan, New York, Oxford: University Press of America, pp. 109-138.

Tettey, W. (2000), "Information Technology, Expertise, and the Politics of Bureaucratic Control in Africa" *Review of Human Factor Studies*, 6(2): 13-32.

Thompson, K. (2002), "Border Crossing and Diasporic Identities: Media Use and Leisure Practices of an Ethnic Minority", *Qualitative Sociology*, 25(3): 409-418.

Tindimubona, A. (1997), "Nation Building in the Age of the Internet: The Phenomenon of "NationaNets", http://www.isoc.org.gh/ans97/alex.htm. Retrieved March 24, 2003.

Tyler, T. (2002), "Is the Internet Changing Social Life? It Seems the More Things Change, the More They Remain the Same", *Journal of Social Issues*, 58(1): 195-205.

Vrooman, S. (2002), "Flamethrowers, Slashers and Witches: Gendered Communication in a Virtual Community", *Qualitative Research Reports in Communication*, 2(2): 33-41.

Walmsley, D. (2000), "Community, Place and Cyberspace", *Australian Geographer*, 31(1): 5-19.

Wellman, B., Haase, A., Wittle, J. and Hampton, K. (2001), "Does the Internet Increase, Decrease, or Supplement Social Capital?", *American Behavioral Scientist*, 45(3): 436-455.

Wellman, B., Haase, A., Witter, J. and Hampton, K. (2001), "Does the Internet Increase, Decrease or Supplement Social Capital?: Social Networks, Participation and Community Commitment", *American Behavioral Scientist*, 45(3): 436-455.

Werbner, P. (2002), "The Place which is Diaspora: Citizenship, Religion, and Gender in the Making of Chaordic Transnationalism", *Journal of Ethnic and Migration Studies*, 28(1): 119-133.

Werbner, P. (1997), "Essentialising Essentialism, Essentialising Silence: Ambivalence and Multiplicity in the Constructions of Racism and Ethnicity", in P. Werbner and T. Madood (eds.), *Debating Cultural Hybridity: Multi-Cultural Identities and the Politics of Racism*. London: Zed Books.

Williams, R. (2002), "Religion, Community, and Place: Locating the Transcendent," *Religion and American Culture*, 12(2): 249-263.

Yang, G. (n.d.), "Information Technology, Virtual Chinese Diaspora, and Transnational Public Sphere". http://www.nautilus.org/virtual-diasporas/paper/Yang.html. Retrieved March 17, 2003.

Chapter 8

Human Factor Decay, American Exceptionalism and the Exclusion of Women and Minorities from Science and Science-Driven Globalization

Randy Moore

Introduction

The United States has long been a leader in developing the science and technology that have driven globalization. Scientific and technological developments from the United States have influenced numerous aspects of globalization, including transportation, engineering, medicine, communications, electronics, engineering, health administration, and agriculture. Scientific societies (such as the American Association for the Advancement of Science) and governmental agencies (such as the National Science Foundation) have repeatedly stressed 'science for all' and the importance of making science accessible to everyone so that the public can appreciate and benefit from the fruits of science and technology (e.g., American Association for the Advancement of Science, 1989). We have often overlooked the human factor (HF; e.g., integrity, accountability, fairness) associated with science, technology, and their globalization. However, science and science-driven globalization have often been impeded by inadequacies related to the HF, which is the spectrum of personality characteristics and other dimensions of human performance that enable social, economic, and political institutions to function (Adjibolosoo, 1999). Indeed, HF-decay has made the United States an exception to its own proclamations, for science and engineering are often hostile neighborhoods to women and minorities wanting to contribute to and benefit from science-driven globalization.

Why has the United States – a country which was founded on democracy and which exports the virtues of democracy and science education – historically excluded large segments of its population from science and engineering? What have been the consequences of such exclusions on globalization? What is being done to remedy the problem? What are the prospects for success?

Science continues to be a hostile neighborhood for women and minorities in the United States. In the 1800s, when many African Americans in the United States were enslaved and when women were denied the right to vote, women and other minorities were considered unsuitable for science. Women were believed to be too emotional for science, or as being needed for other, female-dominated 'caretaker' jobs such as homemakers, nurses, and teachers. Although African Americans were eventually released from slavery and women were given new rights (e.g., the right to vote), the human factor decay that had produced those inequalities persisted in science (and therefore in science-driven globalization) as it did elsewhere in the United States. Women and minorities had virtually no hope for a career in science because the men controlling access to those careers believed that women and minorities were incapable of being scientists. Some people believed (and continue to believe) that minority students could not excel in science (Rey, 2001). As explained by famed Harvard mathematician Benjamin O. Pierce, 'One might as well try to wash out his color as educate the Negro in sciences' (Chemical inaction, 2001).

In the 1900s, women and minorities became more assertive, but were blocked by many of the same stereotypes that had plagued their predecessors. Blacks continued to be segregated from whites and worked in inferior jobs, attended inferior schools, and had fewer opportunities. Women were viewed as mothers and wives rather than as unique individuals, and were often told that their place was in the home, not the workforce. Women who ventured into the workforce were paid less and received fewer rewards than did men. Women who went to college continued to be routed to restrictive caretaker professions such as home economics, nursing, and teaching, not science. Women's careers, if they could pursue them, were usually restricted to low-paying, low-prestige jobs. 'Women in science' was out of the question, as was 'minorities in science'; as one professor noted, 'In those days, one could not estimate the number of times a day academics said to their colleagues, 'The Negro is oriented toward rote memory only'. As noted recently in the *Journal of Blacks in Higher Education*, 'Unquestionably, the established racial opinions of the great men in science have influenced the professional aspirations of African Americans in subsequent years' (Chemical inaction, 2001). The result was that women and minorities continued to be excluded from science and from science-driven globalization.

Despite these barriers, some women managed to pursue careers in science. Although most of these women were routed to support-positions such as technicians, some became successful scientists. For example, Barbara McClintock won a Nobel Prize for discovering transposons ('jumping genes'), and Rosalind Franklin played a critical role in elucidating the structure of DNA.[1] Rachel Carson's *Silent Spring* began the environmental movement and helped make *ecology* a household word. The important contributions of many other women and minorities are well documented, but often overlooked or discounted.[2] In many instances the contributions of women were claimed by men. As noted by the United States Patent Office, it was common 'for a man to receive a patent for an invention that was actually invented by a woman'. This has often persisted. Indeed, in 1993 only 8% of patents granted to Americans included the name of a woman (Showell and Amram, 1995).

Although women and minorities have made many important contributions to science and globalization, they have often been scorned or ridiculed because of their gender or ethnicity. For example, Rachel Carson was labeled a 'priestess of nature' who cared more for birds than people, and James Watson's dislike for Rosalind Franklin prompted him to announce that 'the best home for a feminist was in another person's lab' (Watson, 1980).

In a country that had become a driving force for globalization by exporting science, technology, and the virtues of democracy, and which touted itself as 'the land of opportunity', many people failed to notice that the United States was an exception to its claims; women and minorities in the United States were being denied opportunities to participate in and benefit from science and science-driven globalization. The globalization driven by science and technology was often inhibited by HF-decay involving sexism, racism, and exclusion.

The massive 'reform' of science education that occurred after the Soviet Union's launch in 1957 of *Sputnik I* (the world's first orbiting satellite) made science increasingly competitive; science was believed to be only for the 'best and brightest' students (Moore, 2001a and 2001b). Since many educators continued to believe that women and minorities were not (and in some cases *could not* be) the 'best and brightest', careers in science remained beyond the grasp of most women and minorities.

During the past two decades, there have been several attempts to include more women and minorities in science. Virtually all of these attempts have involved adding more women and minorities to science classes. However, these classes and their traditional pedagogical approaches have often failed to interest women and minorities, for these classes have placed the responsibility for reform on those who have already been marginalized, excluded, and silenced by science education. Although there have been some improvements in the accessibility of women and minorities to science and science-driven globalization, dramatic disparities persist. For example,

1. Women, ethnic minorities, and disabled students are entering math, engineering, and the physical sciences and getting degrees at rates far less than their representation in the population. Most women and minorities in science are in biology and psychology, but even in these fields they remain a minority (Rosser, 1995). Only one-third of the minority students who begin in the sciences end up graduating with a degree in science or engineering (Rey, 2001).
2. Women are less likely than men to choose careers in science and engineering, regardless of their level of education or employment (National Science Foundation, 2000). Women receive only 11% of degrees in engineering and 24% of degrees in physical sciences (Rey, 2001).
3. Young white males have a significantly more positive attitude toward science than do women, African Americans, and Hispanics (Rakow, 1985). Once in the educational 'pipeline', the confidence of males increases while that of

females decreases (Vasquez, 1998); this helps explain why far more women than men drop out of science courses and programs (Lawler, 1999). The disparity in attrition rates of men and women in science is often unrelated to academic ability, for it persists despite the fact that many of the students who drop out are well prepared for college and have high grade-point-averages (e.g., Newkirk, 2001). Poor grades alone do not account for why science is such a hostile neighborhood for many women and minority students.

4. Although blacks and Hispanics make up nearly 25% of the U.S. population, they earn only 13% of the U.S. science and engineering bachelors degrees and 7% of the doctorates (Rey, 2001).

5. Despite some improvements, women and minorities are still underrepresented in graduate and undergraduate education in science and engineering (National Science Foundation 1990 and 2000). For example, there are only 13 African Americans in the nation's 50 most prestigious chemistry departments; these 13 professors represent less than 0.8% of the total faculty in those departments. Of the more than 300 African Americans who have earned doctorates in chemistry since 1991, none are in these prestigious departments (Chemical inaction, 2001). Similarly, there are no African American professors in the psychology departments of prestigious schools such as Harvard University and the University of Pennsylvania (Almost no blacks, 2002).

6. Women constitute 45% of the employed labor force in the US, but only 23% of all employed scientists and engineers (National Science Foundation, 1992; Women make significant gains 2000). Women constitute only 1% of working environmental engineers, 2% of mechanical engineers, 3% of electrical engineers, 4% of medical school department directors, and 5% of physics doctoral degrees. Only 6 out of about 300 tenured professors in the country's top 10 math departments are women (Holloway, 1993). Women constitute about 12% of the employed scientific and engineering labor force in industry. Black and Hispanic faculty 1) are less likely than white faculty to be full professors, and 2) earn lower salaries than white scientists and engineers (National Science Foundation, 2000).

7. Of the more than 1,800 living scientists elected to the National Academy of Science, only 70 are women, and only 2 are black (Rosser, 1995; The most exclusive club, 2001). Women who remain in science are often displeased and transmit their uneasiness to female students and younger female colleagues (Lawler, 1999).

8. Regardless of their discipline, minority students in science have significantly higher attrition rates than do non-minority students. Similarly, scientists who are minorities continue to receive lower salaries than non-minority scientists (National Science Foundation, 2000).

Women and minorities have heeded the many messages – both overt and covert – that they aren't welcome in science, that they are often blocked from entering science, and that they have no future in science (Barton, 1998; Kahle, 1988).

Why is America's Exclusion of Women and Minorities a Problem for Globalization?

The quality of human factors such as integrity, accountability, fairness, and equity is the foundation not only of science and globalization, but of all human progress (Adjibolosoo, 1999). However, HF-decay has often impeded science. For example, and as noted above, poor grades often do not account for the exclusion of women and minorities from science. On the contrary, women and minorities often find science to be a hostile neighborhood filled with HF-related problems such as sexism and racism. This HF-based avoidance, dislike, and distrust of science has incredible implications and consequences. For example, it produces a culturally homogeneous scientific workforce that often cannot appreciate the diverse cultural aspects of science-driven globalization. This has often hindered our ability to effectively address global problems such as the spread of diseases (e.g., HIV).[3] The HF-driven exclusion of women and minorities from science in grades K-16 results in correspondingly fewer women and minorities who obtain graduate degrees and other advanced credentials in science. For example,

1. In 2000, women earned only 16% of doctoral degrees in engineering.
2. In 2000, African Americans earned only 14 doctorates in mathematics; this represents only 1.3% of all doctorates in the field. African Americans earned less than 3% of all doctorates in computer science, physics, chemistry, earth science, and biology, and only 1.6% of all engineering Ph.D.'s (The striking progress, 2002).
3. In 2000, 1765 doctorates were awarded by universities in the United States in the fields of geometry, number theory, topology, computing theory, astrophysics, acoustics, fluids physics, nuclear physics, polymer physics, nuclear chemistry, atmospheric physics, atmospheric dynamics, meteorology, geology, geophysics, seismology, paleontology, mineralogy, petrology, stratigraphy, geomorphology, glacial geology, hydrology, oceanography, agricultural engineering, ceramic science, communications engineering, engineering physics, metallurgical engineering, mining, mineral engineering, oceanic engineering, petroleum engineering, polymer engineering, systems engineering, bacteriology, plant genetics, plant pathology, plant physiology, endocrinology, veterinary medicine, dairy science, poultry science, agronomy, food engineering, soil chemistry, soil microbiology, forest biology, wood science, forestry, wildlife management, range management, econometrics, and psychometrics. Although these disciplines play important roles in globalization, none of the 1765 degrees went to an African American (The striking progress, 2002).
4. Given the current rate of progress, it will be more than a century before African Americans earn doctorates in science and engineering equal to their percentages in the U.S. population. The avoidance of blacks in these disciplines demonstrates the lingering impact of HF-decay (Women are closing the gap, 2002).

The longstanding domination of science by white males (Vasquez, 1998), combined with the ongoing marginalization and exclusion by science of women, minorities, and others, has hindered globalization by producing experiments, data, theories, and conclusions that often reflect the biases of white males (Harding, 1991; Longino, 1990a and 1990b). For example, before 1993, when President Bill Clinton signed legislation requiring the National Institutes of Health to include women and minorities in all of their clinical health studies, there was no federal policy to adequately enforce the representation of these two groups in public health research. As a result, scientists and science teachers often lacked data for a variety of important phenomena that affect women and minorities, such as the contraction of AIDS by women (Link, 1998). Similarly, 1) important new theories (e.g., female-female interactions) and new ideas were discovered about primatology and animal behavior when women were given opportunities to excel in the field (e.g., Fossey, 1983; Goodall, 1971; Hrdy, 1984), and 2) governments that have endorsed inequitable access to science and science education have often widened socio-economic gaps (e.g., South Africa during the apartheid years; see Taole, 1998), thereby impeding the globalization of benefits of science.

Changing the Human Factor to Improve the Access and Contributions of Women and Minorities to Science and Science-Driven Globalization

The globalization of science has been based primarily on the 'science for development' model. This model, founded on Western science, is based on the assumption that 'science literacy and technology are essential for achieving responsible and sustainable development' (Drori, 1998). This model has had a remarkable impact; for example, in many developing countries in sub-Saharan Africa, science and math now consume about one-third of the curriculum in elementary and secondary schools (Benavot, 1992; Lee, 1990; Lee and Wong, 1990). This emphasis on science and science education has often had little impact on economic development (Benavot, 1992; Kamens and Benavot, 1991) because of HF-decay.

A growing number of institutions have realized that their HF-related policies and practices have arbitrarily denied the access of many women and minorities to science and science-driven globalization. These institutions have changed the HF associated with their science programs to provide greater access and opportunities for women and minority students. They've done this by (a) rejecting the longstanding notion that women and minorities cannot succeed in science, and (b) examining the structural, institutional, and HF-related barriers that have blocked women and minorities from science and science-driven globalization (see discussions in Brickhouse, 1994; Moore, 2001a and 2001b). These changes in the HF have typically occurred in several stages as programs embrace teaching science to all students and, in the process, increase the contributions of women and minorities to globalization by increasing their access to science.

The story of women's and minorities' access to science and technology parallels the contributions of women and minorities to science-driven globalization. As will be obvious from the following discussions, minorities of both sexes are often excluded from science and science-driven globalization for the same HF-related reasons that white women are excluded (George, 1982; Matyas and Malcolm, 1991).

Stage 1: No one notices or cares about the absence of women and minority students. These programs represent the most egregious stage of human factor decay and provide the largest obstacles to the participation of women and minorities in science and globalization. In programs at this stage of curricular and human factor development, faculty, administrators, and students are unaware that women and minority students and their concerns are excluded from science programs. Few teachers or administrators ask or care about how their courses, pedagogical techniques, student services, or attitudes contribute to the retention and success of women and minority students. Many programs in math, engineering, and the physical sciences are at this stage of development.

Faculty and administrators in these programs often justify the exclusion and absence of women and minority students from science with the longstanding belief that because science is objective and value-free, factors such as gender, ethnicity, and background are irrelevant to what scientific knowledge is produced or who becomes a scientist. Because these faculty and administrators often reject the notion that ethnicity and gender influence experiments, ideas, results, and conclusions in science, their programs usually perpetuate the hostilities that women and minority students encounter; these are the biases of the white, upper/middle-class males who dominate the programs and who determine what subjects should be studied, what subjects are interesting and important, and what answers and conclusions should be obtained. These biases convince many women and minority students that they are not 'scientific' because they either do not see or are not interested in observing the 'right things' (Rosser, 1995). Although these faculty and administrators acknowledge that students have different backgrounds, they (a) are often unaware that their expectations are based on socioeconomic class, ethnicity, and gender (Stegemiller, 1989), and (b) assume that the students' differing performances are due only to the students' innate abilities and motivations. Few people in these programs think or care much about what it could mean to teach science and science-driven globalization in ways that embrace rather than marginalize or exclude so many students.

Women, ethnic minorities, disabled students, and others often continue to be marginalized by longstanding misconceptions that they are neither fit for nor interested in careers in science, that they make poor risks as graduate students because they are 'unqualified' for science, that they can't contribute as much as white men, etc. These deficiencies in the HF, combined with the fact that women and minorities have traditionally received fewer resources and rewards than white men, have made careers in science especially difficult for women and minorities (see above), and have reduced the impact of woman and minorities to science-driven globalization. When these students avoid or leave science, we often excuse their marginalization and exclusion from science with self-serving excuses such as 'It's probably best for them, anyway' or 'He's a minority – what do you expect?'. These results and excuses are consistent with the beliefs that these students are often obstacles to developing a quality science program; for example, disabled students are often told that they can't do science because of their reduced dexterity or mobility. Similarly, women are often expected to be home with children, whether they have children or not (or whether they want to be there or not). To many people, the phrases *minority scientist* and *woman scientist* are contradictions; if such people exist at all, they are somehow 'unnatural' – either an atypical person, or an atypical scientist (e.g., Rossiter, 1982). Today, as in the past, women and minorities must often overcome the consequences of self-fulfilling prophecies (Doyle, 2000) that dominate science education programs at this stage of curricular development.

 Stage 2: Faculty and administrators realize that there are problems with their program, but implement ineffective changes. Programs at this stage of curricular development typically intervene with compensatory programs that enroll more women and minority students in their courses. This approach to the problem seldom succeeds because (a) the courses and programs in which the women and minority students are placed remain as hostile to these students as before, and (b) it continues to emphasize the alleged deficiencies of students rather than the obstacles and discriminatory practices of science and science education. In these programs, courses remain a 'filter' that excludes students from science rather than a 'pump' that helps ensure students' access to and success in science.

 Moving beyond this stage of curricular development requires that faculty and administrators shift their focus from reactively blaming women and minority students for their alleged failures to proactively identifying and eliminating barriers that block students' access students to science (see discussion in Moore, 2001a and 2001b).

 Stage 3: Faculty and administrators begin to identify the human-factor related barriers in their programs and courses that block women and minority students from enjoying science and contributing to science-drive globalization. This phase of curricular transformation begins with changes in the HF; specifically, it starts when students, faculty and administrators see that women and minorities have been excluded from science and wonder how this has affected science and globalization (see discussion in Moore 2001a and 2001b). Students, faculty, and administrators do not have to look far to find examples of how talented women and minorities are excluded by the current ways that science is taught and practiced (Fausto-Sterling, 1992; Harding, 1986; Moore, 2001b; Rosser, 1995). For example, women and minority students are often not interested in many research topics (e.g., military-related problems) and pedagogical approaches that have been favorites of the white males who have dominated science for generations. Similarly, many women approach science from a different, less competitive, and more holistic perspective than men (Kahle and Meece, 1994; Rosser, 1995 and references therein). For example, many women would rather study interdisciplinary, socially useful problems rather than the hierarchical, reductionist, and dualistic problems that often typify male-dominated science (Belenky, Clinchy, Goldberger and Tarule, 1986; Harding, 1985; Kahle, 1985; Rosser, 1993). Many women do not want to participate in the aspects of science that they consider to be destructive to humans, other animals, and the environment (Halpin, 1989). Although these students are not usually vocal or adamant about their ideas, they are uncomfortable.

Progressing beyond this stage of curricular development requires that faculty and administrators understand that they can increase *all* students' access to science and science-driven globalization by incorporating new ways of teaching and learning based on new experiences and perspectives. These new approaches include the following (Moore, 2001a and 2001b):

1. Encouraging students to become connected with what they study. For example, Nobel laureate Barbara McClintock's insistence on having a 'feel for' her corn plants and Dian Fossey's personalized interactions with mountain gorillas differed dramatically from the 'objective' approaches of men that were based on putting distance between the scientist and his subject (Sapolsky, 2001). The 'connected' approaches of McClintock, Fossey, and others often enhances learning by women, and contrasts the misconception that scientists are isolated and distant from what they study (Hubbard, 1990; Rosser, 1995 and references therein).

2. Encouraging students to view science in larger contexts that include society, justice, and globalization. Although most science programs promote competition, dualistic thinking, and the domination of nature, many ethnic minorities emphasize group cooperation, holistic thinking, and social justice (Anderson, 1988; Caduto and Bruchae, 1989; Hadfield, Martin, and Wooden, 1992). Teachers can make their courses more accessible to these students by making their courses less competitive, emphasizing the social context of science, and showing how science enhances globalization and improves people's lives (Moore, 2001a). Similarly, show students that science is one part of life that is compatible with their other goals; the belief that women in science have added obstacles due to their concerns about marriage and family often causes women to leave science (Arnold, 1987; Gardner, 1986; Matyas, 1985).

3. Offering smaller, more personal classes in which all students have equal access to instructors and which include multiple ways of knowing science, doing science, and using science to contribute to globalization (Barton and Osborne, 1995; Brickhouse, 1994; Roychoudhury, Tippins, and Nichols, 1993 and 1995; Stokstad 2001). The high rate of attrition of qualified women and minorities from many science programs may be due to large, impersonal, and restrictive introductory courses based entirely on monolithic lectures and multiple-choice exams having one correct answer (Rosser, 1995). Effectively teaching women and minority students sometimes requires that teachers use a variety of pedagogical techniques (Moore, 2001b). Merely repeating information slower and louder does not increase comprehension.

4. Designing courses to engage all students in science and globalization. Many women and minority students are apprehensive about science because they have had significantly less experience with science and scientific equipment

(Educational Testing Service, 1988). Teachers can help overcome these concerns by incorporating more time into their classes for hands-on work and observations (Rosser, 1995; Stokstad, 2001). Teachers should also encourage students to gather data themselves, but should not let women and minority students become secretaries while other students operate scientific equipment.

Stage 4: Students learn the unique contributions of women and minorities to science and globalization. The exclusion of women and minorities is strengthened when their work is ignored, misrepresented, discounted (e.g., because of speech patterns and other verbal and nonverbal forms of communication; see Hall and Sandler, 1982; Tannen, 1990), described as nonscience, or attributed to white males with whom they worked (e.g., Ehrenreich and English, 1978; Hynes, 1984). For example, Ellen Swallow's studies of environmental pollution, sanitation, and waste disposal contributed significantly to the birth of ecology, but were described as 'home economics' – and then dismissed as nonscience – largely because the work was done by a woman (Hynes, 1984, 1989). Similarly, the initial rejection of Rachel Carson's contributions to ecology and Barbara McClintock's discovery of genetic transposition were largely due to the fact that Carson and McClintock were women whose empathetic approach to science challenged the prevailing, impersonal, reductionist style followed by most male scientists (Keller, 1983; Moore, 1997).

Teachers can help students overcome these misconceptions by (a) incorporating and validating the contributions of women, minorities, and disabled scientists who have made significant contributions to science and globalization, (b) featuring influential women and minorities who are in decision-making positions in the hierarchy of science and globalization, (c) showing students that women and minorities often have made significant contributions to the work for which men have received prizes and recognition, and (d) encouraging students to uncover biases and stereotypes in human factory deficiencies involving race, class, sexual orientation, etc. (e.g., racism by scientists and the use of science to justify racism are powerful deterrents to minorities' participation in science; Rossiter, 1982). Emphasizing the lives of ordinary women and minority scientists often helps students break the stereotype that scientists are white men and that others are not welcome (see Chambers, 1983; Rosser, 1995).

Stage 5: Science is redefined and restructured to include all students. This is the goal of every science education program: to improve the HF so that all students, regardless of their gender, ethnicity, or social status, have access to science and science-driven globalization. Achieving this goal involves reexamining the attitudes, contexts, conditions, and excuses that we accept as educational norms, and embracing the following (Rosser, 1995):

1. Good science teaching involves teaching science to *all* students. Teachers throughout the program employ teaching strategies that remove barriers to access, learning, and success (e.g., universal instructional design; see Silver, Bourke, and Strehorn, 1998; Waksler, 1996).

2. Good science teaching questions how knowledge and interrelationships are situated within discourses of knowledge, the HF, power, and globalization, as well as how these affects students and teachers.
3. Good science teaching involves using multiple ways of knowing and doing science that reflect social, historical, and political concerns. Science is not isolated from other ways of knowing and doing.
4. Good science teaching must be political because of teachers' important roles and their desire to ensure social justice.
5. Good science teaching immerses all learners in the mediated construction of knowledge in meaningful, relevant, inclusive, and nurturing ways.
6. Effective science teachers teach 'content' as well as the skills necessary for success in school and life.
7. Clearly, achieving these goals depends almost entirely on the HF. As noted by Norman Fortenberry, head of the division of undergraduate education at the National Science Foundation, 'The key lever for change is the faculty' (Mervis, 2001).

Conclusions: Science for All Depends on Improving the Human Factor

It is people, and not objects (e.g., systems, institutions, technology), that make globalization possible. All progress is based on the quality of the HF (Adjibolosoo,1999). Thus, for globalization (or, for that matter, any other program) can succeed, societies must harness the HF necessary for success (e.g., accountability, integrity, equity). It is the level of HF development that either encourages or discourages people to live peacefully and be productive. Without the HF, globalization cannot succeed, because the HF underlies all societal progress. *The HF underlies the link of science, science education, and globalization.*

Our efforts to globalize the benefits of science must be prefaced by programs to strengthen the HF associated with globalization. HF-related problems have impeded science-driven globalization; this is why most people living in Africa, Latin America, and Central Asia are no better off today than they were in 1989 when the fall of the Berlin Wall allowed capitalism to spread rapidly worldwide (Kahn, 2002). As a result, the promised riches and development associated with globalization have not materialized.

Increasing the access of women and minority students to science will increase the number of women, ethnic minorities, disabled students, and others in science-related professions. This, in turn, will help ensure that these students can participate in and benefit from science-driven globalization. This is especially important in light of the fact that 80-90% of workforce growth will be women and minorities – the groups not traditionally attracted in large numbers to the physical sciences and engineering. The status quo – that is, the continued exclusion and marginalization of women and minority students and others – will perpetuate the relative homogeneity of science. This, in turn, will perpetuate similar approaches to the HF, globalization, problem solving and the interpretation of data, thereby restricting creativity and producing bias (Rosser, 1995).

        A variety of educational programs and professional programs want 'science for all Americans'. 'Science for all' requires improvements of the HF and *access and equity* for all. The transformation of science education to include women and minority students will be a big step toward accomplishing this goal.

Notes

[1] Maurice Wilkins, Francis Crick, and James Watson won a Nobel Prize for their elucidation of the double-helical structure of DNA, but they'd not have made their discovery without Franklin's photographs.

[2] For example, Grace Hopper made important contributions to computing, Rachel Brown made important contributions to the invention of fungicides, and Stepanie Kwolek made important contributions to the development of Kevlar (for discussion of these and other important contributions of women to science and technology, see Showell and Amram, 1995).

[3] Minorities account for nearly half of all Americans infected with HIV, but remain less likely than whites to be included in new studies of AIDS drugs (AIDS studies, 2002).

References

Adjibolosoo, Senyo B.-S.K. (1999), *Rethinking Developmental Theory and Policy: A Human Factor Critique*, Westport, CT: Praeger.

"AIDS Studies Include Fewer Minorities" (2002), *USA Today*, (May 2), p. 9D.

"Almost No Blacks in Academic Psychology: Does the Pipeline Defense Hold Water?" (2002), *Journal of Blacks in Higher Education*, 34 (Winter), 48.

American Association for the Advancement of Science (1989), *Science for All Americans*, Washington, DC: American Association for the Advancement of Science.

Anderson, J.A. (1988), "Cognitive Styles and Multicultural Populations", *Journal of Teacher Education*, 39 (1): 2-9.

Arnold, K. (1987), "Retaining High Achieving Women in Science and Engineering", Paper presented at Women in Science and Engineering: Changing Vision to Reality Conference, University of Michigan, Ann Arbor, sponsored by the American Association for the Advancement of Science.

Barton, A.C. (1998), *Feminist Science Education*, New York: Teachers College Press.

Barton, A.C. and Osborne, M.D. (1995), "Science for All Americans? Science Education Reform and Mexican-Americans", *The High School Journal*, 78: 244-252.

Belenky, M.F.,Clinchy, B.M., Goldberger, N.R., and Tarule, J.M. (1986), *Women's Ways of Knowing*, New York: Basic Books.

Benavot, A. (1992), "Curricular Content, Educational Expansion, and Economic Growth", *Comparative Education Review*, 36 (2): 150-174.

Brickhouse, N. (1994), "Bringing in the Outsiders: Reshaping the Science for the Future", *Curriculum Studies*, 26: 401-416.

Caduto, M.J. and Bruchae, J. (1989), *Keepers of the Earth: Native American Stories and Environmental Activities for Children*, Golden, CO: Fulchrum.

Chambers, D. (1983), "Stereotypic Images of the Scientist: The Draw-a-Scientist Test", *Science Education*, 76: 475-476.

"Chemical Inaction: Almost No Blacks in Academic Chemistry", (2001), *Journal of Blacks in Higher Education* (Summer, No. 32): 17-19.

Doyle, R. (2000), "Women and the Professions", *Scientific American*, (April): 30.

Drori, G. (1998), "A Critical Appraisal of Science Education for Economic Development", in W.W. Cobern, (ed.), *Socio-Cultural Perspectives on Science Education*, London: Kluwer Academic Publishers, pp. 49-74.

Educational Testing Service (1988), *The Science Report Card: Elements of Risk and Recovery, Trends, and Achievement Based on the 1986 National Assessment (Report No. 17-S-01)*, Princeton, NJ: Author.

Ehrenreich, B. and English, D. (1978), *For Her Own Good: 150 Years of the Experts' Advice to Women*, Garden City, NY: Anchor.

Fausto-Sterling, A. (1992), *Myths of Gender*, New York: Basic Books.

Fossey, D. (1983), *Gorillas in the Mist*, Boston: Houghton Mifflin.

Gardner, A.L. (1986), "Effectiveness of Strategies to Encourage Participation and Retention of Precollege and College Women in Science", Unpublished doctoral dissertation, Purdue University, West Lafayette, IN.

George, Y. (1982), "Affirmative Action Programs that Work", in S. Humphreys, (ed.), *Women and Minorities in Science*, AAAS Selected Symposia Series, Boulder, CO: Westview, pp. 87-98.

Goodall, J. (1971), *In the Shadow of Man*, Boston: Houghton Mifflin.

Hadfield, O.D., Martin, J.D. and Wooden, S. (1992), "Mathematics Anxiety and Learning Style of the Navajo Middle School Student", *School Science and Mathematics*, 92: 171-175.

Hall, R. and Sandler, B. (1982), *The Classroom Climate: A Chilly One for Women*, Washington, DC: Project on the Status and Education of Women, Association of American Colleges.

Halpin, Z. (1989), "Scientific Objectivity and the Concept of 'The Other'", *Women's Studies International Forum*, 12: 285-294.

Harding, J. (1985), "Values, Cognitive Style and the Curriculum", *Contributions to the Third Girls and Science and Technology Conference*, London: Chelsea College, University of London, pp. 159-166.

Harding, S. (1986), *The Science Question in Feminism*, Ithaca, NY: Cornell University Press.

Harding, S. (1991), *Whose Science? Whose Knowledge? Thinking from Women's Lives*, Ithaca, NY: Cornell University.

Holloway, M. (1993), "A Lab of her Own", *Scientific American*, 269: 94-103.

Hrdy, S.B. (1984), "Introduction: Female Reproductive Strategies", in M. Small (ed.), *Female Primates: Studies by Women Primatologists*, New York: Alan Liss, pp. 103-109.

Hubbard, R. (1990), *The Politics of Women's Biology*, New Brunswick, NJ: Rutgers University Press.

Hynes, P. (1984), "Women Working: A Field Report", *Technology Review*, 38: 37-38, 47.

Hynes, P. (1989), *The Recurring Silent Spring*, Elmsford, NY: Pergamon Press.

Kahle, J.B. (1985), *Women in Science*, Philadelphia: Falmer Press.

Kahle, J.B. (1988), "Recruitment and Retention of Women College Science Majors", *Journal of College Science Teaching*, 27: 5.

Kahle, J.B. and Meece, J. (1994), "Research on Girls in Science Lessons and Applications", in D. Gabel (ed.), *Handbook of Research in Science Teaching and Learning*, Washington, DC: National Science Teachers Association.

Kahn, J. (2002), "Losing Faith: Globalization Proves Disappointing", *The New York Times* (March 21), p. A6.

Kamens, D.H. and Benavot, A. (1991), "Elite Knowledge for the Masses: The Origins and Spread of Mathematics and Science Education in national Curricula", *American Journal of Education*, 99 (2): 137-180.

Keller, E.F. (1983), *A Feeling for the Organism*, New York: Freeman.

Lawler, A. (1999), "Tenured Women Battle to Make it Less Lonely at the Top", *Science*, 286: 1271-1278.

Lee, M. (1990), *Structural Determinants and Economic consequences of Science Education: A Cross-National Study, 1950-1986*, Unpublished Ph.D. Dissertation, Stanford University School of Education.

Lee, M. and Wong, S. (1990), "The Provision of Science Education (1950-1986): Cross-National Patterns", Paper presented at the Comparative and International Education Society Annual Meeting, 1990, Anaheim, CA.

Link, C. (1998), "Attracting More Women and Minorities to the Sciences: A Chautauqua Short Course Points to the Way", *Journal of College Science Teaching*, 28: 26-28.

Longino, H. (1990a), "Can There be a Feminist Science?", in N. Tuana, (ed.), *Feminism and Science*, Bloomington, IN: Indiana University, pp. 45-57.

Longino, H. (1990b), *Science as Social Knowledge: Values and Objectivity in Scientific Inquiry*, Princeton, NJ: Princeton University Press.

Matyas, M.L. (1985), "Factors Affecting Female Achievement and Interest in Science and Scientific Careers", in Kahle, J.B. (ed.), *Women in Science: A Report from the Field*, Philadelphia: Falmer Press, pp. 27-48.

Matyas, M.L. and Malcolm, S. (1991), *Investing in Human Potential: Science and Engineering at the Crossroads*, Washington, DC: American Association for the Advancement of Science.

Mervis, J. (2001), "Getting More Out of the Classroom", *Science*, 293: 1607.

Moore, R. (1997), "Rachel Louise Carson", in L. S. Grinstein, C.A. Bierman, and R.K. Rose (eds.), *Women in the Biological Sciences: A Biobibliographic Sourcebook*, Westport, CT: Greenwood Press, pp. 62-69.

Moore, R. (2001a), "Administering Science Education: Expanding the Pool of the 'Brightest and Best'", *Review of Human Factors Studies*, 7 (1): 44-60.

Moore, R. (2001b), "New Directions in Science Education for Developmental Education", in D.B. Lundell and J.L. Higbee, (eds.), *Theoretical Perspectives in Developmental Education*, Minneapolis, MN: Center for Research on Developmental Education and Urban Literacy, General College, University of Minnesota, pp. 145-153.

National Science Foundation (1990), *Women and Minorities in Science and Engineering (NSF 90-301)*, Washington, DC: Author.

National Science Foundation (1992), *Women and Minorities in Science and Engineering: An update (NSF 92-303)*, Washington, DC: Author.

National Science Foundation (2000), *Women, Minorities, and Persons with Disabilities in Science and Engineering 2000*, Washington, DC: Author.

Newkirk, T. (2001), "A Campus Gender Gap", *Education Week*, 20: 35.

Rakow, S.J. (1985), "Minority Students in Science, Perspectives from the 1981-1982 National Assessment in Science", *Urban Education*, 20 (1): 103-113.

Rey, C.M. (2001), "Making Room for Diversity Makes Sense", *Science*, 293: 1611-1612.

Rosser, S.V. (1993), "Female Friendly Science: Including Women in Curricular Content and Pedagogy in Science", *The Journal of General Education*, 42: 191-220.

Rosser, S.V. (1995), "Reaching the Majority", in Sue V. Rosser (ed.), *Teaching the Majority: Breaking the Gender Barrier in Science*, New York: Teachers College Press, pp. 1-21.

Rossiter, M.W. (1982), *Women Scientists in America: Struggles and Strategies to 1940*, Baltimore: Johns Hopkins University Press.

Roychoudhury, A., Tippins, D. and Nichols, S. (1993), "An Exploratory Attempt Toward a Feminist Pedagogy for Science Education", *Action in Teacher Education*, 15: 36-45.

Roychoudhury, A., Tippins, D. and Nichols, S. (1995), "Gender-Inclusive Science Teaching: A Feminist Constructive Perspective", *Journal of Research in Science Teaching*, 32: 897-930.

Sapolsky, R.M. (2001), "Fossey in the Mist", *Discover*, 22 (2): 73-81.

Showell, E.H. and Amram, F.M.B. (1995), *From Indian Corn to Outer Space: Women Invent in America*, Peterborough, NH: Cobblestone Publications.

Silver, P., Bourke, A. and Strehorn, K.C. (1998), "Universal Instructional Design in Higher Education: An Approach for Inclusion", *Equity and Excellence in Education*, 31: 47-51.

Stegemiller, H.A. (1989), *An Annotated Bibliography of the Literature Dealing with the Contributing Factors of Teacher Expectations on Student Performance*, (Report N. SP 031 604), South Bend: Indiana University at South Bend. (ERIC Document Reproduction and Service No. ED 313 323).

Stokstad, E. (2001), "Reintroducing the Intro Course", *Science*, 293: 1608-1610.

Tannen, D. (1990), *You Just Don't Understand*, New York: Ballantine.

Taole, K. (1998), "Science Education and the Politics of Equity. Part II: An Institutional Perspective", in W.W. Cobern, (ed.), *Socio-Cultural Perspectives on Science Education*, London: Kluwer Academic Publishers, pp. 87-97.

"The Most Exclusive Club of Great Scientists Is Just Two Scholars Shy of Being Lily-White" (2001), *Journal of Blacks in Higher Education*, 32 (Summer): 67.

"The Striking Progress of African Americans in Degree Attainments" (2002), *Journal of Blacks in Higher Education*, 34 (Winter): 100-106.

Vasquez, J. (1998), "Equitable Education: Making Science Accessible to All Students", *The Science Teacher*, (September): 43-45.

Waksler, R. (1996), "Teaching Strategies for a Barrier Free Classroom", *Journal of Excellence in College Teaching*, 7: 99-111.

Watson, J.D. (1980), *The Double Helix* (Norton critical edition), New York: W. W. Norton, p. 15.

"Women Make Significant Gains in Science and Engineering Fields" (2000) *NABT News and Views*, (July): 7.

"Women are Closing the Science Gap; But for Blacks the Progress is Glacial" (2002) *Journal of Blacks in Higher Education*, 34 (Winter): 31.

Pinto, S., (2005), 'Midwife Shortages in Changing Policy Environment 1981-1982', National Association in Science, *Token Changing*, 20 (10), 105-115.

Law, C.M. (2001), 'Making Room for Diversity Makes Sense', *Science*, 294, 1611-1614.

Rosser, S.V. (1997), 'Female Friendly Science, Including Women in Curriculum and Pedagogy', in *Science: The Female Perspective*, Vienna: Garamond 42, 193-220.

Rosser, S. (1995), 'Reorienting the Majority', in Sue V. Rosser (ed.), *Teaching the Majority: Breaking the Gender Barrier in Science*, New York: Teachers College Press, pp. 1-21.

Rossiter, M.W. (1982), *Women Scientists in America: Struggles and Strategies to 1950*, Baltimore: John Hopkins University Press.

Roychoudhury, A., Tippins, D. and Nichols, S., (1995), 'An Exploratory Attempt Toward a Feminist Pedagogy for Science Education', *Action in Teacher Education*, 16, 36-46.

Roychoudhury, A., Tippins, D., and Nichols, S., (1995), 'Gender Inclusive Science Teaching: A Feminist Constructivist Perspective', *Journal of Research & Science Teaching*, 31, 897-924.

Sandler, R.M. (2003), 'Top Gun to the Male', *Discover*, 20, 53-58.

Snowell, E.H. and Ratha, J.P.R. (1995), 'Twin values on Core in Gene Space', *Wooded Spaces in genomics*, Peterborough, NH: Gabbastonne Enterprises.

Short, E, Burke, A, and Farthing, K.C. (1995), 'Relational Instructional Design in Gender Endeavours: An Approach for Individual, Functional Groups and Organisations', *Education*, 51, 47-71.

Sigudilar, L.A. (1984), 'An Annotated Bibliography on the Tolerance of Plating, with the Contributive Factors of Dietary Expectation on Slopes', *Performance Oriented R.SP 0.07.009, South Bend, Individual Grains at Study Bend*, (DPL Operating, Reproduction and Service No. ROS 13.589).

Siekaad, F. 2001, *Wissenschaften Zu John Admir*, Sockney, 555-1998 101.5.

Tannen, D. (1990), *You Just Don't Understand!*, New York: Ballantine.

Pack, B., 1998, 'Service Education and the Politics of Equity: Part II: Archaeological Perspective', in W.W. Cobern (ed.), *Socio-Cultural Perspectives on Science Education*, London: Kluwer Academic Publishers, pp. 87-93.

'The Most Exclusive Club of Female Scientists Is Just Two Scholars Short, Some Think' (1981), *Journal of Women in Higher Education*, 25 (January), 1-4.

'The Shifting Emphasis of Americal America, in Degree Attainment', (2001), *Review of Higher Education*, 24 (Winter), 100-108.

Vasquez, J. (1998), 'Teaching Education, Making Science Accessible: All Standards, The Whole Tradition', (September), 43-45.

Walker, B.C. (1997), 'The Science Debate at a Premier New Experiment', *Journal of Higher Education*, 30 (July), 704-713.

Wilson, E.O. (1998) (ed.), *Intellectual Information Technology*, New York: W.W. Norton, 3-15.

Wonen, Male Significant Gains in Science and Engineering', *Nature* (2001), 20 (March), 1-3, *Nature Daily*.

'Women are Closing the Science Gap, But Are They There Yet', *Prospects in Digital* (2000), *Journal of the Journal in Winter Prospects*, 55 (Winter), 1-3.

PART IV:
GLOBALIZATION, THE HUMAN FACTOR, DEMOCRACY AND GOVERNANCE

Chapter 9

Globalization, Governance and the Human Factor

E. Osei Kwadwo Prempeh

Introduction

Events since the late 1980s suggest a restructuring of the contemporary world economy. In an effort to explain the transformations, many scholars, politicians, journalists and policy makers have tried to capture them under the rubric of 'globalization'. That globalization constitutes a powerful transformative force at the beginning of this new millennium is beyond doubt. Various authors have pointed to the unprecedented economic, social, political, cultural and technological changes that are calling into question the existing architecture of contemporary societies.

This radical change in the social, political, economic, cultural and technological processes is, for better or for worse, akin to the 'great transformation' described by Polanyi (Polanyi, 1975). As noted by Gertler (1997, p. 45):

> It has been taken as an article of faith for some time that we live in a global economy. Frequent pronouncements by academics, journalists, and policy makers alike continue to assert publicly the 'fact' of globalization with numbing frequency. Bound up in such pronouncements are the ideas that globalization both is a reality and, as a process, constitutes an inevitable and inexorable development.

The increasing intensity and extent of globalization has generated a counter-critique. This counter-hegemonic discourse has set the course for a new form of global activism. The anti-systemic resistance is captured in the demand for governance on the basis that globalization left unchecked could become undemocratic or even anti-democratic. The source of this anti-systemic resistance is a grassroots initiated process situated in civil society. Falk (1999, p. 3) refers to this process as 'globalization-from-below' to distinguish it from 'globalization-from-above'. Indeed, it is now commonplace to hear arguments about globalization and a corresponding governance critique, all part of the usual discursive process within the social sciences. Governance is used here to refer to:

the processes and institutions, both formal and informal, that guide and restrain the collective activities of a group ... Governance need not necessarily be conducted exclusively by governments and the international organizations to which they delegate authority. Private firms, associations of firms, nongovernmental organizations (NGOs), and associations of NGOs *[and civil society organizations – emphasis mine]* all engage in it, often in association with governmental bodies, to create governance; sometimes without governmental authority (Keohane and Nye, 2000, p. 12).

In this chapter, I propose to sketch out the confrontation between the economic globalization thesis and the emergence of the governance critique. The reason for this confrontation lies in the argument that the adverse effects of the dominant globalization thesis elicited a counter-hegemonic response and critique. This debate, it is to be pointed out, is cast in quintessential Polanyian terms. My intent is to subject the prevailing wisdoms concerning globalization and governance to critical scrutiny by introducing the Human Factor (HF) dimension. The major claim of this chapter is that any assessment of the globalization/governance debate has to take into account not just the hegemonic and counter-hegemonic forces, but also the HF: those human attributes that ensure enduring commitments and dedication to the governance agenda.

The governance literature has introduced a critical counterpoint to the contemporary globalization literature but the case can be made for widening it. The HF school of thought might seem [to be] well positioned to contribute to this. The central assumptions and ideas of globalization and governance put the issue of human agency on the agenda, hence the need to consider the HF. The chapter moves beyond the globalization-governance polarity. I defend the governance counter-hegemonic process and option as necessary, but with the important addition that such a process and option must also take into account the HF. The governance approach challenges the central claims of globalization, calling for more transparency, accountability, and democratic participation among others. However, this interpretation is itself subject and open to critical scrutiny as this paper will demonstrate. At issue here is whether the governance approach by itself provides a full and incontrovertible alternative.

This critique of the governance thesis is not because of any disagreement regarding the critical importance of the governance elements identified by it. The critique is only secondary. What is argued here is that the HF dimension adds another element to the governance thesis making it a much stronger and more critical, holistic and integrated approach. In other words, including the HF puts the conclusions of the governance approach in a much more critical light. Central to this is the development of a two-step strategy of governance and HF engineering.

The first section briefly reviews the commonly held views on globalization. This is followed by the governance critique to globalization as articulated especially in the works of scholars like Richard Falk, Stephen Gill and others who raise doubts about the predatory nature of the process of globalization. The concluding section considers some critical interventions and contributions from the HF school of thought which, it is hoped, would inject some theoretical and practical insights into the common counter-hegemonic critique to the globalization thesis – namely, the governance approach.

Globalization Unpacked: The Touchstones of the Globalization Thesis

As indicated in the introduction, during the late 1980s, a new and very different language emerged in the academic and non-academic lexicon. The emphasis appeared to be on the impact of globalized networks and processes which tended to suggest that global enterprises were operating in a 'borderless world'. Ohmae is typical of the 'borderless world' interpretation which characterize globalization as leading to the decline of the nation-state. In *The Borderless World*, Ohmae argues that 'today if you look closely at the world Triad companies inhabit, national borders have effectively disappeared and, along with them, the economic logic that made them useful lines of demarcation in the first place' (Ohmae, 1990, p. 172).

Ohmae suggests that the social and political processes are subordinated to economic forces. Above all, the national economy is 'an unnatural, even dysfunctional unit' (Ohmae, 1995, p. 42), a construct which is reinforced by Hirst and Thompson, albeit as a point of critique: "the danger of the rhetoric of globalization is that it tends to ignore these distributions: it treats the world as a single open competitive market and the location of economic activity as dictated by purely commercial considerations (Hirst and Thompson, 1996, p. 102).

For Norris, 'globalization' is understood as a process that erodes national boundaries, integrating national economies, cultures, technologies, and governance, producing complex relations of mutual interdependence' (Norris, 2000, p. 155). This is all part of an emerging global neoliberal hegemonic discourse informed by a strong reliance of market-driven institutional processes and accompanying political, social and cultural practices. This globally dominant discourse with wide political, economic, social, technological and cultural implications is shaping and appropriating the constellation of forces at the local, national and global levels in a way that the global predominates.

While changes in our understandings and attitudes are both affected and reflect the larger changes of globalization, there appears to be no one definition which seems to capture the essence and various facets of the process. In spite of these definitional vagueness and problems, there has emerged some consensus on the core of globalization. For example, Friedman defines globalization as 'that loose combination of free-trade agreements, the Internet and the integration of financial markets that is erasing borders and uniting the world into a single, lucrative, but brutally competitive, marketplace' (Friedman, 1996, p. A15). According to Held et al. (2000, p. 55), globalization is 'a process (or set of processes) which embodies a transformation in the spatial organization of social relations and transactions – assessed in terms of their extensity, intensity, and impact – generating transcontinental or interregional flows and networks of activity, interaction, and the exercise of power'.

What is clear is that globalization is a multifaceted process comprised of dynamic power relations that are reformulating, changing and transforming economic, political, social, technological and cultural boundaries. It also constitutes a stage of capitalism, and the incorporation of larger parts of the world into the world capitalist system.

Contemporary globalization, so defined, has exercised hegemonic control in establishing a new globalized economy. The defining hallmark of this process is a new constellation of market, technological, ideological and civilizational forces with a far reach, a reach beyond the territorial boundaries of current states. Its hegemonic status flows from the unprecedented reach, power and impact of its operative logic and its ideological connotation. This ideological and hegemonic power has been imaginatively interpreted in a powerful way in Gill's sketch of what he terms 'neoliberal market civilization'.

> By market civilization, I mean a contradictory movement or set of transformative practices. The concept entails, on the one hand, cultural, ideological, and mythic forms understood broadly as an ideology or myth of capitalist progress. These representations are associated with the cumulative aspects of market integration and the increasingly expansive structures of accumulation, legitimation, consumption, and work. They are largely configured by the power of transnational capital. On the other hand, market civilization involves patterns of social disintegration and exclusionary and hierarchical patterns of social relations ... Although the governance of this market civilization is framed by the discourse of globalizing neoliberalism and expressed through the interaction of free enterprise and the state, its coordination is achieved through a combination of market discipline and the direct application of political power (Gill, 1995b, p. 399).

Gill's interpretation is useful in the way that it highlights the power dynamic and pretenses to supremacy embodied in the economic globalization thesis. Without mincing words, Gill identifies the encompassing power relations as 'the dominant forces of contemporary globalization are constituted by a neoliberal historical bloc that practices a politics of supremacy within and across nations' (Gill, 1995b, p. 402). While Gill refers to this as 'the politics of *supremacy* rather than hegemony', it is suggested that that is more semantic than substantive. Globalization, thus understood, represents a grand ideological construct, designed to rationalize, reinforce and legitimize a market-driven neoliberal project of global proportions.

In other words, the long reach of the process of globalization is such that the political, economic, social, and cultural impacts it unleashes not only have global implications, but do also affect decisions and policies at the global level. To borrow Held et al.'s words again:

> [Accordingly], the concept of globalization implies, first and foremost, a *stretching* of social, political and economic activities across frontiers such that events, decisions and activities in one region of the world can come to have significance for individuals and communities in distant regions of the globe. In

this sense, it embodies transregional interconnectedness, the widening reach of networks of social activity and power, and the possibility of action at a distance (Held et al., 2000, p. 54).

It is this 'widening reach of networks of social activity and power' that lies at the heart of the contestation and critical counter-hegemonic position, a point to be picked up in the next section. The core of this contestation is the way globalization has altered the basis of policy-making and decision-making in a way, it is claimed, devoid of accountability, transparency and democratic representation. The calls for effective governance that form the basis of the counter-hegemonic discourse is a reaction to this. It proceeds on the basis that this lack of transparency, accountability and representation silences the voices of the people most affected by globalization and is therefore undemocratic or even anti-democratic.

In concluding this section, it should be noted that although the definition of globalization is imprecise and subject to controversy and much disagreement, it is widely accepted that the process has engendered the restructuring and transformation of social, political, economic and cultural processes and forces. Whatever the disagreement, it is important to heed Kofman and Youngs' claim that 'globalization relates as much to a way of thinking about the world as it does to a description of the dynamics of political and economic relations within it. Globalization has opened up new imperatives for investigating power linkages between thought and action, knowledge and being, structure and process' (Kofman and Youngs, 1996, p. 1).

Having now reviewed the fundamentals of the economic globalization thesis, it is important to point out that it contains some fundamental flaws, not least of which is its disempowering effects and tendencies. To quote Scholte:

> The consequences of globalization – arguably one of the most wide-ranging and unsettling systemic trends in contemporary history – remain quite open and will be considerably influenced by the sorts of knowledge constructed about, and fed into, the process. To date orthodox (and especially liberal) discourses have held an upper hand, but ample opportunities remain to salvage notions of globalization for critical theory and associated politics of emancipation (Scholte, 1996, p. 44).

In the following section, I review the governance literature laying the grounds in Scholte's words 'to embrace and enlarge these possibilities' (Scholte, 1996, p. 44) for a politics of resistance, opening up space for political mobilization in opposition to the globalizing logic of the market and finance. The section begins with the general insight that the increasing intensity and extent of globalization has generated a counter-critique.

Counter-Hegemonic Response: The Governance Dynamic

A growing body of critical work has sought to establish an alternative discourse as a counter to the hegemonic discourse of globalization and its globalizing logic of the market and finance. There is an attempt to craft an alternative understanding and response to those currently in vogue in the mainstream globalization thesis. The alternative discourses provide a penetrating interpretation of the dominant, hegemonic discourse, and highlight its limitations and power dynamics. By exposing the limits of its foundations and hidden and not so hidden hegemonic power tendencies and effects, the so-called 'globalization-from-below' thesis shakes the dominant discourse from its claimed timeless pedestal.

The underlying reasons for this new oppositional politics are numerous. The unequal and uneven distribution of the benefits of globalization, a process of such magnitude and scale, has ensured that it will be a highly contested process. Critics have pointed to the inequality and lack of long-term sustainable growth and development. A long line of critics of globalization have reinforced this point. Thus, Kofman and Youngs remind us that '... the issue of inequality remains central to any consideration of globalization. Far from offering positive possibilities for all, globalization signals new forms of oppression for many ... Globalization represents changes in the operation of global capitalism which, if anything, has expanded its potential for producing inequalities' (Kofman and Youngs, 1996, p. 4).

In a similar vein, Scholte points out that 'to date, globalization has often perpetuated poverty, widened inequalities, increased ecological degradation, sustained militarism, fragmented communities, marginalized subordinated groups, fed intolerance and deepened crises of democracy' (Scholte, 1996, p. 53). This is also an argument that Castles (2001) and others like Hurrell and Woods (1995) have extended in their review of globalization. For Castles:

> Globalization [according to critical hyperglobalizers], is the mechanism for the rule of international investors and transnational corporations, who can no longer be controlled by ever-weaker nation-states. Trade unions and welfare systems are collapsing, unemployment and social exclusion are burgeoning, while uncontrolled growth is leading to life-threatening environmental degradation. Thus globalization can lead to social fragmentation, cultural uncertainty, conflict and violence (Castles, 2001, p. 21).

Hurrell and Woods' (1995, p. 447) view is that 'inequalities among states both shape the process of globalization and are affected by it'. In this context, the critiques underlie the impact of analyzing globalization in terms of its tendency to engender profound inequality, power, social upheavals and social dislocations.

The critique of globalization has also unfolded and been expressed in terms of its impact on politics. To be precise, the claim has been made that the globalizing logic of the market and finance is undemocratic and even anti-democratic. The work of Low is symptomatic of this view. Consider this passage from Low:

> 'Globalization', it is usually suggested, disrupts bounded national communities and throws political, economic, and cultural processes out of congruence with one another. From the point of view of much thinking about democracy, therefore, processes of globalization are a matter of some concern: a politics of place no longer seems possible at the scale of the national state, and severe strain is placed upon the efficacy, even possibility, of democracy as usually conceptualized (Low, 1997, p. 242).

In another contribution Gill reinforces the economic, social and political limits of the global, neoliberal hegemonic discourse: 'restructuring along market-driven lines tends to generate a deepening of social inequality, a rise in the rate and intensity of the exploitation of labour, growth in social polarization, gender inequality, a widespread sense of social and economic insecurity, and, not least, pervasive disenchantment with conventional political practice. Such a situation may also open the door to the appeals of extremist political movements, *whilst more broadly giving rise to resistance and counter-mobilisation [emphasis mine]*' (Gill, 1995b, p. 420).

The above-noted limits of globalization are what evoke counter-hegemonic and anti-systemic resistance by social movements and extreme reactions from those disadvantaged by the process. Scholte's again draws attention to this phenomenon: 'debates over globalization relate centrally to questions of social change in the late twentieth century. Discourses of globalization have become a prime site of struggle between, broadly speaking, conservatives who deny such a trend, liberals who celebrate its presumed fruits, and critics who decry its alleged disempowering effects' (Scholte, 1996, p. 43).

The response to the hegemonic economic globalization thesis has come by way of the articulation of a new, discursive logic. Championed by social movements and so-called anti-globalization forces, the new counter-hegemonic challenge has been referred to by Falk (1999) as 'globalization-from-below'. The counter-hegemonic forces and activists seek to reverse and change the direction and impact of what now constitutes the touchstone of contemporary times. As Gill points out in explaining the sources of mobilization, 'there are connections between the processes of economic globalization, and the way the outlook, expectations, and social choices of individuals and groups are being reshaped and reconfigured' (Gill, 1995a, p. 1). And, I might add, reshaped and reconfigured to challenge the dominant economic praxis.

At heart, this challenge constitutes a contestation of the agenda of economic liberalization and the market and financial power of contemporary globalization. How to conceptualize these countervailing forces is perhaps best captured by Lynch in her powerful account in an article titled *Social Movements and the Problem of Globalization*:

The type of normative/discursive contestation of contemporary social, economic, and political practices advanced by the antiglobalization movement at base provides an example of what social movements are able to do most effectively in world politics, that is, delegitimize particular discourse and paths of action in order to legitimize alternatives (Lynch, 1998, pp. 158-159).

As Kacowicz (1999, p. 539) has observed, 'a second and concomitant argument emphasizes the emergence of globalization forces at the 'grassroots' level, or 'from below': the emergence of a global civil society through the transnational undertakings of social forces dedicated to the promotion of human rights, democracy, and sustainable development worldwide'. The goal here is to create progressive local, national and transnational organizations to empower communities and thereby enhance the quality of democratic governance. The way Kaldor sees it, the counter-hegemonic process 'seemed to offer a discourse within which one might frame parallel concerns about the ability to control the circumstances in which individuals live, and about the substantive empowerment of citizens' (Kaldor, 2000, p. 107).

The anti-globalization demonstrations in Seattle and thereafter have been presented as signalling a new form of resistance, 'a new era of contestation in which a reinvigorated civil society attempts to create space for oppositional politics' (Osei Kwadwo Prempeh, 2001, p. 576). In this view, new possibilities for challenge to the status quo provided by globalization has opened up. To reap the benefits of this unique opportunity, Kaldor posits that this 'global civilizing process' would entail:

> The extension of citizens networks who monitor, contest, and put pressure on these institutions. What we might describe as global civil society would be the interaction of these groups, networks, and movements who provide a voice for individuals in global arenas and who act as, to paraphrase a well-known dictum, the transmission belts between the individual and global institutions (Kaldor, 2000, pp. 108-109).

To 'civilise globalization', civil society movements open up spaces for new voices, for empowerment and for a politics of resistance from a grassroots, participatory level. The primary objective is to regulate, monitor and mediate the process of globalization from below and to bring more accountability, transparency, participation and representation to those institutions centrally placed to enforce the rules of the globalization process. In effect, the new movements seek to bring democracy back to the process of globalization. These words from Mazur in describing the accomplishments of Seattle are revealing in this regard:

> The era of trade negotiations conducted by sheltered elites balancing commercial interests behind closed doors is over. Globalization has reached a turning point. The future is a contested terrain of very public choices that will shape the global economy of the 21st century. The forces behind global economic change – which exalt deregulation, cater to corporations, undermine social structures, and ignore popular concerns – cannot be sustained. Globalization is leaving perilous

instability and rising inequality in its wake ... The cacophonous voices on the streets of Seattle represented tomorrow's challenge not yesterday's nostalgia ... The protesters demanded accountability for the powerful and a voice for the voiceless ... The fragile institutions of the emerging global economy will therefore be braced by the democratic tonic that gives working people a place at the economic and political table ... The global market and free trade are not natural phenomena but creatures of state power, 'an end product of social engineering and unyielding political will'. Inevitably, the effort to enforce such a system engenders a democratic response (Mazur, 2000, pp. 79-80).

Henceforth, the counter-hegemonic process of 'globalization-from-below' based on popular mobilization and resistance would be in full force. The political countervailing force to the economic logic of 'globalization-from-above' had been initiated. The challenge was for major reforms of global economic governance under globalization; the objective to open up spaces for contestation and participation.

The counter-hegemonic literature helps articulate a different vision of globalization: it overcomes the overly economic deterministic analysis of the globalization thesis by uncovering the countervailing political dynamics to the process. If the contours of the restructuring of the contemporary global economy is to be understood and challenged, then it is necessary, indeed required, that we explore the political and social forces that are mobilizing to resist it. However, this approach is inherently limited as it does not address the full spectrum of institutional and human factor aspects. The literature opens up new possibilities but needs to go further. The next section explores the ways in which the HF school of thought can be presented as a way to embrace and extend those possibilities opened up by the counter-hegemonic literature.

New Thinking, New Approach: The Human Factor and the Governance Dynamic

As indicated in the previous section, the governance framework introduces an important element in the debate about possible resistance to globalization. These civil society organizations and groups have mobilized at the grassroots level to resist the dominant and hegemonic influences of 'globalization-from-above'. Central to this project is a focus on local, national and transnational normative, political and cultural change and mobilization to include those voices which have been marginalized under existing power structures. This is all part of a grand effort to enhance democratic governance and democratic accountability.

However, this literature is marked by a curious omission, an almost total neglect of the HF dimension: those human attributes that ensure enduring commitments and dedication to the governance agenda and which, can in turn, serve to reinforce those commitments. In other words, the major deficit in the counter-hegemonic discourse which can undermine and scuttle the whole process is the lack of attention to HF attributes. The challenge then is to inject the requisite HF attributes into the process.

This section seeks to widen the prevailing globalization critique offered by the governance framework. The governance literature's conceptualization of the empowering role of civil society is helpful but remains ambiguous; and little scholarly effort has been made to remedy this problem. Central to this is a commitment and dedication to building and nurturing a new two-step governance and HF ethic based upon core values of liberty, justice, equity, integrity, accountability and transparency in both political and human terms.

In seizing up the new possibilities left uncharted by the governance literature, the HF school of thought seeks to address a gap that if bridged would silence critics who question the legitimacy of these anti-globalization forces. The question that is at the heart of the HF approach in this respect is the extent to which these groups which demand democratic accountability and governance of the globalization process are themselves made up of individuals with the appropriate HF attributes of honesty, integrity, responsibility, accountability and dedication to a non-elite driven process of challenge. This draws attention to the actors involved in the counter-hegemonic process. Their legitimacy and claims to democratic governance will be dependent on their ability to articulate and defend the voices of the voiceless. This ability, in turn, depends on the HF attributes of the individuals. This requires that we examine critically the human factor attributes of these actors.

Whether this politics of resistance to 'globalization-from-above' through an engagement with 'globalization-from-below' promotes long-term sustainable democratic governance turns in part on the extent to which the general membership and leadership of civil society develop the human factor capacities for accountability, dedication and commitment to the cause, members and stakeholders. Will such movements provide the needed space for a genuine anti-systemic resistance to globalization? The argument here is that these spaces will enrich and challenge the processes of globalization if the members, actors and leadership are ones that have the HF attributes.

Our effort to understand the critical nature of the HF for 'globalization-from-below' is set in the context of the pioneering work of Senyo Adjibolosoo. The work of Adjibolosoo and others on the HF dimension blows fresh air into a debate that has been subject to overgeneralization. Indeed, Adjibolosoo precisely documents the ways in which the HF provides the foundation for a human-centred and sociological account. In his pioneering study, Adjibolosoo defines the HF as:

> The spectrum of personality characteristics and other dimensions of human performance that enable social, political and economic institutions to function and to remain functional over time. Such dimensions sustain the workings and applications of the rule of law, political harmony, disciplined labour force, just legal systems, respect for human dignity, sanctity of life and social welfare, and many others. As is often the case, no social, economic or political institutions can function without being upheld by a network of committed persons who stand firmly by them. Such persons must strongly believe in and continually affirm the ideals of society (Adjibolosoo, 1993, p. 142).

Elsewhere, Adjibolosoo stresses that:

> No human activity and/or business can be pursued successfully without people who are readily equipped, full of responsibility and accountability, and possessing the willingness to participate in programs aimed at development. In my view, to deny the crucial role of the HF in human progress is to throw the baby out with the bath water because positive human characteristics are the only true media and initiators of all progress (Adjibolosoo, 1995, p. 6).

This statement emphasizing the HF highlights the central and critical importance of human agents and amounts to powerful support for a human agency driven approach.

Consistent with this, the narrative on appropriate HF engineering has typically been based on some basic interrelated assertions neatly summed up by Adjibolosoo (1999, pp. 9-10) as follows:

1. Few trees can survive without well-established root systems. In the same manner, no houses or other buildings can exist without a well-constructed foundation ... Similarly, the creation of excellent plans, policies, programs, and projects will never bring about social, economic, political, cultural, and intellectual progress in the presence of HF decay and/or underdevelopment. The ongoing failure being experienced by those who manage and operate social institutions is not necessarily due to inadequate planning, policy making, program development, project implementation, and financial resources. It is primarily a result of HF decay and/or underdevelopment in society.
2. Continuing HF decay and/or underdevelopment is a vicious venom that spreads at lightening speed in society and then, with devastating blow, decimates the primary foundation on which human progress rests.
3. Every society that desires to experience positive changes must be aware of the fact that personal transformation and/or change is a sine qua non to successful overall social, economic, and political change. This type of change will foster continuing healthy interpersonal relationships.
4. Every HF development program must teach, train, mentor, and educate people to acquire integrity, accountability, responsibility, trustworthiness, commitment, and loyalty. These are critical to long-lasting progress, peace, and tranquility.

Adjibolosoo's arguments concerning the HF theoretical discourse as set up above have been influential in opening up alternative ways of thinking. They have demonstrated the importance of the HF as an added dimension of the theory and praxis of development, world politics and human-centred analysis. In presenting a deep analysis of the human dimension and integrating it into the debate, they have given understanding of this key theoretical concept much more practical substance.

What is the contribution of the HF, so developed, to the globalization-governance debate? The legitimacy of the counter-hegemonic process rests upon explicitly recognizing the HF significance of the politics of resistance as a parallel dynamic driving the critique. This has to go hand in hand with the more technical issues. The focus here is on the dynamics of the individuals and leadership mechanisms that produce and legitimate the actions of the anti-globalization forces in order to ask how far they advance or retard the prospect for achieving democratic governance of globalization. The underlying argument is that the counter-hegemonic process while necessary will not by itself be sufficient to establish a truly effective countervailing force until HF attributes are sorted out.

A strong governance approach needs to be supplemented by HF engineering; the critical factor that will make the governance approach successful or not is the HF. Positive HF traits required in this process include personal characteristics such as dedication, integrity, accountability, commitment, responsibility, honesty, reliability, and determination. Consistent with this, for the anti-globalization forces to remain relevant in the struggle against globalization they have to be made up of individuals and leaders who are not only committed and dedicated to the cause and the grassroots, but also have the integrity and reliability to be accepted by the same grassroots.

A counter-hegemonic process which neglects the human dimension, specifically HF attributes, is bound to fail without realizing its full countervailing potential. The process requires individuals with appropriate HF characteristics to successfully harness the energies of the anti-globalization forces and secure democratic governance of globalization. Successful engagement with, and transformation of, globalization requires people who have successfully acquired and applied the requisite and appropriate HF. In other words, the essential HF traits must be present in the leadership of civil society movements that are engaging with globalization.

Conclusion

The counter-hegemonic process of 'globalization-from-below' opens up new possibilities for contesting the globalizing logic of the market and finance that is inherent in the process of globalization. At issue is the need to bring democratic governance to the process of globalization. These forces seek to reverse and change the direction and impact of globalization. In this respect, the process of globalization has become a site of contestation and struggle between globalizing forces and grassroots civil society organizations and movements who lament not only the hegemonic power of globalization but also its disempowering and undemocratic and even anti-democratic tendencies.

While this critique and counter-hegemonic process is a necessary first step, the prospect for 'civilizing' globalization depends to a large extent on whether the individuals who claim to be representatives of this counter-process have acquired the appropriate HF attributes of integrity, honesty, accountability and commitment to the cause in a non-elite driven manner. The governance critique by itself does not provide a full and incontrovertible alternative to globalization. In this regard, the effectiveness of the anti-systemic resistance groups may well lie in reinforcing the HF. In order to avoid HF reductionism or fetishism, the chapter makes a call for a balance between the effective engineering of HF and governance.

References

Adjibolosoo, Senyo B.-S.K. (1999), *The Human Factor in Nation Building*, International Institute for Human Factor Development.

Adjibolosoo, Senyo B.-S.K. (1995), *The Significance of the Human Factor in African Economic Development*, Westport, CT.: Praeger.

Adjibolosoo, Senyo B.-S.K. (1993), "The Human Factor in Development", *The Scandinavian Journal of Development Alternatives*, 12 (4): 139-149.

Castles, Stephen (2001), "Studying Social Transformation", *International Political Science Review*, 22 (1): 13-32.

Falk, Richard (1999), *Predatory Globalization: A Critique*, Cambridge, UK: Polity Press.

Friedman, Thomas L. (1996), "Revolt of the Wannabees", *New York Times*, (February 7).

Gertler, Meric S. (1997), "Between the Global and the Local: The Spatial Limits to Productive Capital", in Cox, Kevin R. (ed.) *Spaces of Globalization: Reasserting the Power of the Local*, New York and London: The Guilford Press.

Gill, Stephen (1995a.), "The Global Panopticon? The Neoliberal State, Economic Life and Democratic Surveillance", *Alternatives*, 20 (1): 1-49.

Gill, Stephen (1995b), "Globalization, Market Civilization and Disciplinary Neoliberalism", *Millinnium: Journal of International Studies*, 24 (3): 399-423.

Held, David, McGrew, A., Goldblatt, D. and Perraton, J. (2000), "Rethinking Globalization", in Held, David and Anthony McGrew (eds.) *The Global Transformations Reader: An Introduction to the Globalization Debate*, Cambridge: Polity Press.

Hirst, Paul and Thompson, G. (1996), *Globalization in Question: The International Economy and the Possibility of Governance*, Cambridge: Polity Press.

Hurrell, Andrew and Woods, N. (1995), "Globalization and Inequality", *Millennium: Journal of International Studies*, 24 (3): 447-470.

Kacowicz, Arie M. (1999), "Regionalization, Globalization, and Nationalism: Convergent, Divergent, or Overlapping?", *Alternatives*, 24 (4): 527-557.

Kaldor, Mary (2000), "'Civilising' Globalisation?: The Implications of the 'Battle of Seattle'" *Millennium: Journal of International Studies*, 29 (1): 105-114.

Keohane, Robert O. and Nye, J.S. (2000), "Introduction", in Nye, Joseph S. and John D. Donahue (eds.) *Governance in a Globalizing World*, Washington, D.C.: Brookings Institution Press.

Kofman, Eleonore and Youngs, G. (1996), "Introduction: Globalization – The Second Wave", in Kofman, Eleonore and Gillian Youngs (eds.) *Globalization: Theory and Practice*, London: Pinter.

Low, Murray (1997), "Representation Unbound: Globalization and Democracy", in Cox, Kevin R. (ed.) *Spaces of Globalization: Reasserting the Power of the Local*, New York and London: The Guilford Press.

Lynch, Cecelia (1998), "Social Movements and the Problem of Globalization", *Alternatives*, 23: 149-173.

Mazur, Jay (2000), "Labour's New Internationalism", *Foreign Affairs*, 79 (1): 79-98.

Norris, Pippa (2000), "Global Governance and Cosmopolitan Citizens", in Nye, Joseph S. and John D. Donahue (eds.) *Governance in a Globalizing World*, Washington, D.C.: Brookings Institution Press.

Ohmae, Kenichi (1995), *The End of the Region State: The Rise of Regional Economies*, London: Harper-Collins.

Ohmae, Kenichi (1990), *The Borderless World: Power and Strategy in the Interlinked Economy*, London: Harper-Collins.

Osei Kwadwo Prempeh, Edward (2001), "The Politics of One-Sided Adjustment in Africa: A Response to Professor Osabu-Kle", *Journal of Black Studies*, 31 (May): 563-580.

Polanyi, Karl (1975), *The Great Transformation*, New York: Octagon Books.

Sane, Pierre (1993), "Human Rights: An Agenda for Action", *West Africa*, 3978 (December 20).

Scholte, Jan Aart (1996), "Beyond the Buzzword: Towards a Critical Theory of Globalization", in Kofman, Eleonore and Gillian Youngs (eds). *Globalization: Theory and Practice*, London: Pinter.

Chapter 10

Democracy as Political Counterpart to Globalization: Wither the Human Factor?

E. Osei Kwadwo Prempeh

Introduction

As indicated in the previous chapters the transformative process of globalization can be understood as having not only economic, social and technological implications, but also political and cultural ones as well. In fact, the foundation of neoliberalism is provided by an ideological component with political and economic manifestations: democracy and the free market. This multifaceted process of globalization is producing a global political environment in which a particular vision of democracy prevails. Indeed, Western liberal democracy seems to be the political counterpart to globalization. As William I. Robinson aptly points out in his attempts to come to terms with the hegemony of the contemporary global economy and, in particular, the intersection of politics and economics, 'the emergence of a global economy brings with it the material basis for the emergence of a single global society, including the transnationalization of civil society and of *political processes* [emphasis mine]' (Robinson, 1996, p. 4). The transnational political processes Robinson refers to are captured in political systems with a distinct liberal democratic flavour. In this perspective, the globalization of Western liberal democracy provides empirical evidence in support of the emergence of a new global civilization defined by universal norms and standards of political and economic organization. This view has been criticized and the consolidation of democracy can be disputed on a number of grounds. However, this chapter examines another reason for moving beyond this narrow framework, the neglect of the human factor implications of this project.

In the following chapter I profile the political project of democracy that is at the heart of the current debates in globalization. The limitations of that political project are outlined and critiqued with a call for a paradigmatic shift towards increased and greater attention to, and incorporation of, human factor attributes into the analysis to yield a more viable theoretical formulation. This call is made on the grounds that the current discussion about the 'triumph of democracy' in a globalized world is undertaken oblivious to the importance of the human factor

(HF). The argument is that in the presence of human factor underdevelopment and/or decay, political institutions will fail to function effectively and the consolidation of democratic governance would be called into question. The neglect of the HF has important implications for sustaining democracy. Far from being on the periphery, the HF needs to be centrally placed in the discussion about transitions to democracy and democratic consolidation.

The chapter therefore traces this neglect of human factor development and its implications for the process of democratization. The first part examines the political project of globalization and its implications for our understanding of contemporary society. The second section articulates a critical assessment and response to this project from a HF perspective and teases out the broad contours of an alternative to the prevailing discourse with its emphasis on the alleged established connections between globalization and democracy.

The Globalization of Liberal Democracy

Since the end of the Cold War, campaigns to promote democracy have caught the attention of scholars, policy makers and activists alike. Indeed, this transition to democracy which began in the mid-1970s has become especially widespread since the late 1980s with dramatic political changes in Africa, Latin America and Eastern Europe. Thus, Samuel Huntington (1991) speaks of a 'third wave' of democratization and there is talk of the 'triumph of democracy'. Democracy, viewed as a system of government and politics in which individuals and political parties may compete for power in open, free and regular multiparty elections, is on the ascendancy. According to Archibugi, Held and Kohler, 'among the twentieth century's most important legacies to the new millennium [is] ... the assertion of democracy as the legitimate system of government' (1998, p. 1).

The reader gets a sense of the scope, extent and spread of democratization if we consider that in 1973, less than 30 percent of states could be said to be liberal democracies with 40 per cent formally democratic. However, by 1995, the number of formal democracies had risen to almost 60 per cent of the states of the world. Two critical developments have been cited for this: First, the international financial institutions (IFIs), the International Monetary Fund and the World Bank, with the support of the Western governments made political conditionality a component of their loan programs and development assistance. This newfound importance of politics was clearly articulated in the IFIs promotion of good governance, democracy and the role of civil society as a way to foster genuine participation of communities in the choice, design and implementation of projects and as a potentially valuable source of increased accountability (World Bank, 1998, p. 94). The position of the Western governments is captured in former British Foreign Secretary, Douglas Hurds' observation in 1990 that 'in practical terms, it means that we ... will reward democratic governments and any political reform which leads to greater accountability and democracy. The corollary is that we should penalize particularly bad cases of repression and human rights abuse' (Hurd, 1990, p. 2).

Second, there was a clear attempt to establish a relationship between the economic and the political. This was conceptualized in terms of a 'spill over' of economic globalization into the political. Much writing on globalization thus draws attention to the alleged positive effects of economic globalization on political and social organization. Central to the neoliberal tradition, therefore, is the case that we cannot make sense of the contemporary changes in global society without understanding the synergy between the economic and political dynamics of globalization. Concisely expressed, this line of argument highlights the increasing spread of democratization and the global economic forces that have encouraged this process. Hence the more euphoric claim that globalization is a source of the extension of democracy or that democratization is evidence of the widening reach of globalization. The effort to express the interrelationship between globalization and democratization serves a useful point of reference for Robinson when he sets out as one of the main objectives of his book to show how what he terms 'democracy promotion'

> Is linked to the process of globalization and to explore crucial political dimensions of globalization. 'Democracy promotion' [is] inextricably linked to globalization. 'Democracy promotion' in US foreign policy can only be understood as part of a broader process of the exercise of hegemony within and between countries in the context of transnationalization. Polyarchy, or what I alternatively refer to as 'low-intensity democracy' is a structural feature of the new world order: it is a global political system corresponding to a global economy under the hegemony of a transnational elite which is the agent of transnational capital (Robinson, 1996, p. 4).

With transitions to democracy from authoritarian government in vogue, the proponents of this view took to exaggerating the impact of globalization on political processes, even invoking the notion of the 'triumph of democracy'. This euphoric vision of globalization is perhaps best captured in Francis Fukuyama's seminal piece, *The End of History and the Last Man*. In this account the argument that globalization fosters democratization is reinforced in attempts to conflate democracy and capitalism. Before engaging with Fukuyama's thesis in an in-depth manner, it is trite to focus in on the prevailing thought as suggested by David Held on the political significance of economic globalization. Held suggests that:

> [Hyper-globalizers] argue that we now live in a world in which social and economic processes operate predominantly at a global level. According to these thinkers, national political communities are now immersed in a sea of global economic flows and are inevitably 'decision-takers' in this context. For many neo-liberal thinkers, this is a welcome development; a world market order based on the principles of free trade and minimum regulation is the guarantee of liberty, efficiency and effective government (Held, 2000, p. 21).

Similarly, Robinson traces the established links between liberal democracy and economic liberalism. Again, the context for this dynamic is provided by globalization which provides the bosom for the emergence of the globalization of liberal democracy. Robinson outlines the link between liberal democracy and economic globalization thus:

> The etiology of 'democracy promotion' is the historic process of globalization, yet at the same time it is a transnational practice which helps shape and facilitate globalization, particularly crucial political dimensions of the process, such as transnational class formation, the externalization of peripheral states, and new forms of articulation between the political and the economic in a global environment (Robinson, 1996, p. 8).

The end of the Cold War provided the turning point and a decisive move to an explicit and renewed commitment to liberal democracy on a global scale, along with a strengthened belief that economic globalization is a powerful force in this process. The growth of this global capitalist economy is transforming and re-inventing cultures, communities and, above all, acting as a transmission belt for the normative ideas that underpin liberal democracy. In this vein, Sean Lynn-Jones makes the case for promoting electoral democracy and liberal values (Lynn-Jones, 1998). Human rights and global liberal democracy are once again legitimized items on the global agenda with the new globalizing world providing credibility. It is in this respect that one should see Fukuyama's triumphant Hegelian liberalism which explores in an assertive tone the supremacy of Western normative values and a distinctly global liberalism.

Fukuyama's salutary comments in support of the 'triumph of the West' is highlighted in his argument that 'a remarkable consensus concerning the legitimacy of liberal democracy as a system of government had emerged throughout the world over the past years ... Liberal democracy may constitute the endpoint of mankind's ideological evolution and the final form of human government and as such constituted the 'end of history' (Fukuyama, 1992, p. xi). While such bold claims on behalf of Western liberal democracy was bound to evoke considerable criticism and generate controversy, it contained an incontrovertible fact about 'the current lack of competitors against political and economic liberalism in the world ideological market place' (Mortimer, 1989, p. 29).

The new lease of life gained by neoliberalism's long reach provided impetus for the push to globalize liberal democracy. The post-Cold War period thus provided a unique opportunity to pursue the neoliberal aspiration of universal principles through the globalization of the liberal democratic political system. Fukuyama's project is thus set in the context of outlining the foundations for this claim that Western liberal values must or ought to be universalized for the sake of all humanity, thereby asserting globalization as a global ideology with universal relevance. Such an endeavour is again consistent with the whole neoliberal project which claims universal applicability and universal scope and progress.

It is appropriate at this juncture to expand on the political project of Fukuyama as evidence of neoliberal theorizing in a world dominated by the intensification of processes of globalization. His is at once a project of monumental proportions with the objective of making bold and provocative claims about the universality of liberal democracy. Drawing on the link between the economic and political, Fukuyama opines that 'today, by contrast, we have trouble imagining a world that is radically better than our own, or a future that is not essentially democratic and capitalist' (1992, p. 46).

Elsewhere, Fukuyama makes the link between the economic and political, with the economic processes of globalization providing the initial impetus for the homogenizing of the economic and political. He argues that:

> Our Mechanism can now explain the creation of a universal consumer culture based on liberal economic principles, for the Third World as well as the First and Second. The enormously productive and dynamic economic world created by advancing technology and the rational organization of labour has a tremendous homogenizing power. It is capable of linking different societies around the world to one another physically through the creation of global markets, and of creating parallel economic aspirations and practices in a host of diverse societies. The attractive power of this world creates a very strong predisposition for all human societies to participate in it, while success in this participation requires the adoption of the principles of economic liberalism (1992, p. 108).

Here, we see the broad outlines of the economic foundations for the globalized political project of liberal democracy.

Fukuyama also points to what he notes is evidence to support 'a common evolutionary pattern for all human societies – in short, something like a Universal History of mankind in the direction of liberal democracy' (1992, p. 48). The 'End of History' thesis is therefore interesting for its powerful exposition of the hegemonic influence of the discourses of globalization and the argument for the globalization of liberal democracy drawn from the success of democracy in different parts of the world. Thus, Fukuyama indicates that

> The principles of liberty and equality on which they are based are not accidents or the results of ethnocentric prejudice, but are in fact discoveries about the nature of man as man, whose truth does not diminish but grows more evident as one's point of view becomes more cosmopolitan (1992, p. 51).

Here, Fukuyama aligns himself more clearly with an explicit commitment to the globalization of the capitalist economy and its essentially political counterpart of liberal democracy. This is expressly tied to the continued viability and universalization of the values associated with the dual processes of liberal democracy and economic liberalism. Thus, Fukuyama explicitly states that 'indeed, the growth of liberal democracy, together with its companion, economic liberalism, has been the most remarkable macropolitical phenomenon of the last four hundred years' (1992, p. 48). As Gillian Youngs reminds us, 'in its combination of political and economic values and its emphasis on the ways in which individual and social inequalities are accommodated via the liberal path, Fukuyama's thesis could be argued to be the ultimate post-Cold War discourse of globalization' (Youngs, 1996, p. 65).

This triumphalism is also played out more succinctly as a key aspect of US foreign policy as part of an integrated global strategy by the West in general. One is reminded here of Douglas Hurds' musings about promoting good government which translates into promoting and exporting a particular brand of democracy built on neoliberal conceptions of political and economic freedom. In a tone which recalls Robinson's (1996) narrative, but from a different perspective and with a different objective, Sean Lynn-Jones further establishes the links between liberal democracy and the free market in support of US foreign policy goals in these terms:

> Democracies are more likely to adopt market economies, so democracies tend to have more prosperous and open economies. The United States generally will be able to establish mutually beneficial trading relationships with democracies. And democracies provide better climates for American overseas investment, by virtue of their political stability and market economies (Lynn-Jones, 1998, p. 33).

It is this latter point which forms the basis of William Robinson's book. Robinson seeks to explain in more critical terms the change in US foreign policy to 'democracy promotion' in a post-Cold War environment where diverse forces and civil society movements strive for democratization and social change. 'Democracy promotion' is analyzed in 'relation to hegemony and the intersection of politics and economics in the emergent global society and twenty-first century world order' (Robinson, 1996, p. 2).

This analysis of the 'triumph of capitalism' which links the economic and political as mutually beneficial in the context of globalization has gained legitimacy among proponents. By making the case that the liberal democratic changes we are witnessing all around the globe emerges out of globalization, proponents are able, or wish to be able, to stress the empirical and objective nature of their position. The import of this is to claim universal validity and legitimacy for economic globalization's benign nature and predisposition to engender a globalization of democracy.

Notwithstanding these optimistic assessments and analyses, a number of issues have been raised by those who call such analyses flawed. First, the question of what democracy is, and the extent to which its existence is desirable, are highly controversial issues on which a number of authors have offered various insights. For Benjamin Barber, 'there is nothing about McWorld that automatically entails or supports democracy' (Barber, 1996, p. 153). In other words, while the notion of the international spread of liberal democracy is a reflection of globalization in practice, the precise nature and unfolding of this process in different social and cultural milieu as well as attempts to conflate democracy and capitalism require closer scrutiny.

Indeed, scholars and analysts alike have pointed to the obstacles and constraints to democratization some of which can be related aspects of globalization. For example, issues such as the growing economic marginalization of the Third World and the deepening patterns of inequality raise serious concerns about the prospects for democratic consolidation. It is these issues in particular which has led David Held et al., drawing from Samuel Huntington's (1996) *Clash of Civilizations*, to this conclusion: 'such inequality, in the view of many skeptics, contributes to the advance of both fundamentalism and aggressive nationalism such that rather than the emergence of a global civilization, as the hyperglobalizers predict, the world is fragmenting into civilizational blocs and cultural and ethnic enclaves' (Held et al., 1999, p. 6).

If this insight from David Held and his colleagues is not enough to convince the skeptics, consider these claims made by Gills (1997) and Youngs (1996) respectively:

> While the nature of the ongoing liberalization, or globalization processes, constitutes a stimulus to the extension of '*formal* democratic practices', the very structure of the world economy also impedes the development of '*substantive* democratization' (Gills, 1997, pp. 60-61).

> This approach to the liberal paradigm avoids critical discussion of causes of persistent inequalities and a detailed interest in the location, exercise and effects of economic and political power. Its overt preoccupation with claiming a universal relevance for liberal values is distinct from an approach which seeks to investigate in detail the differentiated impact of the exercise of such values in practice in varied social contexts, globally and locally (Youngs, 1996, p. 66).

Youngs and Gills' claims point to some of the more general critiques of the globalization of liberal democracy from the standpoint of highlighting the obstacles engendered by inequalities and hierarchies of power. Youngs goes further to stress the particularities of such encounters and experiences with liberal democracy in the Third World and Eastern Europe which tend to be different from the Western experience. She thus emphasizes that the democratization currently in vogue is associated with democratization of a certain kind, Western liberal democracy, and historically and culturally conditioned and determined. This last point is again reinforced by David Held when he questions some of the underlying issues about Fukuyama's argument. For instance, Held points out that:

> Furthermore, there is, of course, not simply one undisputed form of democracy. Even liberal democracies have crystallized into a number of different institutional types – the Westminster and federal models, for example – which make any appeal to a liberal conception of public life vague at best. Fukuyama essentially leaves unanalyzed the whole meaning of democracy and its possible variants (Held, 1996, pp. 281-282).

For Held, claims about a particular unfolding of economic and political values and principles in future settings is implausible and that 'in all likelihood, the very form and shape of democracy will remain contested for generations to come' (Held, 1996, p. 283). If we accept this postulation, then it implies that the liberal democratic model is but one model whose universal applicability might be questionable and thus unsuitable in different socio-historical contexts.

Furthermore, the universalization of traditional liberal values associated with Western ethos and the Enlightenment presents difficulties of ethnocentrism and Eurocentrism. This controversy is steeped in attempts to claim universal validity and truth of Western values over other values. This narrow interpretation, which affirms universal values over value diversity and pluralism, is what Gillian Youngs refers to when she explains that 'as a discourse of globalization, [Fukuyama's thesis] is fundamentally state-centric, West-centric, and presents an overly idealized view of liberal democracy and economic liberalism, especially concerning their interrelationship ... The 'end of history' is presented as a state-centred celebration of the globalization of the Western capitalist system's capacities to meet economic and political needs' (Youngs, 1996, p. 65).

This critical analysis calls into question the legitimacy and universality of liberal values under the globalization of liberal democracy and, above all, the euphoric claims about the 'triumph of capitalism' and democracy. Hence Jan Aart Scholte's suggestion that 'while contemporary globalization has encouraged some innovations in democratic practices, on the whole the new geography has to date made governance less democratic' (Scholte, 2000, p. 263). While Scholte accepts that the spread of globalization is unfolding in the midst of a revival of liberal democratic governance in various parts of the globe, he questions neoliberal assertions about the links between globalization and democratization. He then outlines four major ways in which the neoliberal account is deficient. These deficiencies are worth restating as a way to conclude this section.

According to Scholte:

First, globalization has by no means constituted the sole force behind the 'third wave' of democratization. Each transition to multiparty regimes with 'free and fair' elections has drawn vital strength from locally based movements for change ... Second, many if not most of the newly installed liberal mechanisms have run only sin-deep. In many cases multiparty elections have not led to wider democratic consolidation ... Third, some critics have argued that liberal constructions of democracy are inherently deficient. From this perspective globalization would need to promote different kinds of collective self-determination in order to be truly democratizing ... Fourth, the state, being territorially grounded, is not sufficient by itself as an agent of democracy in a world where many social relations are substantially supraterritorial (Scholte, 2000, pp. 264-265).

In the above formulation, Scholte highlights the neoliberal dilemma in very bold terms. However, as indicated in the introduction, this chapter seeks to make another bold contribution to the debate about the globalization of liberal democracy. For one thing, traditional liberal democratic frameworks require well functioning political institutions to uphold democratic values, principles and governance. Yet, there is a noticeable absence in the literature as to the importance of individuals and the extent to which they have the necessary attributes and traits to make political institutions functional over time. The next section interrogates the ways in which the development of the appropriate human factor (HF) can help ensure democratic consolidation.

The Human Factor and Democracy

As indicated above the globalists celebrate the 'triumph of democracy' and development as by-products of globalization. Notwithstanding these claims, however, it is quite clear that the consolidation of the 'third wave' of democracy in the post-Cold War period is up in the air. This uncertainty raises fundamental questions: why and what has gone wrong? Why have democratic experiments faltered? How can political institutions be strengthened to ensure democratic consolidation? These questions, it is argued, are not adequately answered in the globalization – democracy debate. This section throws additional light on the inadequacies of current thought with a view to incorporating a neglected dimension: the Human Factor (HF). A disregard and neglect of the HF, it is argued, will lead to institutional decay and ineffectiveness.

The importance of the HF is increasingly being recognized in the debate about economic, political and social development in the less developed countries (LDCs). That such importance is being recognized should not come as a surprise because after all, development is essentially about human beings and a case can be made for establishing a strong correlation between political development and human development. Without the necessary and required HF attributes and a firm HF foundation, democratic sustainability and consolidation would be called into doubt.

From the HF perspective, the performance and effectiveness of political institutions is dependent on the quality of the HF of the individuals involved. The agenda for building effective political institutions and the HF attributes of individuals, leaders and citizens are interdependent and integrated. For one thing, the imperatives of consolidating liberal democracy require strengthening political institutions but institutional effectiveness requires dedicated and committed individuals. Reforming or strengthening political institutions is necessary but not sufficient for consolidating democracy. Particular attention needs to be paid to the importance of appropriate HF and creating effective political institutions. In other words, political institution building needs to go hand in hand with HF engineering and development. Augmenting the effectiveness and efficiency of political institutions requires the empowering of dedicated people, hence the need to look at the HF.

The HF is at heart concerned with fundamental societal and cultural changes in attitudes and beliefs that are critical ingredients for initiating an overall process of economic, political, social and cultural development. In this respect, it is worth noting that the 'HF connotes the entire socio-cultural and political milieu in which the being finds expression, and which defines its identity, institutions, values, needs, rights and duties' (Owusu-Ampomah, 2001, p. 6). The values, identity and the individual's overall sense of being then become critical elements in discussions about effective political institutions and hence democratic consolidation. From this perspective, crucial features of human behaviour as well as culture and social structure need to be taken into account in the globalization – democracy debate. As Haucap points out, 'social norms, customs, and ethics might help overcome problems of organizational failure that hinder development' (1997, p. 13). Furthermore, 'institutions can only work properly if they are well adapted to the underlying culture and ethics of a society' (Haucap, 1997, p. 20).

Again, we need to pay heed to Senyo Adjibolosoo's call for an integrated and interdependent approach to institution-building and HF engineering as the basis for successful democratic consolidation. Adjibolosoo offers these insights to establish the basis for such an approach in unambiguous terms:

> It is the people of a nation who create institutions, develop and assign property rights. When effectively worked through the acquired HF, these institutions evolve and become aids to the development process ... The crucial point is that the availability of the relevant HF provides the necessary leadership qualities for the efficient operation of institutions ... Just as much as all institutions need a well-groomed HF to be effective, so also do people require efficient institutions to perform. However, since institutions are inanimate, they may never be functionally effective without the ingenuity of the nation's citizens. A society may develop institutions and institutional arrangements and/or structures to help in the economic development process, but if the necessary HF is not available to ensure that rewards and sanctions are effectively enforced as stipulated in institutional rules, ... every national institution will be ineffective and inefficient (Adjibolosoo, 1995, p. 82).

The HF is therefore committed to the notion that the development of political institutions per se or in isolation does not guarantee effective functioning because institutions do not function in a vacuum. Effective institutional functioning requires dedicated and committed individuals.

The point to be made here is that the HF paradigm agrees with the argument that building effective political institutions matters. However, the core of their counter argument is that the HF traits and attributes of the individuals in charge of those institutions is crucial to their long-term sustainability and effectiveness. They, therefore, have difficulty, as a practical and policy matter, separating the building of political institutions from the individuals who operate or run them. In other words, institutions remain functional over time if they are operated by individuals who are respected by society as committed to upholding the principles of democratic rule such as accountability, transparency and the rule of law.

From this perspective, the HF school of thought highlights the societal values and personality traits that enhance human performance for socio-political, economic and cultural development. These traits and values include accountability, trustworthiness, transparency, tolerance, diligence, discipline and humanistic ethics, all essential ingredients for sustaining and consolidating a truly democratic ethos. HF scholars also isolate HF underdevelopment and/or decay as the primary source of social, political, cultural and economic problems in societies. By so doing, they establish the importance of the human factor for a sustained people-centred political development in very clear terms.

While this contribution raises some of the same concerns expressed by 'cultural democrats' like Daniel Osabu-Kle (2000) in emphasizing that the culture and traditions of the people and their social and political traditions are essential prerequisites, it also shares important insights with the whole basis of a democratic society which is to uphold the inalienable rights of citizens to participate in decision-making. Consistent with this, political institutions cannot function and remain functional over time without individuals with the requisite HF characteristics and attributes. For Adjibolosoo, such HF attributes 'sustain the workings and application of the rule of law, political harmony, a disciplined labour force, just legal systems, respect for human dignity and the sanctity of life' (Adjibolosoo, 1995, p. 53). More importantly, political institutions cannot 'function effectively without being upheld by a network of committed persons who stand firmly by them. Such persons must strongly believe in and continually affirm the ideals of society' (Adjibolosoo, 1995, p. 53).

Herein lies the importance of the HF for the democracy debate: without individuals committed to the democratic ideals, the whole democratic experiment will falter with dire consequences for society. The failure to capture the importance of the HF as an essential ingredient can unravel the democratization process and call into doubt the political stability of whole societies. At the heart of the globalization – democracy nexus is thus the need to build strong and effective political institutions as a basis for sustaining democratic governance.

The importance of the human factor and human agency in general is clearly articulated in the work of Richard Sandbrook. Writing at a time when the consolidation of democracy in most African countries was in doubt, Sandbrook opined that 'consolidation of democracy involves the institutionalization of organizations and procedures that facilitate the transparency, accountability and responsiveness of governance. And institutionalization means that all the major political actors come to value, and hence defend, the rules that underpin democratic organizations and procedures' (Sandbrook, 1996, p. 85). This view that human factor underdevelopment and/or decay hinders the sustainability and consolidation of democracy finds another clear expression in this nuanced, yet direct statement from Adjibolosoo:

> The necessary and sufficient condition for a successful democracy and economic
> development is a well-developed HF that furnishes every citizen with the
> necessary human qualities, abilities and skills that are *sine qua non* for the

continuing potency of the constitution and its stipulations (Adjibolosoo, 1998, p. 24).

In other words, when citizens and political leaders have acquired the necessary human factor traits it provides a solid basis for defending democratic values and ethics. Thus prioritizing HF development is essential to the long-term viability of political institutions. Positive HF engineering ensures the development of values and corms conducive to nation building and institution building. Democracy and the building of democratic institutions must proceed on a foundation of an elaborate process of human factor engineering. Human qualities such as dedication, responsibility and accountability are relevant to the pursuit of democracy because it is these traits and attributes, or their absence, which determine the success development or otherwise of societies. The relevant HF ensures a careful blending of societal values and other skills for the consolidation of democracy. Well-developed HF attributes will engender and sustain effective and efficient political institutions. And, developing strong and resilient political institutions in support of democracy begins with the HF which can help generate rules and principles for the rule of law.

In a powerful contribution to the democracy and the human factor debate, the renowned Ghanaian political scientist, Kweku G. Folson, concludes that a democracy 'entails a good deal of self-restraint by those wielding political power (incorporating the instruments of violence) and the citizens who ultimately control the government. Both the government and the electorate must accept that they are limited in the way they do things and the powers they wield. These conditions clearly have implications for the quality of human beings who operate the delicate political machinery of liberal democracy' (Folson, 1995, p. 29).

The point being emphasized here can be brought into sharper focus if we examine the important role of astute political leadership in a democratic dispensation. After all, democratic consolidation does not occur in a vacuum. For political institutions to be functional over time, selfless and dedicated leadership is required. The recognition of such leadership is reflected in Folson's views elaborated above, but also highlighted in Karl Deutsch's (1961) view that effective leadership will generate public enthusiasm and support for political, economic and social development efforts thus mobilizing the citizenry for political, social and economic modernization. Such a leadership would necessarily be committed to upholding democratic values and ethos. The point is that it is a leadership with the relevant HF that can generate support for democratic institutions and the rule of law and ensure democratic consolidation.

In this respect, a new kind of enlightened leadership is a *sine qua non* for democratic consolidation. Such a leadership must exhibit a commitment to building a tolerant society and seek to realize the aspirations of its people and, above all, seek to serve as opposed to being served. This contribution is essential because of the failure of prior democratic experiments in various parts of the Third World. From a HF point of view, the failures can be attributed to the fact that these societies have experienced HF decay and/or underdevelopment. The HF is thus presented as being a critical ingredient for the effective performance of individuals and leaders. This point is buttressed by Husain's observation that 'the development of the individual enriches and improves society, and a well-organized, free, and just society provides wider opportunities for the individual to grow ... We want to create a new social order based on justice, equality, freedom and the dignity of the individual' (Husain, 1969, p. 365).

Consider also this declaration by Mike Oquaye about the prospects for sustaining liberal democratic experiments in Africa:

> Democracy comprises a set of values and attitudes. It is not only a compendium of principles but also a way of doing things. Human beings cannot achieve any goal without being guided by a fountain of ideas. Before a democratic system of government can take root in Africa, a mental liberation is imperative. This can be realized through political education. It has been feared that since most people are politically inept and unrestrained in Africa, democratic governance is unsuitable. Such a defect, however, can be cured through the development of the people's moral, intellectual and civic sense of responsibility (Oquaye, 1996, p. 56).

The HF, with its emphasis on political accountability, ethics and responsibility looms large in Oquaye's analysis both implicitly and explicitly. A citizenry and political leadership imbued with the HF has the capacity for ensuring effective and efficient operation and functioning of political institutions and upholding and guaranteeing political, administrative and judicial sanctions.

In a more direct way, it can be said that HF development can help shape and lay the foundations of a democratic political culture. Effectively developing and applying HF attributes such as integrity, accountability, responsibility and consensus-building could constitute the necessary framework that unites and successfully engages democracy and leads to its consolidation. Liberal democratic institutions cannot function effectively without the necessary HF development and engineering. Hence Adjibolosoo's suggestion that:

> Although the successful running of a democracy requires legal, social and political institutions, sound and workable cultural norms, ethos and efficient police and military forces, these may not perform their duties efficiently as expected without the HF. Similarly, the transformation of ideas into practice requires people who have acquired the HF to do so. All institutions of social transformation and popular movements cannot achieve their intended goals without a group of people who are readily available and willing to be responsible, accountable, committed, honest and trustworthy (Adjibolosoo, 1998, p. 20).

In this account the HF school is making the case that it is the HF that makes a sustained and vibrant constitutional democracy possible. While a constitution is a good blueprint, it is inanimate and cannot operate and implement itself. Upholding that constitutional blueprint requires individuals with the requisite HF through a process of human-centred development.

A note of caution is appropriate at this juncture. The argument about the need for HF engineering and individuals with positive HF attributes is by no means an attempt to imply that societies that are undemocratic have defective social structures. Such a position would move the HF school of thought perilously close to the intellectual terrain of modernization theorists. The conceptualization of the HF widely drawn upon here is meant only to highlight one, though important, aspect of the human quality debate that reinforces the role of human agency in the democratization process. As Wisdom Tettey perceptively points out in his contribution to this book, there is a need to examine the interrelationships between the normative and prescriptive aspects of HF theorizing and link them with a 'critical analysis of the socio-economic and political dynamics that define and shape human actions, attitudes and behaviour'. In making the case for the integration of the HF into the analysis, therefore, care must be taken not to overemphasize its contributions or reify it. The HF is one important and crucial aspect in the process of democratic consolidation. Furthermore, the HF is not static but dynamic and changes over time.

The HF school's contribution is in reminding scholars, activists and students alike that effective political institutions building is affected by the values and structures of the individuals tasked with ensuring its operation. Political institutions evolve in response to their environment and the individual's perceptions and understandings of that environment. Herein lies the need to address the HF by outlining the contours of the relationship between the individual's identity, values and purpose and institutional performance.

Conclusion

This chapter has critically interrogated the globalization of democracy debate in prevailing thought and has made the case for extending that debate. It has been argued that in the absence of positive human factor engineering the political project of globalization, democracy, will not be realized. Without the HF, political institutions cannot be functional over time. To sustain democracy, therefore, requires individuals, leaders and citizens who possess the HF necessary for the efficient and effective functioning of democratic institutions. This requires that we pay close attention to the political, social, cultural and institutional factors that relate to, and also affect, the HF.

References

Adjibolosoo, Senyo B.-S.K. (1998), "The Human Factor Foundation for Development and democracy", in Victor G. Chivaura and C.G. Mararike (eds.) *The Human Factor Approach to Development in Africa*, Harare: University of Zimbabwe Publications.

Adjibolosoo, Senyo B.-S.K. (1995), *The Human Factor in Developing Africa*, Westport, CT.: Praeger.

Archibugi, D, Held, D. and Kohler, M. (1998), "Introduction", in D. Archibugi, D. Held and M. Kohler (eds.) *Re-imagining Political Community: Studies in Cosmopolitan Democracy*, Cambridge: Polity Press.

Deutsch, Karl (1961), "Social Mobilization and Political Development", *American Political Science Review*, 14: 493-514.

Folson, Kweku G. (1995), "The Human Factor and the maintenance of Democracy in Ghana", in Senyo B.-S.K. Adjubolosoo (ed.) *The Significance of the Human Factor in African Economic Development*, Westport, CT.: Praeger.

Fukuyama, Francis (1992), *The End of History and the Last Man*, New York: The Free Press.

Gills, B. (1997), "Whither Democracy? Globalization and the New Hellenism", in Thomas, S. and Wilkin, P. (eds.) *Globalization and the South*, New York: St. Martin's Press.

Haucap, Justus (1997), "Institutions, Development, and the Human Factor: The German 'Miracle'", in Senyo B.-S.K. Adjibolosoo (ed.) *International Perspectives on the Human Factor in Economic Development*, Westport, CT.: Praeger.

Held, David (2000), "The Changing Contours of Political Community: Rethinking Democracy in the Context of Globalization", in Barry Holden (ed.) *Global Democracy: Key Debates*, London and New York: Routledge.

Held, David and McGrew, A., Goldblatt, D. and Perraton, J. (1999), *Global Transformations: Politics, Economics and Culture*, Stanford, California: Stanford University Press.

Held, David (1996), *Models of Democracy*, Stanford, California: Stanford University Press.

Huntington, Samuel (1996), *The Clash of Civilizations and the Remaking of World Order*, New York: Simon and Schuster.

Huntington, Samuel (1991), *The Third Wave: Democratization in the Late Twentieth Century*, Norman, Oklahoma: University of Oklahoma Press.

Hurd, Douglas (1990), "Promoting Good Government", *Crossbow*, (Autumn): 2-4.

Husain, Z. (1969), "The Never-Ending Pursuit of Learning", in D. Toppin (ed.) *This Cybernetic Age*, New York: Human Development Corporation.

Lynn-Jones, Sean M. (1998), "Why the United States Should Spread Democracy", *BCSIA Discussion Paper*, 98 – 01, Kennedy School of Government, Harvard University.

Mortimer, E. (1989), "The End of History." *Marxism Today*, November:

Osabu-Kle, Daniel (2000), *Compatible Cultural Democracy: The Key to Development in Africa*, Peterborough, Ontario: Broadview Press.

Oquaye, Mike (1996), "Preparing for Effective Constitutional Democracy in Africa: Political Education and Training", in Senyo B.-S.K. Adjibolosoo (ed.) *Human Factor Engineering and the Political Economy of African Development*, Westport, CT.: Praeger.

Owusu-Ampomah, Kwame (2001), "The Human Factor in Social Policy Formulation and Implementation in Emerging Democracies", *Review of Human Factor Studies*, 7 (1): 1-43.

Robinson, William I. (1996), *Promoting Polyarchy: Globalization, US Intervention and Hegemony*, New York and Melbourne: Cambridge University Press.

Sandbrook, Richard (1996), "Transitions without Consolidation: Democratization in Six African Cases", *Third World Quarterly*, 17 (1): 69-87.

Scholte, Jan Aart (2000), *Globalization: A Critical Introduction*, New York: St. Martin's Press.

Youngs, Gillian (1996), "Dangers of Discourse: The Case of Globalization", in Eleonore
    Kofman and Gillian Youngs (eds.) *Globalization: Theory and Practice*, New
    York: Pinter.
World Bank (1998), *East Asia: The Road to Recovery*, Washington, D.C.: The World Bank.

Index